Lundy

The Loss of H.M.S. Montagu Lundy 1906

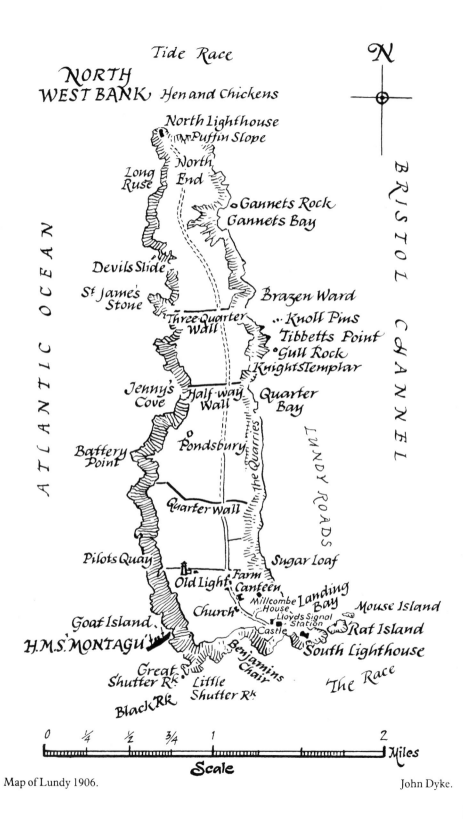

Map of Lundy 1906.   John Dyke.

The Loss of H.M.S. Montagu Lundy 1906

Compiled by G. M. DAVIS

Cover designed and drawn by John Dyke
Lettering by Robin Tanner

Published by GM&RC Davis,
Atworth, 1981

Reprinted 2006 by the
Landmark Trust in agreement with
GM&RC Davis

ISBN 0 9507391 0 3
© G. M. DAVIS 1981

Printed by Short Run Press LTD

Respectfully dedicated to the memory of
Captain T. B. S. Adair of H.M.S. Montagu,
without whose unwitting help this book
would not have been possible.

Contents

Introduction and Acknowledgements

The incidents recorded here took place seventy-five years ago on May 30th 1906.

To mark the 75th anniversary I have compiled this record of the wreck and subsequent attempts at salvaging of H.M.S. Montagu at Lundy.

My grateful thanks to Myrtle Langham for her kind help and her contribution "Lundy: a Brief History" and "setting the scene" so to speak prior to the incidents recorded here.

The dramatic events which ended with the almost total loss of this battleship, the Court Martial and the almost impossible task of salvaging have been vividly brought to life by John Dyke for which I thank him most gratefully, also for his splendid art work of Captain Adair, the map of Lundy and for the cover illustration.

My thanks to the Ministry of Defence (Navy Department), National Maritime Museum, London and the Imperial War Museum for permission to reproduce photographs of H.M.S. Montagu in happier times.

To F. E. Gibson of the Scilly Isles for his fine photographs taken at the time of the wreck.

My thanks also to Miss Eileen Heaven for the loan of the photograph of the Rev Heaven, and to Col R. C. Gilliat for the photograph of the Crest of H.M.S. Montagu, and to those friends who have found time to assist me in various ways in the production of this book, although not mentioned by name, nevertheless their help is gratefully acknowledged. The remainder of the photographs used, where not recognized, have come from my own large collection of post cards issued at the time of the wreck and after. Many of the post cards had to be rejected as unsuitable for reproduction owing to the passage of time.

The photographs of S.S. Ranger were a lucky find, being the personal photograph album of the Captain of the Ranger prior to Captain F. W. Young (who took the S.S. Ranger to Lundy in 1906 to assist in the salvage operations) and record salvage operations that the Ranger performed in 1902. Over the years many items have been recovered from the sea bed by underwater exploration of the wreck, and hopefully will one day be on view in the proposed museum on Lundy. The very fine wood panelling (complete with open fireplace!) all in bird's eye maple that lined the Captain's cabin was recovered during the early salvage operations and now adorns a room in a house in Ilfracombe, together with the cabin door.

Jill Davis, Atworth, 1981.

The Rev. Hudson Grosett Heaven, owner of Lundy in 1906.

Lundy: a Brief History

By Myrtle Langham

The remains of prehistoric settlements tell us that Lundy has been inhabited at least since Neolithic times. There are evidences of Iron Age and Dark Age occupation before the first written reference to Lundy is found in the *Orkneyinga Saga*, when it is mentioned as the refuge of ". . . that Freeman from Wales . . . who ran away to that Isle which is called Lund". Very little more is known about Lundy until about 1150 when it was in the possession of the de Newmarch family, from whom the de Mariscos held it.

In 1235 the island was the refuge of William de Marisco, who fled the displeasure of the king and who used Lundy as an outlaw base and centre for Bristol Channel piracy. After William was suspected of having been implicated in an attempt upon the king's life in 1238, efforts were made to bring him to justice. Fourteen of the king's men eventually managed to land in 1242 and William was captured, imprisoned in the Tower of London, tried, and subsequently put to death, despite his protestations of innocence. Once having possession of Lundy, the king immediately reinforced it by providing a garrison of men and the building of a "good tower with a bailey wall", which was then held by a succession of Constables and keepers until the de Marisco family were allowed to re-possess the island in 1281.

Lundy passed from the de Mariscos to the de Wyllentons and then, in 1332, to William de Montacute (1st Earl of Salisbury) from whom it was passed down by family inheritance for the next four hundred years until it was sold to Sir John Borlase Warren in 1775. There is evidence that during this long period the island was frequently the resort of pirates and, on at least one occasion, the victim of them. With the outbreak of the Civil War, Lundy's position across the Channel and the approaches to Bristol would account for its having been garrisoned for the king, whose stronghold was in the west.

The king's man in charge of the island was Thomas Bushell, a remarkable man, who at that time was engaged in mining and in minting coins for the king. Lundy was the last Royalist stronghold to capitulate to the Parliamentarians; Bushell did not surrender it until February 1647. At the Restoration he petitioned Charles II for reimbursement of his costs in fortifying the island, garrisoning it, and rebuilding the castle. His claim was supported by John Grenville, 1st Earl of Bath, to whom the island had reverted in 1660, and from whom it passed by marriage to John Leveson, Lord Gower, in 1711. During this time there was another lengthy period of pirate activity and, as previously the island was leased to tenants.

In 1748 Lord Gower leased the island to Thomas Benson, a wealthy merchant, who was Sheriff of Devon in 1746 and became M.P. for Barnstaple in 1747. He contracted with the government to carry convicts abroad, but instead of fulfilling the assumption that "abroad" meant America, Benson removed the convicts to Lundy, where he employed them in labouring. He also engaged in contraband, using Lundy as a hiding place, but finally he was forced to flee the island and escape to Portugal when his attempt to carry out an insurance fraud miscarried. He had heavily insured the cargo of one of his ships which was destined for America, and then secretly unloaded the cargo on Lundy before setting the ship on fire in such a way as to make it look an accident.

Lord Gower died without an heir in 1754, and after some interval Lundy was sold to Sir John Borlase Warren, who immediately set about improving it. He imported labourers and built a quay and a house, but unfortunately he went off to serve his king in the American War of Independence and Lundy was again sold, this time to John Cleveland, from whom it passed in 1803 to the Vere Hunts. During their ownership the Lighthouse on Beacon Hill was completed by Trinity House and was put into operation in 1820; it was the highest lighthouse in Britain. The hazard which Lundy presented to shipping, particularly in fog, made the lighthouse a necessity, but its height proved to be a disadvantage since the tower was very often obscured by mist; it was augmented by the Fog Signal Station on the West Side in 1863, and finally superceded by new lighthouses at the north and the south end in 1897.

Sir Aubrey Vere Hunt apparently gambled Lundy away and it passed to a Mr Matravers and a Mr Stiffe, who sold it in 1834 to William Hudson Heaven, gentleman, of Bristol. Mr Heaven intended to use it as a summer resort and shooting estate, and he built the house in Millcombe for his own residence. His son, the Rev Hudson Grosett Heaven, later built the Church of St Helena which, with the Old Lighthouse, provides Lundy with its landmarks. In 1863 the part of the island not reserved for Mr Heaven's use was leased, and a granite works was established on the East Side which was only operative until 1868, the difficulties of transportation making the enterprise uneconomic. Although the granite company was not on the island for very long, much of the present aspect of the "village" is the result of their work.

Mr Heaven and his family were unique among the owners of the island in that they made the island their permanent and only home. This permanent residence lasted from 1851 to 1905, when ill-health and old age forced the Rev Hudson Heaven and his cousin, Anne Mary, to spend their winters on the mainland; by this time these two were the only members of the family remaining in residence. Walter Charles Hudson Heaven, the Rev Heaven's nephew, took over the island in 1916 on his uncle's death, but in 1917 he was forced to offer it for sale, as he had insuperable financial difficulties. From then to 1925 the owner of the island was Mr Augustus Langham Christie of Tapeley Park, Instow, who was a descendant of the John Cleveland who had held it from 1787 to 1803. For the greater part of this period the island was leased by Mr C. H. May, who farmed the island but did not live there himself. In 1925 Mr Christie's unfortunate illness caused the island to be offered for sale again, and the purchaser was Mr Martin Coles Harman, a London business man.

Mr Harman took great pride in Lundy's peculiar legal status, and he also had a very keen interest in its wild life and natural beauty. He was determined that Lundy should remain independent of the mainland and in his agent, Mr F. W. Gade, he found a man who shared these feelings completely. The Post Office was "dismissed", and any encroachment on Lundy's rights, including the uninvited landing of officials of any kind, was vigorously resisted. At the same time Mr. Harman was a courteous man who joyed in sharing his island with others who appreciated it as he did. In 1929, to help offset the cost of transporting mail to the mainland, he introduced his own local postage stamps, denominated in "Puffin" values; these, the longest established of the local issues, are still in use. He also minted Puffin coins, but was brought to trial and convicted of infringement of the Coinage Act of 1870, so that the coins were withdrawn. In 1946 he sponsored the founding of the Lundy Field Society and gave it the use of the

Old Light; the Society is devoted to the study and preservation of the wild life and the habitat, and is still active today.

After Mr Harman's death in 1954 the island became the property of his three surviving children, who strove hard to succeed in bringing it to economic independence, but the death of Mr Albion Harman in 1968, and the serious collapse of the Beach Road in 1969, forced them to put it up for sale. It was hoped that the National Trust would be able to buy it, but although the purchase money was donated by Mr Jack Hayward, the Trust was prevented from buying because there were no funds with which to maintain the island. Not until the Trustees of the Landmark Trust undertook to lease the island, administer it, and institute a programme of repair, was the National Trust able to complete the purchase. Lundy became the property of the National Trust on September 29th 1969, since when the Landmark Trust has been responsible for its upkeep; the island farm is maintained, and Lundy is open to holiday visitors, who may go over just for the day, or to stay there and enjoy its great tranquillity.

Lundy in 1906

The owner of the island was the Rev Hudson Heaven, then aged 80, who had inherited it from his father in 1883. He was unmarried; a man of bookish disposition always called "Phi" by his family, a name that was a shortened version of their reference to him as "Philosopher". He had been educated at Oxford and became headmaster of a school in Taunton; when the school closed in 1864 he had returned to live on Lundy, both to attend the spiritual needs of the population and to help his father in the management of the estate.

Services were conducted every Sunday afternoon, and on all days of religious observance, but, until the little iron church was built at the head of Millcombe Valley in 1884, there had been no church for the congregation and services were held in a "Church room". The iron church was a dedicated, not a consecrated, building and consequently its functions were limited, and it was replaced in 1897 by the granite church of St Helena which stands in a prominent position on the plateau. The building of this church was the realisation of a long-cherished ambition for the Rev Heaven and the source of much gratification to all the Heaven family and their close friends, who each donated particular items to its fabric and furniture. In addition to the services Sunday School was held for the island children, who were taken to the mainland by the Rev Heaven for the ceremony of confirmation. The Rev Heaven, his sister and his cousin had also given lessons to the island children, but by 1906 both these and the Sunday School had been given up, although the services were continued.

The Rev Heaven's health was sometimes uncertain, and as he got older he found both the administration and the expenses of the estate too much for him, and so the island farm was leased to tenants, while a portion of the south-east corner of the island, including Millcombe, was reserved for the Heaven family. The tenants were Mr Thomas Wright (1885-1891), Mr Ackland (1891-1899), Mr Taylor (1899-1908) and L. and W. Saunt (1908-1912).

Thus the tenant in 1906 was Mr George Taylor, who was responsible for running the farm and the Store, and for the accommodation of visitors. By 1906 he seems to have been largely an absentee holder of the title and to have left the day-to-day running in the hands of his employees. The farm supported sheep, pigs, cattle and poultry, and there was a dairy where considerable quantities of butter were produced; hay and cereal crops were grown, as well as potatoes and other vegetables to provide for the island population. Fuel, fertilisers, building materials, additional foods and goods of all kinds had to be brought across from the mainland, but supplies for the family and for the tenant were always separate, as were the mails. The Heaven family and the Post Office were served by Capt Dark and the *Gannet*, which made the crossing once a week, weather permitting, and Trinity House supplied their stations by their own vessels which called at regular intervals. In addition to these it was easy to charter vessels from Ilfracombe and other neighbouring ports, for which the charge was 25-30 shillings per day. The shipping about Lundy was busy and there were tug boats in the vicinity, to which the islanders resorted for transport when the need arose; there were also the pilot boats which used Lundy as a base to wait for ships needing their services to travel up-channel. In the summer season the pleasure steamers called once or twice a week, as well as occasional private enterprise excursionists and yachtsmen.

Apart from Mr Taylor, leases had also been granted to Trinity House, Lloyds, The Admiralty, the G.P.O. and the Board of Trade, while a Mr Miles leased the Old Light, which he used for holiday visits. Trinity House was responsible for the North and South Lighthouses, which in 1906 had been in operation for nine years. Lloyds had a Signal Station and two cottages near the Castle, from where a watch was kept on all shipping and messages transmitted to and from all kinds of vessels. The Admiralty had the lease of the Semaphore Station; the G.P.O. of the Cable Hut; and the Board of Trade the lease of a piece of land on which was built the shed where the Rocket Life-Saving Apparatus was housed. The Admiralty had also contracted for the building of premises for the Coastguards.

The population of the island in 1906 thus consisted of the Heaven family and their employees; Mr Taylor's employees; Trinity House employees, and Lloyd's personnel. Their sub-agent was Mr F. W. Allday, who lived at a Signal Cottage with his wife and daughter, and who was also Postmaster and in charge of the telegraph station. This gentleman lived on Lundy for over twenty years without going ashore, and he asserted that he would not have gone when he did, had he not needed to consult a doctor! Although the islanders were separately employed, labour was "lent" in times of need, such as haymaking; they all contributed to the island community and the Rev Heaven was referred to as "The Squire" generally.

The presence of Trinity House, Lloyds and the Admiralty all serve to underline the importance of Lundy to shipping, and to remind us that at times there were large numbers of vessels about the island. The crews of the ships greatly extended the volume of trade at the Store, and they often augmented the island congregation in Church.

The Rev Heaven had spent the winter of 1905-6 on the mainland, following the death in October 1905 of his dear sister, Amelia Anne; he was accompanied by his cousin, Anne Mary Heaven, who had lived with the family on Lundy since 1873 and who was then 75 years of age. They were joined later by her niece, Helen Heaven, who came to help care for them, and they were visited on Lundy by the other members of the family who lived at Bristol and Abbotsham. At the time the *Montagu* went aground the island was up for sale, but although the disaster brought Lundy into the forefront of the news, the required price was not reached and no sale was made. The particulars of sale detail all the buildings on the island, and it is mentioned that one of the three Quarter-Wall cottages was occupied, and one of the four Castle cottages, and that George Thomas was still living in the bungalow which he built near the Castle (now Hanmers).

In a letter to his niece dated 5.6.06, the Rev Heaven says that ". . . the island has been much excited about the wreck of the *Montagu*, and the consequent visits of various battleships etc. There are three of these and a cruiser here in attendance, besides a fleet of salvage craft. If the weather continues fine as at present, they may refloat her, but should it come in rough and stormy, I think it is very problematical . . ." On 15.6.06 he writes: ". . . The steamers are now in full swing with their trips. The Barry or "Red-funnelled" boats at present come here on Tuesdays and the *Brighton* on Fridays. The former, however, are running every day "Channel" trips, sometimes twice a day to view the wreck and the other Battleships in attendance on it . . . We have been simply swarming with photographers and their Kodaks, snapshotting in all directions . . ." In October 1906 the Rev Heaven left Lundy to spend the winter ashore; Mr Taylor shut the Manor House for the winter, and the *Montagu* was left in the care of the Coastguards who were sent to the island to guard her.

Capt Fred Dark (standing with single oar) landing stores at Lundy. His father Capt William P. M. Dark, stated in his affidavit to the Court Martial on behalf of Capt Adair, ". . . that the tides, from his own observations, were very irregular in the set of the current, and ran at different angles at different states of the tide, sometimes . . ."

The men employed in salvage operations were housed in the Marisco Castle cottages. South Light can be seen to the right of the picture.

North Light, Lundy, mistaken for Hartland Point by the two officers from the stranded "Montagu".

994.1. Hotel & Farm, Lundy.

The Automatic Photo Printing Co. Ltd.

View of High Street with Manor Hotel and Farm in the foreground.

18

Marisco Tavern and General Store with Church of St. Helena.

The Automatic Photo Printing Co. Ltd.

19

T.B.L.Adair. CAPTAIN

John Dyke.

The wreck of the "Montagu"

By John Dyke

The following account of the wreck of the "Montagu" was originally written in 1957 for publication in the first issue of the "Lundy Review", a magazine published by Mr Stanley Smith, then resident on the island. It has been brought up-to-date by the inclusion of additional material which has since become available, not the least interesting being the Log of Midshipman Nelson Clover, serving on the fated battleship, which gives a first-hand account of the stranding and subsequent attempts at salving the vessel.

On May 30th 1906, an event took place which focussed world-wide attention on Lundy. H.M.S. "Montagu", one of the most recently commissioned battleships and pride of the Channel Fleet, surrendered her massive armour-plate to the treacherous Shutter Rock at the south-western corner of the island. Here she was doomed to end her days, despite every device known to salvage experts of that period.

The "Montagu" was a first-class twin-screw battleship of 14,000 tons belonging to the "Duncan" class, which were named after famous admirals. Launched at Devonport in 1901, she had a complement of 750 officers and men, carried 16 guns, and engines of 18,000 horsepower, which gave her a speed of 19 knots. The battleship had been assigned an important part in manoeuvres, and on the day previous to grounding was patrolling the entrance to the Bristol Channel on the open side of Lundy, where Captain Adair had been carrying out wireless signalling trials with the Scilly Isles. The signals proved unsatisfactory owing to the distance and it was decided to move in closer to obtain better results, but visibility was poor and during the night dense fog developed. To add to the difficulties a strong prevailing current drove the "Montagu" off course. Soundings were taken at frequent intervals, and at 1.07 a.m. showed 70 fathoms; at 2.00 a.m., 19 fathoms, and just before 2.12 a.m., Lundy loomed up with startling suddenness.

The ship grounded by the bows before any evasive action could be taken. Although the "Montagu" was steaming very slowly, the impact was so great that several of the crew sustained injuries. The captain tried going astern, but without success, as there was no room to manoeuvre. The ship struck at flood tide and the swell had carried the stern around to the rocks, with the result that both propellers were carried away. The "Montagu" lay firmly across a ledge of rock about 15 feet from the almost perpendicular cliffs, and parallel to the island, with a large hole in her starboard bottom, a heavy list to starboard, and water rising above her torpedo nets. The engine room, boiler room and stokehold were badly flooded—wireless telegraphy was also damaged, but fortunately the sea remained comparatively calm and there was no loss of life.

A contemporary press report states: "The ship's company behaved splendidly and went about their work as though they were at ordinary drill. All the electric lights were on during the time the boats were being got out. Despite the water-tight compartments in the ship, the fore boiler room was soon flooded to a depth of 15 to 20 feet, and whilst the various orders were being executed calmly, the peril of the position was fully realised and fires were drawn in time to avert a probable explosion. After this had been done the electric light went out and the ship was in absolute darkness. The completest discipline was maintained and there was no suspicion of panic."

Immediately on striking, distress signals were fired and minute guns continued until 6 cases of ammunition had been expended. In the meantime, Lieutenant S. P. B. Russell, together with a junior officer, left the vessel in a gig and pulled under the lee of the island in the direction of the North Light, the approximate position of which was indicated by continuous fog signals. In this manner the two officers proceeded for about 2½ miles along the western coastline, and, after making a landing, climbed up the face of the cliffs to the top of the island—a very difficult matter on such a dark night. They presented themselves at the North Light at 5.40 a.m., 3½ hours after the "Montagu" struck, and were very surprised to hear they were on Lundy, being quite convinced in their own minds that they had struck Hartland Point. In fact, a contemporary report indicates that a sharp exchange of words took place, and the argument was finally resolved by the Lundy keeper assuring them that ". . . he did really know which lighthouse he was in charge of." This, of course, was the first intimation on Lundy of the mishap.

As soon as the news reached the mainland, tugs and salvage vessels literally swarmed to the scene and the battleships "Exmouth", "Duncan", "Dido" and "Albermarle" arrived to give assistance. The Paymaster from the "Montagu" was sent ashore, taking with him all sick men, also ledgers, money, and confidential papers, the latter being placed for safe keeping in Millcombe House, residence of the Reverend Heaven, a guard being placed over them for additional security. On the "Montagu", bags and hammocks belonging to the crew were brought on deck, as well as officers' gear, all of which was later transported to the "Duncan". Finally, everybody left the ship for the night, apart from the Captain, First Lieutenant, and sea-boat's crew. As the shock of the grounding had broken the aerial of the wireless telegraphy apparatus, no signals could be made, but this difficulty was overcome with the assistance of Lloyd's Agent on the island, who kept watch on the cliff top to pass any urgent messages. Although Lundy never supported an H.M. Coastguard Station, Lloyd's of London had operated an agency on the island for many years, then in 1883 the island was up-graded to a full agency under the Reverend Hudson Grosett Heaven. An Admiralty/Lloyd's agreement enabled the former to open a station staffed by Admiralty Signallers at the south-eastern end of the island on June 1st, 1909, and this establishment may have been a direct result of the stranding of the "Montagu". The Agent at that time, Mr. Frederick William Allday, despatched the first report of the casualty to Lloyd's of London, and then to the Admiralty, and it is said that he was afterwards censured for not having given the Admiralty first priority in the messages!

During the hours of daylight the crew of the "Montagu" were employed salving stores and transferring them to the "Duncan" and "Dido"; also a life-saving apparatus was rigged from the forecastle to the cliffs. During Sunday, June 3rd, two main deck 6 in. guns were hoisted out and lowered into a lighter. It was impossible to do much work at high tide as the upper deck was knee-deep in water, and it was waist-deep on the main deck; however, by the following day all the guns were out of the ship, with the exception of the turret guns. By this time the whole ship's company had been transferred to the "Exmouth" and "Dido", returning each day as working parties, whilst a Watch was left aboard during the hours of darkness. A number of men from Pembroke Docks had arrived and were working on the air pressure plates, removing rivets, gun turret covers etc.

At first the Admiralty had great hopes of saving the "Montagu", and ordered a floating dock to be towed across the Atlantic from Bermuda. It was then thought that it would be possible to refloat her in July, when the tides would be at their highest for the year. However, after a while it was obvious that Lundy would become her grave, and work was put in hand under the direction of Admiral Wilson, to remove remaining guns, arms, torpedoes and all possible stores, which were transferred to lighters and Government vessels using Lundy Roads as their anchorage.

The salvage operations proved a great attraction for sightseers, and passenger-carrying craft from the nearby coastal resorts did considerable business. It must have been an impressive concentration of shipping, with the warships "Cornwallis", "Duncan" and "Mars" in attendance, and numerous salvage craft in support.

A contemporary Midshipman's Log bears witness to the difficulties under which the salvage crews were working due to adverse weather conditions, and it was necessary to cease work many times on account of the heavy seas. On these occasions it was reported that the men used their free time in "scrubbing hammocks and washing and mending clothes."

His report of the disaster on May 30th reads: "2.5, stopped—hard a starboard. 2.10, full speed astern. 2.12, grounded by the bows. When the telegraphs were put over again the engines raced round as the propellers were broken. As soon as we grounded closed W.T. doors and so people had only time to put on very scanty clothing. As soon as possible we hoisted out the pulling boom boats and three steam boats; the steam boats being very dangerous as the ship was rolling heavily, both the picket boats had their bows stove in . . . the fog was so heavy that although the rocks and cliff were less than eighty yards away yet we could hardly make anything of them at all. 7.5, ship surged astern—8.0, tried to lay out sheet anchor, but failed . . . flooded the port engine room to keep the ship as steady as possible. 11.0, both picket boats here took the advantage of watering alongside the "Monarch", cable-laying steamer, and we also managed to get some breakfast, which was a great boon."

An historic entry appears on May 31st: "Dressed ship with masthead flags in honour of the marriage of King Alfonso XIII and Princess Ena of Battenburgh." On Friday, June 1st: "During the forenoon, a lighter, which had in it four 6 in. guns and the starboard nets, carried away the tow-rope and passed over the Shutter rocks and sank. During the afternoon the "Ranger" and "Linnet", salvage steamers from Liverpool, arrived."

On Friday, June 22nd, an entry appears: "Dressed ships with Masthead flags—Norwegian at main. At noon the ships present fired Royal Salute of 21 guns in honour of Coronation of King Haakon and Queen Maud." Another for Wednesday, June 27th, reports: "No-one went on board ship on account of bad weather—make and mend clothes. In the evening an impromptu sing-song took place on the Quarter deck. The Dockyardmen and some of our seamen contributed to the singing."

On Monday, July 23rd, more difficulties presented themselves, as the entry reads: "All night the Captain was going round the passages (myself with him) superintending operations. 3.45, Tug escort came alongside, but sheered off as there was rather a heavy swell. "Mars" and "Duncan" took up appointed positions—the "Duncan" in getting out of the way of "Mars" drifted on top of outlying rock and made a hole in aftermost double bottom compartment. 4.30, ship started to bump very heavily—4.45, stopped all pumps and air compressors on account of ship bumping too heavily—allowed ship to flood to main deck. "Duncan" and "Mars" picked up their old billets. In the afternoon gave hands a make and mend clothes . . . cleared up decks and secured all gear on the upper deck."

More misfortune was reported on Thursday and Friday, July 26th-27th. "Towards the evening (Thurs.) a heavy swell came on, and ship was working very heavily; standing right forward one could see the bow moving considerably, mostly towards the cliffs. The salvage men all went aboard the "Ranger" for the night. (Fri.) Found ship had shifted—her bows going 13 ft. to starboard . . . she had a degree more list to port and her stern appeared to have sunk considerably. 12.30, H.M.S. "Vengeance" arrived from Berehaven bringing cork. Parties from "Exmouth", "Duncan" and "Vengeance" getting in cork and putting it on Main deck—it is to be placed afterwards in compartments which cannot be pumped out, or are open to the sea." Then on Tuesday, July 31st: the ship was "Bumping very heavily" and worse was to come, as shown by the following entries for August:—

August 1st
"When Dockyardmen were piped to fall in, 63 of them refused to go over to the ship as the weather was very threatening. 9.30, all hands left ship."

August 3rd
"It was too rough again to go near the ship, so hands had another make and mend clothes. In the afternoon gave leave to C.P.O.'s from 1.30 till 6 p.m. Looking from the cliffs, the seas seemed to be coming over worse than they had ever done before."

August 4th
"The ship's stern had sunk a great deal more. This was very evident in the Ward-room, where the deck had a pronounced slope; also in the port battery all the planks had started, and the coal shutes had risen noticeably, above deck. 12.30, sent hands to "Mars"—2.00, no-one left in ship.

August 5th
"Admiral made signal to the effect that he had decided to abandon the attempt to refloat the ship and that he was waiting for the Admiralty's permission to hoist out pumps and gear.

Copy of signal from C. in C., intimating their Lordships' appreciation of the efforts of all concerned to salve the ship:

"The Admiralty having directed me to communicate the following telegram to all those who have zealously assisted in the efforts to save the "Montagu": The same is communicated for the information of the officers and ships companies of the ships here, the Dockyard officers and men who have been engaged on the work here and at Pembroke and Devonport Dockyards; the Captain and crews of the tugs and the employees of the Salvage Company—although the efforts to save the "Montagu" have not been successful, their Lordships recognise with satisfaction the untiring energy and skill and courage displayed by all concerned, and the zealous endeavours to bring the operations to a satisfactory conclusion."

August 10th
"Sent hands aboard to save gear at 5.50, but as weather was bad we came off at 7.30, bringing everything away with us."

Following this entry all ships weighed anchor and proceeded in company for Portsmouth; all the Dockyardmen returned to Pembroke in the tugs "Alligator" and "Volcano". Midshipman Clover, now aboard H.M.S. "Mars", writes: "1.00, entered

Solent—1.40, we passed the "Britannia" R.Y.S., with H.M. the King on board—fired salute of 21 guns." His last entry on the subject of the "Montagu" appears on Monday, August 13th: "Capt. Gamble, H.M.S. "Canopus", held court of enquiry on loss of gear in wreck of H.M.S. "Montagu". In the afternoon all midshipmen not required for court martial went on leave."

The Court Martial opened at 10 o'clock on Wednesday morning, August 15th 1906, taking place aboard the "Victory", with Rear-Admiral Charles Cross presiding. The officers put on trial were Captain Adair and the navigating officer, Lieutenant Dathan. There were two charges against the prisoners, the first alleging that the accused, being persons subject to Naval discipline, on the 30th May 1906 did negligently, or by default, hazard, strand, or lose H.M.S. "Montagu"; and second, that on the same date the prisoners negligently, or by default, suffered the said ship to be hazarded, stranded, or lost. The report of the Captain to the Admiralty was read, and other officers gave evidence as to the movement of the "Montagu" during the six hours preceding the disaster. All witnesses agreed that there was no reason to think she was off her course. No fog signals were heard from Lundy or Hartland Point, though the Officer of the Watch was listening for them in between the intervals of sounding the "Montagu's" own siren. Following further evidence, Commander G. E. S. Petch said he turned out of his bunk when the ship grounded and was on deck 5 minutes later. Immediately after striking, the bower anchor was got out and the capstan manned by hand, as the compartment working the steam engine was flooded. The behaviour of the crew was exemplary in all respects—in fact, the grounding might have been all part of the daily routine. When Captain Adair was asked if any officers and men had especially distinguished themselves, he replied "I do not wish to make distinction, where all did so well. The conduct of Artificer Eng. Marchant, who was the Officer of the Watch in the engine room was admirable, but I do not consider it necessary to mention anyone else in particular. The behaviour of the officers and crew was in all respects what it ought to be."

During the course of cross-examination, the Navigating Officer, Lieutenant Dathan, admitted that he was several miles out in his reckoning.

The trial concluded with the court finding the charges proved against both prisoners; ordering Captain Adair to be severely reprimanded and dismissed from the "Montagu"; and Lieutenant Dathan to be severely reprimanded, dismissed from the "Montagu" and to forfeit two years seniority as Lieutenant of the Fleet. Part of the sentences might be regarded as distinctly quaint under the circumstances; the force of the wind and sea having already effectively anticipated the decision that both officers should be dismissed their ship!

The press gave a sympathetic report on Captain Adair's career and future. One paper said "He is universally regarded as a rising officer and, at the Admiralty, where his ability and professional record are well known, there will certainly be no disposition to dispense with his services. That he may not get command of another ship is probable, if only in deference to public opinion, but that staff employment will be found for him until he attains flag rank may be regarded as more than probable." Public opinion did not consider the punishment meted out to be unduly severe. It was thought that the loss of the "Montagu" was particularly due to the amount of attention Captain Adair had devoted to his wireless telegraphy experiments, which was considered detrimental to his command of the ship. The blot upon his career was all the more regretted, for the service contained no more devoted servant, who, in addition to his scientific proficiency, was one of the leading experts in naval gunnery. He had spent 32 of his 45 years in the Navy and he had a first-class record, especially in gunnery, serving as Assistant to the Director of Naval Ordnances, and being a member of the Ordnance Committee. Captain Adair was a qualified interpreter in Hindustani, and was a member of the class of the Spanish Naval Order of Merit; he had previously won the Egyptian Medal and the Khedives Bronze Star for his service with the Naval flotilla in the Egyptian War of 1882.

Of Lieutenant Dathan, the press treated him thus:— "He has a highly meritorious record and comes from a well known Naval family. Not least amongst the personal virtues which fit him for his responsible post is the fact that he is a staunch teetotaller." (Something of a Naval rarity, one would imagine).

The battleship was officially considered as being paid off on August 20th, the date on which the Court Martial dissolved. Sanction was received from the Admiralty to abandon operations on the "Montagu"; the Navy withdrawing in favour of more experienced salvers led by Captain Young of the Liverpool Salvage Association. The announcement by Admiral Wilson was received with tremendous cheering. The heavy and incessant work and lack of sleep had put a considerable strain upon the nerves of the men—they had been working like Trojans, labouring continuously for as much as thirty hours at a stretch. These conditions had already led to some disorder aboard, and the final "down tools" resulted in a few thirsty workers breaking into the island canteen and helping themselves to Mr Pennington's liquor. Several of the imbibers suffered injury through falling over the cliffs and paid for their misdemeanours in broken limbs and bruises!

Admiral Wilson must have been very happy to relinquish his unfamiliar task directing salvage operations on the "Montagu"—apart from coming in for a good deal of criticism from the press and public opinion over his handling of the operation, he very nearly lost his life whilst in charge. A heavy sea swept him off his picket boat when returning to the flagship, and he was rescued with considerable difficulty—and some loss of dignity!

Another catastrophe was averted by the timely action of Petty Officer Cosh of H.M.S. "Duncan", who rescued a seaman thrown overboard when a "camel" broke loose. The "camel", weighing 6½ tons, was rolling within 5 ft. of the ship, and Cosh, at the risk of being crushed, jumped into the narrow space and succeeded in saving the man, who had sustained head injuries. Petty Officer Cosh later received the Royal Humane Society's Bronze Medal.

Captain Young's primary task was the salvaging of the four 12 in. breech guns—of the latest Mark X wire wound pattern, these cost £9,049 each, measured 40 ft. in length, and weighed 48 tons apiece. The Admiralty attached great importance to their successful recovery for, apart from the monetary value, the reserve of big guns was very low, having been drawn on to replace defective ordnance in the "Majestic" and "Canopus" classes.

Eight shipwrights were engaged to work on the "Montagu" and it was reported that they had revealed serious defects in the construction of the battleship. It was alleged that rivets in the bulkheads had been driven in too far apart to secure watertightness; that joints had been passed over uncalked, and tack rivets to join two thicknesses of plating where armour plate bolts pass through, had been omitted. In some places the removal of cement revealed that wooden plugs had been driven in instead of rivets. The allegations brought an indignant denial from the officers and men at Devonport, who stated that scamped work was impossible. There was no undue haste in her construction, over 15 months having been taken in bringing her to the launching stage—the usual time being a little over a year. She was the fourth modern battleship to be built at Devonport. Probably there was truth in the allegations, since it would have been to no one's advantage to put out false reports on the constructional work.

Salvage operations vastly improved under the expert guidance of Captain Young. In fact the success which attended the efforts of the salvage men when they were given an absolutely free hand lent colour to the suggestion that had they been allowed to do their own work in their own fashion the results might have been much better. "The Mercury" commented "They undertook to recover the four 12 inch guns and this has been done. Why was it not done during the three months that Admiral Wilson was superintending affairs on Lundy? It is the old story of each to his kind. As a strategist Admiral Wilson is 'par excellent', as a salvage authority he is a bit of a novice." The newspaper suggested that an official enquiry should be held into the conduct of the "Montagu" salvage operations.

Captain Young certainly knew his job; by the end of September his men had recovered, in addition to the 12 inch guns; the foremost gun cradles, the remains of the starboard propeller weighing about 10 tons, and the slide and fittings from the after barbette; also divers had picked up a quantity of small gun gear. Although a good deal of time had been spent in trying to locate the second propeller, it was not until nearly 18 months later that it came to light in rather curious cicumstances, when the anchor of the salvage steamer "Zephyr" became entangled with something on the sea bed. Repeated efforts were made to move it, but without success; finally it was decided to send a diver down to investigate and he returned to report that the object was no less than the long lost and much sought after propeller. Dynamite was used to dislodge it, and the "big screw" was salved in two pieces, together weighing nearly 13 tons—at the prevailing price of £60 a ton it had proved to be a very profitable hindrance. The metal was landed at Ilfracombe and sent to Devonport for resmelting; ten horses were used to haul it to Ilfracombe station—an uphill task for the team—prolonged by the breaking of one of the trolley wheels, which had to be replaced.

With the approach of winter, work on the "Montagu" ceased, and the Admiralty guardships returned to base. The salvage ship "Ranger", with Captain Young aboard, left Lundy on October 15th. Six of the "camels" or tanks prepared for the salvage work were sold and the remainder were filled with concrete and utilised in the repair of Plymouth breakwater.

It was now proposed to use the "Montagu" for target practice before submitting her to the auctioneer's hammer, and H.M.S. "Doris" was detailed to carry out the experiments. The Admiralty were anxious to try out some of their latest weapons, and since the "Montagu" contained a belt of "Krupp" steel 14ft. deep and 7ins. thick amidships to 3ins. at the bow extending 286ft. from 5ft. below water, what better than to try their modern projectiles on the future enemy's armour plate!

However, the Admiralty had not reckoned on strong objections from the owner of Lundy, the Reverend Heaven, who feared for his property on the island, much of which lay in the direct line of fire. Also the Trinity Brethren were apprehensive regarding the fate of the South Light should such a plan be put into operation, and it was made quite clear, therefore, that the Service would be held responsible for any damage done. The risk was too great and experimental firing was stopped. In pursuance of more recent instructions a boarding party from the cruiser "Doris" blew out the side of the wreck with the object of facilitating the removal of her machinery, but were not entirely successful, for they only managed to make a small hole in her port side and a large dent in the armour belting about 15ft. long by 7ft. deep. Westerly gales sprung up during this time and on November 18th, 29 steamers were sheltering in Lundy Roads. When the weather improved, two torpedo warheads were fastened to the stern, the result of which has not been recorded, but very soon after, on November 22nd, the "Doris" and "Vixen" left for Plymouth and the Admiralty put out a statement that no further experiments would be made on the "Montagu".

Severe gales in December 1906 did a lot of damage to the wreck, which settled considerably during this time. The 'tween deck stanchions were forced through the main deck, and heavy ground swell helped to wash adrift many of the battleship's bottom plates. Water was now pouring through the vessel at every tide, and in a rough sea she was completely buried in the waves.

On January 28th, 1907, the Admiralty announced their intention of putting the "Montagu" up for auction, and Lundy was visited by representatives of ship-breaking firms from all over England, eventually being purchased for £4,250, with possible risk of the ship disappearing bodily in a gale. In fact, by the time the purchase was effected, the ground sea had played havoc with the hull, armoured plates had parted in places under the severe strain, and a portion of the bridge was washed away. However, the speculation proved profitable to the purchasers—romantically described by contemporary papers as a "Syndicate of South Wales Adventurers".

A large number of men were employed on this phase of salvage operations. Like most of their predecessors they were housed in the Marisco Castle cottages, and an aerial footway over 500 feet long was constructed from the top of the cliffs to the roof of the charthouse on the "Montagu". Also a path was made down the cliff sidings, on the lower part of which granite slabs were set in to form steps, and then footholds cut into the rock itself. Iron handrails were provided for additional safety on the more hazardous sections of the descent. This approach, known as "Montagu Steps", is still visible from the cliffs above, but has become very dangerous with the passing years.

Work was only possible for a short while at low tide and speed was essential. Every day, weather permitting, lighters were brought alongside the wreck and, piece by piece, huge sections of armour plating were removed and brought ashore. A vast quantity of copper and brass was also salvaged. The company continued blasting and carrying away metal and parts of machinery from the engine room well into the Autumn; the bulk of this was taken to Ilfracombe and disposed of.

A dramatic incident took place during these operations. The chain of a derrick used on board the wreck became jammed, and one of the men climbed up the chain to clear it. By some mischance, the block and chain became detached and fell to the deck, leaving the man hanging by his hands to the end of the derrick 40ft. above the jagged iron plates of the broken deck. Before help could reach him he was forced to let go but, in falling, fortunately deviated slightly to one side, escaping the ironwork and certain death by falling through a hole in the upper deck. The force of his fall broken, he miraculously escaped with a few bruises and temporary shock.

Towards the end of October, heavy ground seas, among the most severe ever experienced on Lundy, battered the wreck continuously and she settled down forward. A large quantity of valuable diving gear was washed overboard and lost, and further salvage work abandoned. Half the vessel, which formerly listed to starboard, now inclined towards the port side—this meant that the "Montagu" had practically broken her back; fulfilling the pessimistic predictions in the contemporary local press during June, 1906: "The prevalent opinion amongst Bristol Channel mariners is that the ship must inevitably break up . . . the battleship is practically doomed   if the "Montagu" can be refloated it will be little short of a miracle."

The "Montagu' was soon to be engulfed by the ocean upon which she might have won great battle honours at Jutland or Zeebrugge—perhaps witnessing the final surrender of the German fleet at Scapa Flow. Instead she was destined to become a monument to the tremendous power and force of the sea surrounding the shores of Lundy. Before the last war it used to be possible, during calm weather, to make out her rusty plates resting on the sea bed, but all that now remains as a positive reminder are the few surviving steps of the cliff path leading down to the scene of one of our great peacetime Naval disasters.

However, in recent years the Bristol Channel Divers Ltd., present owners of the salvage right on the "Montagu", have raised a number of interesting and unique items which form part of a collection of underwater discoveries in store on the island, and, hopefully, it may be possible to place these on view to the public at some future date.

H M S Montagu

M. o. D.

M. o. D.

National Maritime Museum, London.

National Maritime Museum, London.

F. E. Gibson, Scilly Isles.

33

"The Fog had become very thick, but after weighing the matter in my mind I decided to continue towards Lundy, hoping that the explosive fog signal would give me due warning of my approach." Capt Adair's defence. *(Court Martial, The Times, Monday, August 20th, 1906.)*

"Charles W. Hugh, signalman of the middle-watch on the fore-bridge, said that he heard sound signals about 1.40 a.m. four times right ahead. He thought that they were from a steamship. He could not see beyond the bows of the ship." *(Court Martial, The Times, Friday, August 17th, 1906.)*

"Captain Adair.—Is the South Light explosive fog-signal audible to the westward?—No, it is well-known at Lundy that there is an area of silence to the westward, and although close to the island the fog-signal is inaudible."   *(Court Martial, The Times, Tuesday, August 21st, 1906.)*

H.M.S. MONTAGU ASHORE AT LUNDY.   PUBLISHED BY TWISS BROS., ARCADE, ILFRACOMBE.

H.M.S. MONTAGU ASHORE AT LUNDY
PUBLISHED BY TWISS BROS., ARCADE, ILFRACOMBE. N.B.

H.M.S. "Montagu" on the rocks at Lundy Island, May, 1906.

"The engines worked so erratically as to cause him to come to the conclusion that the starboard propeller had either broken off or that the shaft was fractured. He had just come away from the voice pipe when he received a message from the port engine-room to say that the port propeller had gone too." Artificer-Engineer Marchant's evidence.

(Court Martial, The Times, Friday, August 17th, 1906.)

This post card, postmarked Pembroke Dock, July 30th, 1906, records that "this is the 'Montagu' with her funnels off".

HMS MONTAGU
ashore at
Lundy

"The first thing reported was that the water was leaking into the starboard side bunker of No. 1 boiler-room. He immediately proceeded there, and found that a seam was leaking about 18″ long. He had the plates removed. He examined the bilge and found the door leaking. They tried to tighten it but could not succeed. They then tried to shore it down. While they were doing this work there was a rush of water, evidently from a large hole." Engineer-Commander Baker's evidence. *(Court Martial, The Times, Friday, August 17th, 1906.)*

S.S. Ranger at work pumping. *c* 1902.

S.S. Ranger. 12 inch "full bore".

The 12″ guns on the Quarter Deck.

The last 12″ gun being removed, September 30th, 1906. Figure to the left of the picture is probably Capt Young.

Roger E. Allen.

44

The comment on the back of this post card reads "Don't you think it a great pity for so splendid a ship to be lost".

Salving the 12" guns.

Salving one of the four 12" breech guns which measured 40 feet in length and weighed 48 tons.

Removal of one of the four 12″ guns into a lighter waiting alongside.

H.M.S. MONTAGU, WRECKED AT LUNDY
SALVING THE BIG GUNS.
BROS., ARCADE, ILFRACOMBE   No 48

Work in progress de-coaling the coal bunkers of H.M.S. Montagu. Duncan class battleships had a capacity which varied between 900 and 2240 tons of fuel.

Roger E. Allen.

PUBLISHED BY TYBBS BROS., ARCADE ILFRACOMBE.

DIVER AT WORK ON H. M. S. MONTAGU

A rare postcard of a diver at work on H.M.S. Montagu.

Note the aerial footway over 500 yards long stretching from the top of the cliffs to the roof of the charthouse.

F. E. Gibson, Scilly Isles.

A view showing the effects of salvage work, c 1907.

52

A splendid view of the aerial footway. A good head for heights must have been needed to negotiate it.

F. E. Gibson, Scilly Isles.

Work in progress on Nansen's *Fram*

6303. H.M.S. Montague Landing, Lundy, in rough weather.

"Montagu" landing in rough weather. Only the railings remain in this photo, the wreck being submerged beneath an angry sea.

The Automatic Photo Printing Co. Ltd.

The floating dock with which it was hoped to extricate the "Montagu" from her watery grave, but never used.

Ilfracombe Museum.

This rare post card shows various items removed from H.M.S. Montagu and bears the cryptic legend "I aint no sailor bold, and never been upon the sea".

Crest of H.M.S. Montagu.

The two post cards shown here are of H.M.S. Duncan, which tried unsuccessfully to assist the stranded "Montagu" on Lundy, herself became grounded and the resultant damage to her taking 72 days to repair, after which she joined the Atlantic Fleet in February, 1907.

Further Reading

Farr, Graham E. Wreck And Rescue In The Bristol Channel. D. Bradford Barton, 1966.

Larn, Richard. Devon Shipwrecks. David & Charles, 1974.

Langham, A. & M. Lundy. David & Charles, 1970.

Langham, Myrtle. A Lundy Album. Published privately, 1980.

Loyd, L. R. W. Lundy: Its History & Natural History. Longmans, Green & Co., 1925.

Bouquet, Michael. A Watery Grave on Lundy's Rocks. Country Life, October 1st, 1964.

The Times 1906

Tuesday May 29th, Thursday May 31st, Friday June 1st, Saturday June 2nd, Monday June 4th, Tuesday June 5th, Wednesday June 6th, Thursday June 7th, Friday June 8th, Saturday June 16th, Tuesday June 19th, Monday June 25th, Tuesday June 26th, Saturday June 30th, Tuesday July 3rd, Saturday July 7th, Monday July 9th, Friday July 20th, Monday July 23rd, Tuesday July 24th, Friday July 27th, Saturday July 28th, Wednesday August 1st, Thursday August 2nd, Monday August 6th, Tuesday August 7th, Saturday August 11th, Monday August 13th, Tuesday August 14th, Friday August 17th, Saturday August 18th, Monday August 20th, Tuesday August 21st, Wednesday August 22nd, Monday August 27th, Monday September 10th, Saturday September 22nd.

MRS. THATCHER'S
GAMBLE

DAVID J. KENNEY

Contents

Acknowledgements

Robert Headland is the Keeper of the Flame for South Georgia's history and its people. Jim Mandelblatt retains more knowledge about diesel submarines than anyone else I know. He can retrieve the little gems about World War II boats that make a narrative. Keith Paul Mills recalled his military feat on South Georgia with accuracy and modesty. Nick Vaux's book, *March on the South Atlantic: 42 Commando Royal Marines in the Falklands War* informs even the least of us how and why Royal Marines win. Guy Sheridan and Chris Nunn were ruthless fact checkers—rather like my parents correcting assignments in Latin grammar. This book would have been an arid and mistake-filled try without their often demotic help. Dr. Max Goepp edited poor logic out of the book with a combination of charity and malice. Captain Horacio Bicain of the Argentinian Navy helped enormously with his honest telling of his ship's cruise and the needless death of crewman Felix Artuso. Secretary of Defense Caspar Weinberger, RIP, was the ghost on my shoulder. If we all fought the good fight as he did the world would be a far better place. Pam Owens has put order into my collection of pictures, charts and maps, designed the covers and put the book together with insight and good humor. Without her I was helpless in these matters. Dr. Amy Davis instructed me in matters that I did not know that I did not know. She edited this book from cover to cover and made the narrative flow where I had inserted words from my own store of trivia. Her unusual patience, learning, and skills, which range all over the scholarly map, beguiled me and have saved the reader from needless head scratching. Without her this book would have been laced with errors and bad rhetoric. And perhaps never finished.

Writing this dramatic sliver of history is like feeding a racehorse. It does all the work; it only needs feed, water, sunshine, and a jockey hanging on for dear life.

David Kenney
Upperville, Virginia
Autumn, 2012

v

Foreword

Margaret Thatcher almost fell in April of 1982. Perhaps that is why the events around South Georgia Island in the spring of that year have been buried and exhumed so often. Professor Lawrence Freedman has written an excellent official history of the entire Falklands War, Nick Vaux's book is the best on the combat, and Robert Headland remains the undisputed master of all things South Georgian. The white paper written at Thatcher's request after the war, however, is a model of smarmy expiation. No help there! Moreover, few egregious lessons spring out of the decayed viscera of a battle that turned out a dud. The ensuing years have fetched up precious few bits of tantalizing gossip. A few sullen cabinet ministers here, some misplaced equipment there made up the rocks on Thatcher's path. The blood that might have flowed and the political earthquakes that might have rent alliances and divided parties did not happen. Finally, I concluded that the most puissant character in the drama was not a human adversary but that malign and hostile chunk of ice and snow called South Georgia Island. But there is drama here, of misguided military adventures that could have brought Thatcher down and of how the sailors, pilots, and junior infantrymen who executed the missions they had been sent to complete managed to overcome the paralytic lethargy of a critical few and so to save the campaign.

This tidy affair birthed other larger events that held or broke a few taller dams of history. In the end, the Argentinian Junta fell, and the world saw its vulgar brutality. Thatcher rescued her future by the thinnest strands of fate to become a major figure in European, if not global, history. This author stands by the notion that broad events cannot occur without a diverse cast of supporting players well lacquered with good luck or ill fortune. Buffoons and heroes, mostly nameless, dispense the lubricant that lets history grind away. Their triumphs and failures pepper *La Longue Dur*ée.

In March and April of 1982, South Georgia hosted a Saturday night pub full of all that. I have spoken with many of the characters who appear in this narrative. In the main they are intelligent, funny, professional, thoughtful, open, and honest. Their stories check out. A few major actors did not speak, and their reluctance to open their careers to an American is understood. It would be better for us all if they had. Those who helped, and there are some very unusual individuals among them, know who they are. The footnotes often tell their side. More than a few Argentines declined to speak on the record, and their accounts are woven into my words without attribution. Yet a few, betrayed by their rulers and defeated by their enemies, have told their tales.

Major J. M. G. Sheridan's brief stopover in South Georgia ended a singular scrap of British and Argentinian history. It should be recalled. It is a good story.

One

"I shall never be easy until I have seen some of these places."

Jane Austin, *Emma*

On his homeward voyage from a trading expedition along the West Coast of South America, Antoine de la Roche, a Huguenot merchant from London, missed his tacking and got blown off course. The year was 1675. He had just rounded Cape Horn, and his immediate goal was Salvador, Brazil, just far enough north to escape the northeasterlies and not so far as to cause a knackered crew to mutiny a battered ship. His goal once in the Atlantic was to set the ship on a base course of approximately three hundred degrees, roughly towards the Argentinian and Brazilian coasts. Contrary to his wishes, his ramshackle ship did not pass through the Le Maire current that ran six knots out of the Magellan Strait in a northeasterly direction ninety degrees or so to the east of his intended course.

That route would have afforded some safety; instead his ship was quickly shunted eastward. Once into the South Atlantic, the prevailing winds, current, and possibly some badly executed tackings by a sickly crew ran the ship east-northeast into the southern fifties, there to carry its unfortunate hostage even further towards northwest Africa. Once there, de la Roche's ship bobbed in the midst of one of nature's geologic and climatological freaks where, despite its tropical track, its ragged sheets and spars still suffered the Antarctic's freezing temperatures and awful storms. The yardmen, almost certainly exhausted by repeated changes and replacements of sail in the strait, had little choice in the matter. Far from hugging the South American coast and its supply of cordage, linen, and timber, de la Roche found himself in the middle of a frozen nowhere whose mysteries included a fabulous ice-covered island. After inspection of his sparkling discovery from afar, he declined to assay his findings on foot and contented himself with only a distant glimpse of the icy freak before heading north for home. Three hundred years later, the same weather that trumped de la Roche also battered the Royal Navy's task force with its cargo of Major J. M. G. Sheridan's Royal Marines on their way to retake this geological oddity.[1]

Comes now Captain Edmond Halley, who closed the same island in 1700 but failed to land owing to fog and icebergs. A prominent astronomer as well as a sailor, he had received command of the ship *Paramour* in order to investigate differences in the earth's magnetism, an understanding of which was critical to accurate navigation.[2] His researches were spectacularly successful, and he was the first to publish isogonic lines on naval charts. Yet curious as he was, Halley's exploratory instinct did not extend to a frozen-footed tramp about the island, and he remained on his bridge—never to be awed by a chain of glittering icy mountains and never to feel the island's cold through his boots.

It is almost certainly true, but not established to a certainty, that the Spanish merchant Captain Gregorio Jerez of the ship *Leon* got blown off course on his way from Callao to Cadiz and saw the same rocks in 1756. He, too, failed to claim his eerie discovery for any sovereign state. The reasons were clear; no ships' records show any desire, commercial or otherwise, to make South Georgia as it then was. Getting there remained an accident of navigational incompetence or foul weather. If compensating sailings were not exactly computed and executed at the east end of the strait, ships were thrust into the South Atlantic well off the Patagonian coast. Once on that base course, there was no easy tacking for Buenos Aires or the Falkland Islands, 800 miles to the northwest. The current carried ships steadily up to and off the Uruguayan coast, where they met the warm, easterly Brazilian current.[3] Such forces of nature were almost undeniable; any challenge to them put exhausted top men and their cranky bottoms at risks that few homesick captains forced on their sullen crews.

Eons earlier, the seismic forces that split South America from Africa had forced layers of material upwards from the earth's crust; a few broke the ocean's surface. One such piece of land is South Georgia, a mountainous mass of 1450 square miles shaped like a banana, running northwest to southeast and half-covered by ice. Captain James Cook's discovery, or rediscovery, of South Georgia thrust the island into international life, not least because his sighting had been freighted with the chicaneries and quibbles that infested court life. On Sunday, January 15, 1775, after a two-and-one-half-year passage, Cook, aboard *Resolution,* saw land, or what he could glimpse of it under its icy coat at S 54°, W 38°. Two days later, on January 17, he made the earliest recorded landing at Possession Bay.

By Friday, January 20, Cook had also sailed around this oddity, ending at the point where he had begun and concluding that his discovery was not part of a continent. "A great fall happened while we were in the Bay," he wrote. "It made a noise like a Cannon. The inner parts of the Country were not less savage and horrible; the Vallies lay buried in everlasting snow. Not a tree or shrub was to be seen. . . . I landed in three different places, displayed our colors and took possession of the Country in his Majestys name under a discharge of small Arms."[4] In fact, after circumnavigating the entire island, reconnoitering ashore at three points, and finding that none of them was connected to Antarctica, Cook named the southern tip *Cape Disappointment*. He admitted chagrin in his journal: "I may now venture to assert that the extensive coast, laid down in Mr. Dalrymple's Chart of the Ocean between Africa and America . . . does not exist."[5] Cook was not pleased. His published account did, however, note the vast numbers of elephant and fur seals on South Georgia. Coincidentally, he also reported that there were markets for seal pelts in China. Merchants in Boston, Salem, New Bedford, and London took the authoritative navigator to heart, and sealers soon started to exploit, indeed overexploit, this novel biological resource.

Then as now, adventurers' fictive goals secured governments' funding as long as the pleaders' rhetoric made diaphanous promises sound halfway reasonable. In search of the fabled Aurora Islands, but not of South Georgia itself, Captain Benjamin Morrell, on the schooner *Wasp,* claimed to have made South Georgia on November 18, 1822. Morrell and the *Wasp* then circumnavigated South Georgia, allegedly in only four days, and saw snow-covered mountains whose sheer often fell into the water. There were low valleys with dense tussock. Morrell did not say where he had learned of the bogus Auroras or of South Georgia or how he knew that de la Roche had discovered that same South Georgia in 1675. Historians since believe Morrell's work to be partly, perhaps wholly, fiction.[6] To be sure, ship chandlers, sail makers, navigators, and merchants had, for centuries before steam, informal intelligence systems, the better for being unwritten, that proved more effective in many cases than complex modern systems of discovery.

Still, it was enough that diminished and sickly crews found themselves unable to fight nature's dangers, the winds, and currents that haphazardly brought ships to South Georgia. It is not known how many skippers declined to note, for fear of embarrassment in the waterfront pubs and jails of England, that they had seen South Georgia due to sloppy navigation or just bad luck. Few set a determined mind to such a bizarre passage. At S 54°55', W 36°38', South Georgia falls victim to some of the world's worst weather. Cook's described its barrenness, as well: "The wild rocks raised their lofty summits till they were lost in the clouds and the valleys laid buried in everlasting snow. Not a tree or shrub was to be seen, no not even big enough to make a toothpick."[7] Thatcher and her circle had never seen a place from which not even a toothpick could be harvested. Major Sheridan and friends had.

Pitiless weather and jagged topography—some mountains exceed five thousand feet—make the island impassable for most of its length to all but the most intrepid. Storms with winds of one hundred miles per hour are common. Violent drafts swoop down from peaks to ground level with little warning and savage one part of the island while leaving others in frigid calm. Icebergs calved from steep cliffs compete, in both size and menace, with their larger cousins floating up from the Antarctic. Because these formations do not always show on radar screens, navigating inshore, especially at night when chunks of ice slink in unnoticed, is a hazardous affair. In the Falklands War, Lieutenant-Commander Horatio Bicain, who commanded the Argentinian submarine *Santa Fe,* and Captain Nicholas Barker, of the British Navy's *Endurance,* used this feature to hide their ships.[8] Wind-borne rubble scours mountainsides. The constant freeze-thaw cycles render this geological debris especially unstable underfoot. Climbers are few. Food crops do not grow. Tussock grass feeds and hides rats and a few thousand reindeer, while seals, penguins, and several dozen species of other birds live off the riches of the sea. The Special Air Service [SAS] patrols that landed in April 1982 had to discover all these oddities anew. For until the late twentieth century, only the ink-stained clerks of Whitehall's lower regions coveted the island, and the name and implicit British ownership stuck. Every kind of man and woman visited the South Atlantic, most on voyages of escape. Exotically rich in rare flora and fauna, South Georgia was a beautiful bolt-hole in which to contemplate one's transgressions in safety.

Yet a vast change in the island's history had begun in 1904, when Norwegians started whaling in the Southern Ocean and established stations on South Georgia. Since that year, the island has had a continuous, although very variable, population. Accompanied by some other enterprising souls, Captain Carl Anton Larsen began hunting the huge mammals and processing their blubber in Grytviken, the island's principal settlement, in 1904.[9] By then the settlement was sufficiently large that a small Norwegian Lutheran church was built. Larsen formally founded the settlement circa 1904, named it, and populated it with a crew of Norwegians who then built crude but effective stations that transformed their oily trophies into hard European and American cash.

A Chilean pastoralist, Richard Lion, tried in 1905 to rent the island for sheep grazing, though no sheep had been seen there before or have been since. His project died a silent bureaucratic death. The island and its waters offered open season for petty malefactors and their often not-so-petty misdemeanors. More than a few outcasts sought refuge from serious crime. Equipment and food vital to lifeboats were stolen or consumed often enough that owners hid these supplies. The island was one of those singular places where, upon encountering another rifle-bearing stranger, it was better not to enquire into his background. Though some hardy souls sought scientific knowledge in this unlikely place, few tried actively to preserve *Pax Britannica* over Britain's frozen properties.[10] Distant kings ruled with light-handed sovereignty.

Later still, the British and then the Japanese brought a spirited rivalry for real financial profit to the awful smells of South Georgia's whaling stations. In 1911, Norwegian sailors felt optimistic enough about their future to bring reindeer from their homeland; their transport ship got battered by seven cows and three bulls thumping the bulkheads in rough seas. But far from home, the workers had familiar meat to eat. During World War II, Captain Victor Marchesi of the Royal Naval Reserve prosecuted Operation Tabarin, which was designed to protect British interests and property from predations by the Axis powers in the deep southern Atlantic. The genesis of this bizarre enterprise is, by design, lost in the Admiralty's danker records, but there remains no doubt that Captain Marchesi was an intrepid man and a first-class bureaucratic operator. The whole enterprise was probably his alone. He and his Hull-built trawler, the Royal Research Ship *William Scoresby,* headquartered inside a dormant volcano on Deception Island, a fair distance from South Georgia. *Scoresby* had a very light caliber gun on her forward deck, and Marchesi, her captain carried a pistol. He established research outposts in remote places and fought no engagements ashore or at sea.[11] He disappeared from history after World War II, but his boat's name lives on to this day as a well-visited hulk.[12] William Scoresby, Sr. was the inventor of the barrel crow's-nest, still the highest lookout station on many ships.

Most of the region's post-World War II history is undramatic. The *Queen of Bermuda*, an armed merchant ship, patrolled Antarctic regions in 1941 and found nothing of hostile intent. Two four-inch guns were deployed on South Georgia ostensibly to thwart German capture Grytviken's safe harbor but were never used in anger. No records show that a qualified crew was equipped and trained to resist whatever seaborne enemy London thought might lay covetous eyes on a wooden church and malodorous pot stills.

By 1960, crowds had come, and their modern methods of capturing whales *en masse* diminished South Georgia's sole economic raison d'être; there were few whales left to kill and little blubber left to be rendered in Grytviken's giant pots. By 1964, the whalers' profits fell to naught, ending an unusual commercial era during which 175,000 whales had been flensed and rendered. The factories began their forlorn turn to rust. A benign if unintended consequence of this sad overexploitation occurred here because killing whales beyond their rates of reproduction caused an overabundance of krill, a nutritional bonanza for South Georgia's seals and penguins, whose numbers soared. By 1965, the whalers, mostly Japanese by then, had left for good. For enough years to become the stuff of sailors' lore, seals, birds, and little else had sustained the whalers who came in search of wealth, endured unforeseen hardships, and left the wiser. Mostly they left some strange-sounding place names, a few shacks, and the occasional scientific outpost.[13]

The British Antarctic Survey [BAS] began basic scientific investigations of the island in 1943 and in time became Britain's corporate keeper of South Georgia's records and memory. After whaling ended, BAS scientists occupied the government's station and began the research that took them out of their warm shacks into some of the most remote and inhospitable places on earth. The odd lost mariner and a few daring travelers hived around Grytviken, Husvik, Leith, and Stromness, all clusters of buildings abandoned by the whalers and nearly derelict, but still the only settlements worth the name. The variations of nature at its hardest shaped the scientists' existence. The Survey's head came to be the island's de facto magistrate, constable, port captain, postmaster, and immigration agent. All in all, South Georgia was not a fortuitous or a likely place to live, let alone to begin or end a war.[14]

NOTES

1- Captain Cook took his own view: "I too doubt if either de le Roche or the ship *Lion* ever saw the Isle of Georgia." James Cook, *The Journals of Captain Cook.* (New York: Penguin Books, 1999), 411.

2- *The Oxford Companion to Ships and The Sea. (*New York: Oxford University Press, 1994), 370.

3- Nathaniel Bowditch, *The American Practical Navigator* (1802; revised, Bethesda, MD: National Imagery and Mapping Agency, 2002), 437.

4- Cook, *Journals,* 409.

5- Cook, *Journals,* 411.

6- Benjamin Morrell, *A Narrative of Four Voyages* (Upper Saddle River, NJ: Gregg Press, 1970, reprint of 1832 original). Morrell (1795-1839?) was born in New York and, after colorful youthful experiences, took command of the sealer, *Wasp,* in 1833. It is certain that he trolled the South Seas in *Wasp* and returned alive. He composed tales that are difficult to disprove, but historians like Simpson-Houseley has accused him of plagiarism, and Sir James Clark-Ross has been unable to find Morrell's New South Greenland at Morrell's position. In conversations with the author, a noted historian of the period called Morrell "a scoundrel" and worse. See *The Oxford Companion to Ships and the Sea*, which lets Morrell off as being "Hyperbolic." Simpson-Housley, Paul (1992). *Antarctica: Exploration, Perception and Metaphor*. New York: Routledge. ISBN 978-0-415-08225-9. Retrieved December 17, 2008.

7- Captain James Cook quoted in Richard Hough, *Captain James Cook: A Biography* (New York: W. W. Norton, 1997), 251.

8- See J. Goebel, *The Struggle For The Falklands Islands* (New Haven: Yale University Press, 1927) for a fine description of early navigation in these waters.

9- Grytviken means *pot harbor* in Norwegian. Old sailors have recalled to the author the town's foul smell.

10-For a down-to-earth description of everyday life on South Georgia, see George Sutton, *Glacier Island* (London: Chattow and Windus, 1957).

11-Obituary, "Captain Victor Marchesi," *Telegra*ph February 13, 2007. In 1943, Lieutenant (soon to be Captain) Victor Marchesi took command of the *William Scoresby,* an unusually fragile craft for such tumultuous waters. His charge was to protect the Falklands from Argentinian incursions and to prevent German submarines from using the Falklands and the South Orkneys. For three years, he scoured the islands in search of others' hostile intent. He found none: "just as well because my one handgun and William Scoresby's puny bow-mounted gun would hardly have put the fear of death into anyone." Marchesi, a fine intelligence officer ahead of his time, unearthed caches left by Argentinian naval ships in order to claim sovereignty and replaced them with two operating post offices, themselves proof of British sovereignty. During the war Marchesi wrote letters, franked by his Falklands' post offices, to countries around the world proclaiming British sovereignty and practical control over the Falklands. In his spare time, Marchesi stood watch on the *Scoresby's* exposed and icy bridge. Marchesi's work went well beyond his remit but was covered by the almost nonexistent terms of Operation Tabarin.

12-Marchesi enjoyed for many years a seaman's delight—great distance from headquarters during a war while staying alive. He trawled some of nature's greatest wonders and got paid for it.

13-During his circumnavigation of the globe, the Russian Otto von Kotzebue, commanding officer of the small Brig *Rurik,* left his name on South Georgia, probably in 1822.

14-Captain Carl Anton Larsen having founded Gryvtken in 1910 led the charge to farm reindeer in 1911. Five more reindeer landed later that year and died in an avalanche, but seven more landed and throve around Husvik. Larsen organized the village's construction with a team of sixty Norwegians, became a citizen of the King and moved his wife, three daughters and two sons to Gryvtken. Over the years many thousands more reindeer than people came to be born. In the summer cull of 2013 twenty-five hundred animals existed in two distinct herds. Their numbers made them a nuisance and Sami herdsmen from Northern Norway culled the entire population. No reindeer herds exist today on South Georgia Island.

Two

Asleep or Not Interested

South Georgia enjoyed "Letters Patent" issued by the Crown in 1908, and the Falklands and South Georgia were, in British eyes, not colonies but dependencies administered from London.[14] Despite this condition, Argentina had laid claim to the Falklands for decades before World War I and diplomatic scribbles sent between London and Buenos Aires fill little-visited crates. In 1971, Great Britain and Argentina agreed to a process whereby any Argentine who wished to visit the Falkland Islands needed to obtain a "White Card" from the Foreign and Commonwealth Office [FCO]. When presented to the Falklands' magistrate, the card allowed its bearer entry under terms to be determined by the magistrate.[15] It remained for Governor Rex Hunt of the Falklands to remind the FCO in 1981 that South Georgia, a dependency of the United Kingdom, not of the Falkland Islands, was specifically exempted from that act.[16]

The events surrounding South Georgia in the spring of 1982 belong to historians and storytellers disposed to accept the close identities of fact and fantasy. It is barely possible to introduce order into what was a very untidy series of political and military events and so to tell a coherent story. Each event was often related to the others in very bizarre ways, and together they built to a final outcome. Each piece of the conflict presented its own difficulties of resolution by either side in the face of governmental bungling, terrible weather, and enervating climate. How, in the end, can one explain the scant attention paid by the British intelligence services to prophesies of war with Argentina?

The first discrete precursor to war could be entitled the "Davidoff Affair," as the British and Argentinian governments contrived to heap more notoriety upon that adventurous gentleman, Constantino Sergio Davidoff, than he either deserved or had bargained for. He claimed to have obtained in December 1981 a contract from Salvesen and Company, the owners of several whaling stations, to dismantle and remove the disused whaling facilities on South Georgia, retrieve the scrap, and resell it on the world market. Whether Davidoff moved in concert with the new Junta's plan to retake the Falklands or simply sniffed around enough to recognize that he might profit under the military protection of General Leopoldo Galtieri, then the president of Argentina, remains a mystery. There is little doubt that the Junta, always open to the grotesque and the seamy, used this spotted trader to gild its territorial claims. Either way, his assertion was a patent subterfuge, as was the pretty tale that he could fetch a higher price on the world scrap market for the kettles, cranes, and so forth than he would pay for their salvage. Davidoff's venture seemed a feckless gambit and appeared even more so as the world's price for scrap fell during 1982.[17] His legal contract included provisions that he and his salvage workers report to the magistrate on the island for permission to enter South Georgia.

On December 18, 1981, Davidoff arrived at Stromness Bay and Leith Harbor aboard the Argentinian naval ship *Bahia Buen Suceso*. Without contacting either Hunt or the local magistrate, he landed at Leith with a party of civilians and Argentinian marines led by Lieutenant-Commander Alfredo Astiz, more commonly known as a war criminal and brutal interrogator. Davidoff scanned his putative prize of rusted metal and then left for Ushuaia at the continent's southern tip, but not before his accompanying party of marines had raised the Argentinian flag and fired shots. Even though *Bahia Buen Suceso* had sailed covertly and kept radio silence, its presence was detected by the British Antarctic Survey. The British Magistrate, Peter Witty, alerted Hunt, who sent a dispatch to the BAS field party's Trefor Edwards and Neil Shaw. They then warned Captain Gaston Briatore, *Bahia Buen Suceso's* skipper, to leave, bag and baggage. He replied that his party had permission from the Foreign and Commonwealth Office to land. Years later, it appears almost certain that Davidoff's violation of British sovereignty was supported, informally but genuinely, by the Junta—or at least the naval part of it.

Suspicions of probable landing irregularities were rekindled when Peter Witty inspected Leith Harbor on December 23, 1981 and found both detritus left scattered by the departed Argentinians and a scrawled note, dated December 20, that claimed Argentinian sovereignty over the island. Years later, at the University of Virginia Miller Center's 2003 roundtable on the war, US Navy Admiral Harry Train recalled: "We picked up on our intelligence, and the British picked it up also, that when the scrap dealer [Constantino] Sergio Davidoff was making plans to go to South Georgia to dismantle old whaling factories, that the Argentines were going to put commandos in that party. . . . The Argentines called it *Operation Alpha*. The British picked up on it. [US Navy Admiral] Tom Hayward probably saw it but didn't recognize it as anything significant."[18]

On the ground, BAS members kept as watchful an eye on Argentinian activities around Leith as any satellite could have done from the heavens. By March 21, Peter Stark, Robert Headland, and Neil Shaw of the BAS were manning an observation post, keeping visual sighting of the Argentinian ship, monitoring radio transmissions, and sending reports to Hunt, who in turn kept the HMS *Endurance,* an ice patrol ship, and London informed. "The observation party was not at Leith but near Jason Peak on the Busen Peninsula, about 7 km away across Stromness Bay. It occupied a high pass with a good view of all the whaling stations in Stromness Bay. Activities at Leith were observed through powerful binoculars and Argentine VHF communications were monitored on 21 March by a Survey officer who understood Spanish."[19] Its crew having re-ordered the ship, avoided heavy weather, and awaited new orders, the *Bahia Buen Suceso* left Leith without fuss on the night March 22. It had unloaded stores for a substantial force's wintertime needs.[20] "The BAS Observation Post reported that six to ten Argentines could be seen on the jetty at Leith after the *Bahia Buen Suceso* had departed and that they had heavy plant, two boats and other heavy gear."[21] The British press did take small notice of this incident on March 23, but no discussion of it occurred in Parliament.

On March 23, the Cabinet, prodded by Admiral Sir John Fieldhouse, ordered *Endurance* and Lieutenant Keith Mills RM to eject the remaining Argentinian marines from South Georgia.[22] Mills and his men were not an established garrison, but a landing party put ashore on the spur of the moment.[23] The reasons for the government's change from utter passivity to something approaching normal military prudence remain obscure. That there were no other minatory measures against what was shaping up as a full-scale Argentinian invasion remains a matter of conjecture, if not of wonder. No one except the BAS party had seemed to care that Davidoff had arrived in an Argentinian naval vessel from which he had not sought or received clearance to land and that, upon his departure, he had left a small party of combat troops.

The details fascinate. Hours after the Argentines had put their heavy gear ashore, the BAS warning message from Grytviken fell on appreciative ears. "I was there with [Admiral RN] John Fieldhouse. . . . we were walking around the lake [in the American Midwest]. . . . This young Navy lieutenant ran up with his hair on fire and handed him a message. Fieldhouse read the message and handed it to me. . . . 'Look at this. . . . The Argentines have landed.'"[24] The report came from the British Antarctic Survey Team in the South Georgia Islands and not from a military or diplomatic source. That single sentence led Fieldhouse to have his lieutenant call for Royal Navy headquarters in London to send *Endurance* and its Royal Marines to seize Davidoff's party on South

Georgia Island. His order was the first "British military response to any Argentinian provocation. Fieldhouse took his decision not knowing that *Operation Alpha*, the full Argentinian occupation of South Georgia, had been cancelled. That was the step that led to the next series of steps, any one of which . . . had it been interrupted, the war wouldn't have occurred."[25]

While Davidoff skulked about Ushuaia, his son remained in Buenos Aires, and rumblings from the Argentinian press and Foreign Office grew more frequent and more ominous. Jesus Iglesias Ruoco, the press leak of the Commander of the Argentinian Navy, Admiral Jorge Anaya, wrote in January that Argentina would surely take military steps if Great Britain refused to surrender sovereignty of the Falklands. This statement, if taken at face value, menaced. Yet in March, the Junta had cancelled the immediate execution of its Plan Alpha to take possession of South Georgia because its naval staff reported that its amphibious force could not mount a successful landing of a distant South Georgian beach and simultaneously perform a landing substantial enough to secure Port Stanley, the capital, on East Falkland. That no such beaches existed on South Georgia seemed not to have entered the Junta's logic when it made its initial plans to seize the island. In London, none outside of Admiral Fieldhouse's immediate circle knew or seemed aware of his decision to send British troops to South Georgia. It was a routine order soon forgotten.[26]

Few if any in Whitehall seemed concerned, let alone worried, about this convergence of events. Peter Lord Carrington, Thatcher's Minister of Foreign Affairs, was concerned about the Junta's military initiatives but could not bring his colleagues in the cabinet to an equal level of interest. "Unless and until the dispute is settled, it will be important to maintain our normal presence in the area at the current level. . . . Any reduction would be interpreted by both islanders and the Argentines as a reduction in our commitment to the Islands and in our willingness to defend them."[27] In Carrington's defense, he had inherited no policy towards the Falklands except the government's history of temporizing on a minor matter which the Junta saw as critical to its electoral promises to regain sovereignty over the Falklands and, more pointedly, to ensure its own survival. Worse, Carrington was hostage to the earlier decisions of Defence Minister John Nott and Thatcher to reduce the size of the navy and to withdraw *Endurance*. The Treasury rebuffed Carrington's request for funds to keep *Endurance* at Port Stanley. Anthony Williams, the British ambassador in Buenos Aires, sustained his masters' composed mood by repeatedly counseling against any public measure or statement that would awaken the not-so-dormant Argentinian outrage about British ownership of the Falklands.[28]

Peter Lord Carrington's role in removing *Endurance* as the station ship at

Port Stanley needs explication. On March 24, 1982, he wrote to John Nott a last plea for support in gaining funds for *Endurance*. He cited "Secret Sources" who had suggested that Argentina might cut services from the Falklands and that the best remedy for so drastic an action would be to have kept *Endurance* on station. Carrington's letter was copied to the Chancellor of the Exchequer and to the Prime Minister.[29] In reply, Leon Brittan of the Treasury claimed that contingency funds from the Exchequer were not available and that such funds as might be needed to keep *Endurance* on station might be better sought from the Navy's contingency funds. Brittan copied his letter to the prime minister and to other members of the Overseas Defence Committee.[30]

Carrington found this reply unsatisfactory and on March 31, 1982 sent instructions from Tel Aviv to the FCO. Carrington wanted the Americans kept out of negotiations lest they propose a negotiated solution politically unacceptable to Britain. He advised against saber rattling and any mention of nuclear submarines heading south. He hope still to find a diplomatic solution, with negotiations continuing at the working level—although he thought a "A Special Envoy" might enter into the mix.[31]

It is difficult to find, in modern times, the head of one of the great offices of state who was so out of touch and, sadly, so wrong. The records show that he was days behind events. Henderson, the British Ambassador to Washington, had sought American help two days prior, and Thatcher had already telephoned President Reagan for assistance. US Navy Secretary John Lehman had diverted two tankers of fuel oil to Ascension Island. After April 1, the SAS was put on standby and later began to receive a spate of unique equipment from their American counterparts that flowed until war's end. Yet no contingency plans were made. Why continue working-level discussions with the Junta when such talks had failed for a decade? Why downplay British naval intentions when threat was all they had at that point (and, ironically, it was the sea services who would ultimately win the fight)? Moreover, in the end, it would be the US Secretary of State, not Carrington, Nott, or Pym who told the Junta face-to-face that the British would fight and win. Carrington had forgotten his lines. The lion's roar that in earlier days would have warned off a tertiary power like Argentina was not vented. The Foreign and Commonwealth Office protested the presence of *Bahia Buen Suceso* and Davidoff in British waters with more of a meow than a bark and was rewarded by the Argentinian Foreign Office's smarmy denial of any knowledge of the incident.

It is not known if the British Joint Intelligence Committee, under the chairmanship of Sir Antony Acland, took notice then of the camel's nose under the tent. If it did, it did not act or sufficiently articulate its cautions to Thatcher's

government and so failed to induce her and her cabinet to act in direct propor-
tion to the Argentinian provocation. Nor was any part of the British military
establishment put on alert. By the evening of April 1, the last of the subordinate
units tipped for possible operations, mainly 40 Commando, a battalion-sized
unit of the Royal Marines 3 Commando Brigade, had been stood down. Julian
Thompson, the commanding officer of 3 Commando Brigade remembered later, "I had therefore gone to bed under the impression that no British reaction
to Argentine military moves was being contemplated and, even if it was, my
Brigade would not be involved."[32] Indeed *Endurance* continued its bureaucratic slide towards final withdrawal and becoming scrap.

For Davidoff, his reconnaissance of Leith validated the private contract
he claimed to have signed. The rusting scrap was indeed there for the taking,
however skimpy his legal rights. For the Junta, Davidoff's scheme and his
presence at Grytviken, which could be seen as having occurred in lieu of the
aborted Project Alpha's full occupation of South Georgia, constituted a military triumph of sorts that compromised the element of surprise for the main
invasion of East Falkland but established *de facto* Argentinian sovereignty
over British territory. The ten or so Argentinian marines left behind after Davidoff's departure guarded his scrap with no British armed presence in sight
and none even over the horizon. The Falklands War did not begin with tanks
rolling across the North European Plain or missiles falling on London; it simply yawned into existence.

The bizarre indicators of impending conflict did not fit the classic mode
of preparations for war as taught at the North Atlantic Treaty Organization
[NATO] or Warsaw Pact's staff colleges. The signals that might have been
noticed had they occurred during the emergence of a great-power conflict involving the possibility of nuclear conflagration flew by unheeded in the great
buildings on the Thames. Yet the day-to-to-day clumsiness and misadventures
of the Argentinian government, described daily on page six of the world's
newspapers, might have been understood to suggest that similar abnormalities
would characterize its military initiatives. All told, any habitué of the Southern
Cone or its waters could sense that the South Atlantic was about to enhance its
reputation as a troubled and unstable area.

British officials at the time offered up contradictory arguments about the
war. The first was that it "was very sudden. No one predicted the Argentine invasion more than a few hours in advance."[33] Yet many British government employees had sensed that Argentinian military action was imminent, as evidence
abounded. Especially notable was Prime Minister Thatcher's meeting with the
Argentinian Minister of the Economy, Martinez de Hoz, on June 5, 1980 in her

room at the House of Commons. It must be assumed that de Hoz, an Etonian, spoke perfect English. Miscomprehension of the exchange by either party was unlikely. This meeting was not mentioned in either the *Falkland Islands Review* (the commonly labeled *Franks Report*) or the *Official History of the Falklands War* by Sir Lawrence Freedman.[34] Thatcher received a gift from de Hoz and wrote the usual note in return. As described in the Thatcher Archives, that note states only that trade matters were discussed and that Thatcher scrutinized the letter carefully. Only Thatcher, Nicholas Ridley (the Foreign Office secretary for the Falklands), and de Hoz were mentioned as having been present. During the same visit to London, de Hoz also met, either individually or jointly, with Lord Carrington, Chancellor of the Exchequer Geoffrey Howe, and Defence Secretary John Nott. The subject of these discussions has not been disclosed. Shortly afterwards, Ridley sent Ian Gow, Thatcher's secretary, a request to see Thatcher about the Falklands, saying "I know that the Prime Minister is very concerned about the whole subject."[35] It is hard to argue that war came out of the blue given that Thatcher had been briefed before Ridley's failed mission to Port Stanley of April 1980, when he tried to negotiate a transfer of sovereignty of the islands to Argentina and a leaseback to the Falklanders.[36] On March 3, 1982, Thatcher saw a telegram from the British ambassador in Buenos Aires that reported indications of a military move against the Falklands. Thatcher penciled in: "We must make some contingency plans."[37] None were made. Moreover, the Latin America Current Intelligence Group, which met eighteen times between 1981 and March 1982, failed to mention the Falklands in any of those meetings.[38] The voices of Captain Nick Barker of the *Endurance* and Colonel Steven Love, the British military attaché in Buenos Aires, both raised in warning, were never heard.

The other claim was that "we have been preparing for this for a long time."[39] Perhaps Nott recalled menacing language from his chat with de Hoz; if so, the bad omens never reached the official record. Finally, the Junta made good on old threats that few had believed would come to fruition. It is clear that Nicholas Ridley received permission from the Defence and Overseas Policy Committee for his attempted solution of transfer and leaseback, but when he visited the island, both he and his proposals were loudly refused. After his return to London, his already wounded proposal to reach agreement died a dramatic and noisy death in the House of Commons, which showed no sympathy for any agreement that would peck away at the islanders' control of their own affairs. In fact, neither claim is correct even in part. The Franks Report, commissioned by Margaret Thatcher after the war, contained enough inculpatory evidence to indict and convict Lord Carrington's Foreign Office of reckless neglect, but the silken volte-face at the document's end exonerated all who had ever heard the name Galtieri.

On December 15, 1981, a new regime took charge of Argentina. Although Galtieri was its nominal head, its intellectual force came from Anaya, a man of mixed Spanish and Indian heritage and passionate anti-British beliefs. The regime's goal was the preservation of the Junta's power by any means in order to fulfill an ill-defined if bloody national purpose. In the clear light of reason and practicality, their options were few. Within hours of its election, the Junta had turned to a time-honored choice: war with a despised foreign power—a fight on behalf of a unifying issue that would galvanize the electorate in favor of Galtieri long enough for him to resolve the economic and social horrors that were tearing Argentinian society apart. On the very evening of December 15, after his election had been assured, Galtieri, at Anaya's insistence, ordered the establishment of a five-man cell in Buenos Aires's Libertad Building to plan the seizure of the Falkland Islands. The planning was complete on February 23, although no certain date was set for the invasion.

Argentina did not signal its immediate intent with a dropped handkerchief, nor did Great Britain's foreign affairs community sense that military rather than diplomatic initiatives impended. US Ambassador Harry Shlaudeman lamented years later that: "I have spent a great deal of time beating myself up for not having foreseen this crazy endeavor."[40] In 1982, the foreign offices of both countries had no inkling of likely bloodshed, despite the many ambassadors, attaches, and delegations they exchanged. By the end of the affair, Argentina and Great Britain had finally found true intimacy, but only in war. Each had lived in black holes of ignorance about the other, and those were separated by a high wall of inertia. Even after the war began, neither had a firm idea of how the other would proceed.

There was only a barely remembered but telling precedent for the belligerencies. Late in 1976, approximately fifty Argentinian technicians, probably marines, had established a station on South Thule, an uninhabited British possession in the Southern Ocean. A British research ship, the *Bransfield*, reported the island's new inhabitants to the FCO, whose minister, Dr. David Owen, decided to do nothing for fear of disturbing relationships between the two countries. The Argentines would remain on South Thule, in fact, until after they were evicted from South Georgia in 1982. Then the British forced them out. Into this petri dish of innocence, non-commissioned and middle-ranking officers (the latter including Sheridan, Mills, and Captain Christopher Nunn) were ordered to jump. Brigadier Julian Thompson, their military boss, had spent his professional life preparing his commandoes to resist a Warsaw Pact invasion across the plains and snowcaps of northern Europe rather than invading the frozen unpleasantness of fifty-nine degrees south latitude. The laudable task they had been trained for was now to be put aside in favor of a wretched job in a wretched place to fulfill a nebulous plan with scanty resources, one that could topple Thatcher and finish Britain as a great power if it did not succeed.

What follows is a partial list of indications in the winter of 1982 that war menaced at the tip of the southern hemisphere. Each apart from the others meant little. But their occurring over so short a time augured almost certain hostilities to even the drabbest mind.

1. In December 1981, a Soviet intelligence officer who spoke English and Spanish arrived at the Soviet Antarctic base.[41]
2. On December 20, Argentinian forces, probably both civilians and marines, made a clandestine landing on Leith.
3. On January 22, 1982, Argentinian Captain Russo told British Captain Nick Barker that Argentina would initiate war with Great Britain and that Admiral Anaya had ordered him not to fraternize with the British.
4. On January 24, *La Prensa*, the Buenos Aires newspaper that served as the outlet for the Junta and Anaya's leak, published hypothetical plans for an invasion of the Falklands.
5. Robert Headland of the BAS noted to South Georgia's magistrate that the Argentinian ship *Caiman* had radioed Buenos Aires as it inspected Leith Harbor.
6. In February, Colonel Steven Love, the British military attaché in Buenos Aires, visited the Falklands at his own expense. He reported back in great detail and concluded that war with Argentina was almost certain. His report was not read beyond the lower levels of the British Intelligence service.
7. In March 1982, just prior to the Argentinian invasion, crew from the *Bahia Buen Suceso* looted the BAS house in Leith and posted signs that said in English and Spanish: "Entry Prohibited." Shots were fired.[42]
8. On March 11, an Argentinian C-130 plane reconnoitered South Georgia. This was the third such flight that year.
9. On March 19, Trefor Edwards and Neil Shaw of BAS found *Bahia Buen Suceso* at Leith. Its commanding officer claimed that permission to land had been granted by the British Foreign and Commonwealth Office. An incident report was filed with *Endurance*, which sent it to London.
10. On March 18, Captain Cesar Trombetta, the commanding officer of the Argentinian Navy's Antarctic squadron, refused to meet Captain Nick

Barker, the commanding officer of *Endurance*, an unusual violation of naval etiquette.

11 On March 22, Peter Stark of the BAS reported an Argentinian crane unloading cargo onto the jetty at Leith.

12. On March 25, *Bahia Paraiso* arrived at Leith and unloaded Argentinian Special Forces and heavy cargo.

13. On March 29, the Russian oceangoing tug *Storki*, operating far from its normal Antarctic haunts, prowled South Georgian waters and invited the Royal Marines aboard.

14. On March 31, the Argentinian warship *Guerrico* joined *Bahia Paraiso* in Leith Harbor.

15. Late in March, the BBC reported five Argentinian surface warships headed for South Georgia.

16. Also that winter, the voices of Argentinian academic and political circles weighed in. As summer turned to winter, the declamations of academic and political voices that had long nurtured the belief that the Southern Cone nations of Argentina, Brazil, and Chile belonged to those nations alone crescendoed into full-throated roars. They wanted those nations stripped of any hegemonic influences from the outside, especially from northern English-speaking cultures. The published articles of Jesus Iglesias Ruoco, now clearly Admiral Anaya's public voice, became increasingly inflammatory and predictive of war.

17. The French yacht *Cinq Gars Pour* sailed, in disregard of the Magistrate's orders, to Stromness Bay, where she met and assisted the six Argentines already there.

For a nation that had compensated over the centuries for its small size and paucity of natural resources with astutely collected and well-employed intelligence, the British Secret Intelligence Service (SIS) and its customers displayed an almost catastrophic lack of prudent and timely judgments about this new threat. Even noticing a few warning signs would have suggested the swift and deliberate dispatch of a nuclear submarine to the Falklands in order to warn Vice Admiral Juan José Lombardo that his fleet would be sunk if it menaced the islands. Until the British marines landed on East Falkland, British commanders had no grip on the entire affair. "On our way South Admiral Woodward flew around the fleet giving his pep talk and asking if there were any questions. On HMS *Glasgow* the question was put to him as to what we might be up against. To this he replied that the army was mostly conscripts and probably demoralized, and that the Navy probably wouldn't put to sea and as for their Air Force, well, they did have a couple of missiles but mostly 'iron bombs' not much threat there!"[43] Few assessments of opponents' capabilities in modern times have been less accurate.[44]

Neither did American sources predict the war. It must be remembered that the Falklands were not labeled by the US State Department as a British and, therefore, an American vital interest. Nor were they mentioned in the transition papers compiled for President Ronald Reagan before he took office. In fact, the British government had never declared the Falklands to the US as being of any interest to it. None of that really mattered. Any kind of conciliation between Argentina and the UK foundered on the belief of the Kelpers [the Falklanders] in self-determination, on the British government's clear inability to defend the islands, and on Anaya's blind enthusiasm for an adventurist foreign policy. The confluence of these factors in spring 1982 assured a military confrontation. The US was so blind to the area, however, that Defense Secretary Caspar Weinberger later lamented, "We had to turn the satellites" [to gather data on the Argentinian invasion of East Falkland].[45] Others did find interest in these frigid goings-on, however. Beginning on April 2, the day that the Argentinians seized the Falklands, the Soviet Union orbited a record number of reconnaissance and strategic early warning satellites. At least eight of the strategic warning satellites were put up through early June.

Nonetheless, had the American intelligence services surmised Argentinian intentions, the US would almost certainly have informed its British partners, for the establishment of global stability, not to say comity, had come since the onset of the Cold War to be an overriding bilateral goal. He or she who winkled out perfidious designs on the other would receive vendible medals and green-eyed praise, or so the thought went. Yet when the time came, the opposite happened. In the winter of 1982, Colonel Steven Love, Britain's military attaché in Buenos Ares, sent to his bosses the finely researched and prescient claim mentioned above concerning the likelihood of an Argentinian invasion. That report, by accident or design, got him and his analysis buried. Yet the depth of his foresight became clearer as April 1 approached, although it still evoked a dead silence from Whitehall.

One slight to British sovereignty over South Georgia's ownership would by itself not have caused alarm. Together they shouted that some kind of Argentinian military action lay in the offing. It is useful to note here the enormous part played by the British Antarctic Survey before, during, and after the conflict. The BAS occupied five posts for scientific investigation and logistical support. They knew the mountains and the four named abandoned whaling stations of Leith, Grytviken, Stromness, and Husvik. These very practical scientists had all along sensed that trouble lay in the offing, and they had set out at various places caches of food needed for their survival. This close-knit and very competent band had, without prodding from the government or anyone else, prepared for disaster. In the large outflow of literature that followed the war, the BAS contribution to the conflict has not gotten its due.

Far to the north of those BAS practical measures, different threads of American concern and foreknowledge were emerging from different sides of the US government. As Train noted later, "The British picked up on it, we picked up on it. [US Admiral] Tom Hayward [probably saw it but didn't recognize it as anything significant." And then, too, another layer of confusion emerged since "there were no satellite photographs to support those nugatory concerns [voiced by BAS staff, Love, and from Barker to the Pentagon]." Years later, it still rankled Hayward that the US Mission in Buenos Aires had failed to predict the war. "I think it was an enormous intelligence failure. All the military people we had, my God. We had a full milgroup there plus the attaches, and never had the slightest indication that any such thing was in the works." Admiral Harry Train was also irked: "they offloaded my [US Navy] exchange officer who was on the *Belgrano* [an Argentinian light cruiser], put him on the pier. He went home and never reported it." Both human and technical intelligence failed at the same time. When at last the US and UK intelligence apparatuses delivered useable intelligence to their masters in early April, the US government began to spew aid and never stopped.

There were emotional responses too. The suddenness of the war, amplified by the fog of Argentinian military incompetence, induced a kind of horror in foreign observers. UN Ambassador Jeane Kirkpatrick summed up her colleagues' reactions at the UN, "Every conversation I had with [the Argentinian diplomats] confirmed my sense that they really didn't know what they were doing . . . they had no notion of what the world they were getting into was like. I tried to persuade them that they were making a terrible mistake."[46]

An agreed and immediate response to Argentinian military action was nonexistent, because there had been no Anglo-American policy for the Falklands. Yet there had been an extraordinarily prescient essay written a few years before Port Stanley's fall. Upon retiring from the British Foreign Service in 1978 (although Thatcher would later recall him to service as ambassador to the United States), Sir Nicholas Henderson had written to the FCO in his farewell essay: "At the present time, although we still retain certain extra-European responsibilities, e.g., in Rhodesia and Cyprus, we are unable to influence events in the way we want because we do not have the power or will to do so. It is true that we may have a special relationship with America, and based as this is upon certain shared traditions and responsibilities, it will continue."[47] Henderson's Solomonic remark stated the obvious. The Falklands were a dim shadow on everyone's radar, but whatever nastiness befell the UK, the United States would probably help out.

In the end, other than the wailing of the Buenos Aires press and ineffective grunts from the bowels of the British intelligence services, few people in either Britain or Argentina had heard or knew much about the Falklands. Centuries after being claimed for the Crown, frozen fingers had scrawled, on an uncertain date, a mute notice of British sovereignty that stood at Leith Harbor: "British Antarctic Survey, Leith Harbor Depot. Unauthorized entry prohibited." The last line was repeated in Spanish, Russian, Polish, and French.

In the torpid negotiations with Argentina over the sovereignty of the Falklands, Margaret Thatcher had put the wishes of the Falkland islanders first; that is, they would remain British for as long as they wanted. Thatcher's *sotto voce* stance was correct morally and legally. Nonetheless, her decision, if that is what it was, created a trap by making the prewar negotiations a three-cornered affair in which 1,800 Kelpers held veto power over their principals' decisions. Thatcher's midnight gloss was a distant goat's bell in the night in comparison to the Falklanders' noisome lobby in Parliament. Moreover, the lobby's well-articulated positions had military implications that she either did not consider or chose to ignore. In fact, the prime minister and her Secretary of Defence had not provided for the islands' protection should Argentina stop talking and invade. Repossession of the islands, if conquered by force, was believed by her military to be impossible and indeed, no signal had been given to the Argentines that a tripwire was in place that, once broken, would set off an immediate military reprisal. In a masterstroke of poor timing, the opposite occurred when John Nott's Ministry of Defence declined to fund the overhaul and continued stationing the *Endurance* in the South Atlantic. Nott's refusal came about from a curious defect in British procedures for funding defense. In the US and in the USSR, monies for ballistic missiles were debated, appropriated, and spent separately from the Army, Navy, and Air Force budgets. In contrast, the British Ministry of Defence considered British ballistic missile submarines an integral component of the Royal Navy's budget, even though they operated under a distinct and separate command structure. Their huge operating and construction expenditures stripped other parts of the Royal Navy of appropriations sufficient to support its other missions, such as keeping the English Channel and the North Atlantic open in time of war.

When soon after her election Thatcher gave Nott permission to cut the military budget, conventional forces bore the brunt, and *Endurance* was set to be stricken from the Navy's list. The argument was put: "Shall we have a frigate to help keep open the North Atlantic sea lanes or shall we keep that antiquated, hideous looking non-combatant in the South Atlantic?" Robbing Peter to pay Paul was not an unheard of bureaucratic move, but it invited disaster as long as the Falklands remained British soil that had to be defended. By 1982, Nelson's descendants sailed on the thin skim of a hobo's stew. Even worse, a calamitous rift opened between the Foreign and Commonwealth Office and the Ministry of Defence. The FCO, then led by Peter Lord Carrington, failed to muster the depth of support from the civil service that might have overcome the budgeters' misplaced zealotry to scrap *Endurance*. Then, too, there was the personal side of the politics of the Defence Ministry. During the negotiations over the defense budget, Thatcher refused to see Sir Henry Leach, the head of the Royal Navy, who accused the prime minister of prejudicing Britain's national security. Nott was put off by what he thought were intellectually unsatisfying encounters with Vice Admiral Staveley, his naval briefer, and said, "I liked him as a person . . . but I quickly lost respect for his intelligence, as I received one inadequate briefing after another. I was asked to accept ideas which even a layman like myself could see were pure nonsense."[48]

NOTES

14-See Henry Campbell Black, *Black's Law Dictionary*, edited by Bryan A. Garner, 8th ed. (St. Paul, MN: Thomson/West, 2004), 925.

15-Anglo-Argentine Communications Agreement 1971. See also *Falkland Islands Review: Report of a Committee of Privy Counsellors* [Franks Report] (London: HMSO, 1983), paragraph 26.

16-Franks Report, paragraph 57.

17-During the war Captain Paul Badcock, the Royal Navy Fleet Marine Engineer, used scrap that remained, steel plates from the stills, to repair battle damage to Royal Navy ships.

18-Admiral Harry Train in Ronald Reagan Oral History Project, "The Falklands Roundtable," Miller Center of Public Affairs, University of Virginia, May 15-16, 2003. http://web1.millercenter.org/poh/falklands/transcripts/falklands_2003_0515.pdf.

19-Robert Headland letter to the editor, *Times* (London), April 5,1985.

20-BAS Chronology, Rev. January 7, 1985. In the author's possession. This document is the collective effort of most of the BAS personnel on South Georgia during its occupation and recapture.

21-Robert Headland letter to *Times* (London), October 22, 1982. Unpublished. In the author's possession.

22-Franks Report, para 179.

23-Mills was technically a department head on *Endurance.*

24-Admiral Train, "Falklands Roundtable," 16.

25-Admiral Train, "Falklands Roundtable," 16.

26-Thatcher told US Secretary of Defense Weinberger that "all the military people in Great Britain, all of her professional military leaders told her that the military attempt could not succeed." Caspar Weinberger in Ronald Reagan Oral History Project, "The Falklands Roundtable," Miller Center of Public Affairs, University of Virginia, May 15-16, 2003, p. 7.

27-Memorandum, "Defence Programme," FCS/81/70, June 5, 1981,

http://www.margaretthatcher.org/
document/867ab473a1e542a4b51218d34228ed6e.pdf

28-Franks Report, seriatim.

29-FCS 82/55.

30-Letter, Brittan to Carrington, March 29, 1982. Received. April 1, 1982.

31-FCO 311240Z, March 1982.

32-Julian Thompson, *No Picnic: 3 Commando Brigade in the South Atlantic, 1982* (London: Leo Cooper, 1985), 3. Thompson commanded 3 Commando Brigade Royal Marines that conquered the Falklands.

33-Margaret Thatcher, *The Downing Street Years* (New York: HarperCollins, 1993), 173.

34-Franks Report and Sir Lawrence Freedman, *The Official History of the Falklands Campaign*, 2 vols. (New York: Taylor & Francis, 2005).

35-Letter, Nicholas Ridley to Ian Gow, June 11, 1980, http://www.margaretthatcher.org/document/79622496734E46649EFCEB9848CF75EC.pdf

36-Arthur L. Gavshon and Desmond Rice, *The Sinking of the Belgrano* (London: Secker & Warburg, 1984), 27.

37-Hugo Young, *The Iron Lady: A Biography of Margaret Thatcher* (New York: Farrar Strauss Giroux, 1989), 263.

38-Young, *Iron Lady*, 262.

39-Minister of Defence John Nott, Official Report, April 2, 1982, column 667.

40-Harry Shlaudeman in Ronald Reagan Oral History Project, "The Falklands Roundtable," Miller Center of Public Affairs, University of Virginia, May 15-16, 2003. http://web1.millercenter.org/poh/falklands/transcripts/falklands_2003_0515.pdf.

41-Nicholas Barker, *Beyond Endurance: An Epic of Whitehall and the South Atlantic* (London: Pen and Sword, 1996), 111.

42-Robert Headland letter to South Georgia magistrate, March 23, 1982. In the author's possession.

43-Rear Admiral Woodward speaking to crew of Glasgow, "HMS *Glasgow* – May 12th 1982," Royal Naval Association (RNA) Number 10 Area, http://www.rna-10-area. co.uk/glasgow.html

44-This captures the assessment of one member of the Glasgow crew. "HMS *Glasgow* – May 12th 1982."

45-Weinberger, "Falklands Roundtable," 17.

46-Jeane Kirkpatrick in Ronald Reagan Oral History Project, "The Falklands Roundtable," Miller Center of Public Affairs, University of Virginia, May 15-16, 2003. http://web1.millercenter.org/poh/falklands/transcripts/falklands_2003_0515.pdf.

47-"Britain's Decline: Its Causes and Consequences," *Economist*, June 2, 1979. This dispatch was an FCO document that fell into the *Economist's* hands and was published over the FCO's objection.

48-Nott won the budget battle, whose consequences Thatcher had failed to foresee. It is fair to say that in return, the navy and its senior officers loathed Nott. When war came Nott put Admiral Fieldhouse as CINC, Rear Admiral Woodward as Battle Force commander, Captain Young as Commander of the South Georgia task force, and Major Sheridan as the Land Force Commander.

Three

The Fog of War

Too often, failed intelligence induces military action that could have been avoided. On March 22, 1982, Captain Nick Barker was roused from his bunk on *Endurance* with the news that Argentinian marines and substantial supplies had landed at Leith. He prepared forthwith his two helicopters and Lieutenant Keith Mills's marines to land and to retake Leith from its Argentinian occupiers. Mills was that rare and fortunate junior officer of the Sea Services who was assigned to a watery posting thousands of miles from his headquarters. He would subsequently be appointed the Officer in Charge, Royal Marines [OCRM] on board *Endurance* in June 1982, a position that necessitated considerable time on that ship. His Royal Navy boss aboard *Endurance*, Barker, was a cheerful, experienced, and hospitable skipper. Although Mills was a department head on board, he was as close to being his own boss as ever happens in military service. Mills and his men fell easily into the ship's routine and became functioning members of the crew. One marine served as the ship's butcher and another as a ship's cook. Mills could also glimpse firsthand the machinations of both his own and the Argentinian foreign offices.

Despite support for Fieldhouse's initiative to remove Davidoff, but all too much all of a piece with the Foreign Office's cumbersome handling of the entire Falklands' affair, Barker's prompt and suitable military response achieved nothing when a signal from the Defence Ministry "scuttled the anticipated pleasure of throwing the Argentines off the island."[49] The message to Barker, which was sent at almost the same time as the Fieldhouse order, emended the original directive with a simple: "*Endurance* should not, repeat not, enter nor [sic] conduct any naval operation in the vicinity of Leith Harbor."[50] Still, as Mills landed, he continued to plan for the ejection of a small number of Argentinians illegally remaining at Leith. Admiral Fieldhouse's original order to eject the occupiers, albeit somewhat modified, was still in play, and it remained Mills's governing document when *Endurance*'s helicopters ferried the twenty-two marines ashore on the last day of March and first of April. Simultaneously, Military Operations Command at Northwood came to know, but Mills was not told, that an Argentinian task force of five ships, later shrunk to three, had sailed for South Georgia with a company-sized force of Argentinian marines who were to seize and hold the island. By the time Mills landed, the Argentinian patrol ship *Guerrico* and transport *Bahia Paraiso* had anchored in Leith Harbor.[51] To Mills's advantage, *Guerrico's* 100mm gun was the only weapon that posed a standoff threat to the British marines.

Mills's marines bore weapons more suitable for Admiral Fieldhouse's intended police action than for a proper war. All carried the 7.62 SLR, a serviceable, if not universally favored, rifle. They carried a modest suite of one medium and two light machine guns, one 84mm anti-tank launcher with twelve rounds, and twenty 66mm anti-tank launchers. They had no crew-served weapons. Among them, the men stocked twenty thousand rounds of ammunition and enough explosives to mine jetties, structures, and possible enemy landing sites. But immediately upon landing at Grytviken, Mills's tactical situation deteriorated markedly when *Endurance* was sent north to Stanley. With it went the helicopters that were to have provided him with reconnaissance both of Leith and of seaborne threats to his tiny force. Captain Nick Barker's moral force sailed away, too. That deficiency, along with his belief that he might be forced to act in self-defense against the Argentinian troops at Leith, quickly centered Mills's thoughts. He was alone in a geographical and military void.

Just before landing, he had received orders that seemed strange to him then and still do to us three decades later.

Maintain a British presence on the island.

Protect the BAS personnel at King Edward Point in the event of an "emergency."

Continue surveillance of Leith Harbor.[52]

The British marines immediately dug defensive positions around the BAS headquarters and Shackleton House, and they also manned a lookout at Jason Point. After the British marines arrived at King Edward Point, Governor Hunt announced a state of emergency covering the entire Falkland Islands.[53]

As Lieutenant Mills put it after he landed, "I only began to formulate a plan when I realized that the Falklands had actually been invaded and that we were most likely to be next. . . . I had no instructions about what action I should take in the event of an Argentine invasion, because up to this point an invasion was considered highly unlikely."[54] Mills had been well briefed by Barker about South Georgia's topography and weather while still aboard *Endurance* and by members of the BAS ashore, but his seniors in London did little to clarify his mission once he had dug in. A mild scuffle ensued between those on the

Fieldhouse side, who wanted action, and those like Nott, who believed that no military action would succeed in retaking the Falklands. Mills and Barker had no knowledge of the Junta's plans and scant appreciation of how Thatcher might compel them to act in the next few days.

Thatcher and her cabinet had not yet sorted out their options for dealing with South Georgia, let alone come to hard decisions. Unfortunately for Mills, strictures from London about closing with the Argentinian occupiers could be said to have thwarted the collection of the tactical intelligence needed to protect his forces. In lacking a broad operations plan for events beyond NATO's sphere, Thatcher and Nott had trapped themselves into the micromanagement of a distant, platoon-sized war. Neither Nott nor Barker knew the precise numbers and equipment of potentially hostile forces that Mills was meant to surveil. They did take comfort from knowing that the Argentinian troops had neither air nor heavy gun support and were unlikely to receive it in the foreseeable future. On the other hand, London's squeamish replies to requests for clarification of their orders left Barker's storm-tossed crew and Mills's forsaken troops on their own as no hard data came from London or from the British embassy in Buenos Aires to inform their actions over the next few days.

What Mills and Barker did know was that they should not take steps that might provoke the Argentinian invaders into open war. At least ten thinly disguised Argentinian military persons, almost certainly marines or special forces, were still on South Georgia, having stayed when Davidoff's ship departed on March 22. Davidoff himself had not gone to South Georgia with *Bahia Buen Suceso* on this visit, although his son was aboard. Along with the initial landing force of marines, about one hundred additional Argentinian troops landed from *Bahia Paraiso* on Leith at dawn on March 25 with their equipment and stores. The Argentinian force now numbered about 150 men, all but a dozen or so marines and members of the *Buzo Tactico*, the Argentinian special forces. The Junta's publicly unsubstantiated belief that Britain would force the original Argentinian landing party out of Leith by military means was offered at that point as the reason for the additional Argentinian marines, despite the fact that the Royal Marines' tiny force had no air, artillery, or naval support and was outnumbered six to one.

The Argentinian staff's belief that Britain would not fight to regain the Falklands but would, rather, try to expel the Argentinian workers and marines from South Georgia demonstrated the helter-skelter logic that permeated their entire operation. Working from the assumption that Thatcher would not fight, Anaya directed the first-rate troops who had made the original invasion onto East Falkland during the first two days of April to return to their mainland garrisons immediately after the landing. Almost none of them engaged the British, and all returned to stand guard in the Andes against their traditional enemy, Chile. Moreover, this sequence of events and the reasoning behind them confused the Argentinian Navy's entire chain of command as much as it did the operational head, Vice Admiral J. J. Lombardo, who was not told about the military insertion onto South Georgia as it occurred but was only advised to plan for an October invasion of the Falklands themselves. Anaya, the Junta's intellectual force and cheerleader, worked outside the normal chain of command, but his grip on the navy's operational units still trumped Lombardo's. Mills observed this landing of Argentinian troops and reported it to London, whose reaction was not to fire but only to observe. Whatever each side's assumptions about the other's conduct or intentions, the simple act of putting armed men within rifle shot of each other almost guaranteed a military event between Great Britain and Argentina.

Years of civil discourse between the two nations' foreign offices had accomplished little but to provide a string of good lunches at expensive hotels and reports from both that successful negotiations were just around the corner. Why did matters come to this impasse given the complex web of negotiations? Argentina's Junta needed respite both from the scandal of the Disappeared Ones, who had been tortured and murdered at the "Mechanics School" (in 1982 a focus of global opprobrium) and from a faltered economy. These proximate causes fell into the corporate notion that the Southern Cone should exclude what was perceived as undue North American leverage on the region's financial and political affairs. To no one's surprise, this sensitivity failed to preclude the Junta's continued reliance on London and New York banks for seemingly permanent credit. The Junta had inherited a finance minister's nightmare because Argentina depended on soft-currency payments from its exports of wheat to Russia to repay its massive hard-currency debts in London and New York.[55] Sheridan, his small troop, and the soldiers of 3 Commando Brigade knew little of international economics but unknowingly began the redemption of that dog's breakfast.

Galtieri's refusal to install the classic remedies for a hyperinflated economy left him few attractive options for its management. Defeating or humiliating Great Britain would tilt the balance of national pride in Buenos Aires's favor and, the Junta believed, lessen Argentina's image as a bit player on the world stage. On a more palpable level, chopping off some of the lion's tail would increase the Junta's credibility in the credit markets. After all, if Galtieri savaged his prime lender, what fear could he have in approaching the world's banking community for cash to keep him afloat until the next big wheat crop?

The Junta's most impalpable but also most nettlesome problem lay in the Argentinian political promise to its electorate that the Falklands be returned to their rightful owner. For decades already, no map of Argentina could be locally published without inscribing the Falkland Islands as the *Malvinas*. All Argentinian regimes issued postage stamps declaring the Falklands to be part of the mainland state. That enervating pathology had slumbered restlessly for decades, deep in the national will, only to surface occasionally in odd ways. Anomalies abounded. Then Commander Jorge Anaya, for example, refused as a naval attaché in London to learn to speak English *en poste,* even while a spirited, homogenous, and influential British society of banks, newspapers, clubs, and English-speaking schools throve in Buenos Aires. As Winston Churchill noted of another place in an earlier era, "gratitude perhaps may fade but revenge does not."[56]

For its part, the UK had delayed settlement of the Falklands' long-term ownership in the face of Buenos Aires's sometimes-passionate insistence. The FCO's culture of keeping the ball rolling while never coming sufficiently to grips with the guts of a problem so as to resolve it was never better practiced than in the decades-long lunches, cables, and letters that passed between the two countries. Then too, as if to show disinterest in the islanders' ultimate governance, the British government had denied citizenship to certain categories of them. It was clear to all that after the winter of 1982, the economic imperatives of any British government foreclosed the possibility of a *Fortress Falklands* policy. From his prison cell, Admiral Anaya explained his reasoning about going to war to the visiting US Admiral Harry Train. Anaya went back to the 1966 Dennis Healy Defence White Paper, which had announced that Great Britain had no strategic interests east of Suez. Then, Train recalled, Anaya pointed out that the next thing the British did was to withdraw from the Mediterranean. "Malta, gone," Train related Anaya as remembering, and also that "then they declared that they were going to decommission all their aircraft carriers." Also, in November of 1981, John Nott, declared that he was going to decommission twenty-four percent of all the service combatants in the Royal Navy. Anaya said, "What am I supposed to believe with that history? What I believed was that we were dealing with a country that had neither the national will nor the capability—were that will to be resurrected—to defend their interests 8,000 miles from home."[57] Post hoc justifications did little to assuage the anxieties of Barker and Mills's very competent, but tiny force. Indeed, threadbare British diplomatic activity those spring days of 1982 preempted Admiral Fieldhouse's military resolve. In the first week in April, the entire affair seemed lost to the Secretary of Defence and Whitehall's ken. Mills's marines were kept aboard

Endurance. The diplomatic exchanges between Great Britain and Argentina, disingenuous and opaque as they were, are fully described elsewhere and reflect unsubstantiated hope on the British side that peaceful agreement might be reached without bellicose posturing.[58]

Although it became clear that last week of March 1982 that the Argentinian invasion was on, the British could do nothing about it because useable military force was eight thousand miles away. Moreover, Thatcher and Nott knew nothing about the weather, the terrain, or the enemy on South Georgia. Nor did any of the straw men around them. Thatcher had little idea about how to establish a military administration that might recover the islands and save her job. Barker would soon receive this message from Admiral Fieldhouse, his commander in London, who had become more cautious than he had seemed to be earlier: "The present situation remains extremely delicate and every effort should be made to avoid any encounter which could be construed by the Argentines as escalatory."[59]

NOTES

49-Nicholas Barker, *Beyond Endurance: An Epic of Whitehall and the South Atlantic* (London: Pen and Sword, 1996), 137.

50-This message misled its recipient because it was not inclusive. Could the inference be drawn that action could be initiated anywhere but Leith?

51-BAS Chronology, March 31, 1983, p. 3

52-Keith Mills, correspondence with author, May 16, 2009.

53-Mills, correspondence, May 16, 2009.

54-Mills, correspondence, May 16, 2009.

55-The Argentinian financial establishment sought an early invasion out of a belief that success would rearrange its foreign debt obligations, increase its standing in the credit markets, and finally help fill the country's nearly empty coffers. See Juan Carlos Murguizur, "The South Atlantic Conflict: An Argentinian Point of View," *International Defense Review* 2 (1983): 135-40.

56-John Colville, *The Fringes of Power: Downing Street Diaries, 1939-1955* (London: Hodder and Stoughton, 1985), 504.

57-Admiral Harry D. Train, Ronald Reagan Oral History Project, "The Falklands Roundtable," Miller Center of Public Affairs, University of Virginia, May 15-16, 2003. http://web1.millercenter.org/poh/falklands/transcripts/falklands_2003_0515.pdf

58-The best recounting, especially as it affected the British on and around South Georgia, is in Barker, *Beyond Endurance*.

59-Barker, *Beyond Endurance*, 150.

Four

Mills's Defense of South Georgia

ndurance, technically an ice patrol ship, lacked major combat equipment
and could do little but cruise the South Georgian waters to which it had returned and send its two Wasp helicopters to observe Argentinian activity at
Leith.[60] The islands had, after all, no economic or symbolic value for a country
that made it a practice to shed the bits and pieces of a long-ago empire, even as
the Junta claimed through both leaks and public announcements that oil was to
be had offshore and that Argentina was its rightful owner.

On March 31, as the Argentinian invasion fleet was about to put its troops
on the beaches, Margaret Thatcher sent an "urgent message" requesting that
President Reagan intervene with General Galtieri. A storm had delayed the
Argentinian landing by twenty-four hours, and that interlude gave Galtieri and
Anaya sufficient time to halt the invasion should they have chosen to do so. In
fact, a concerned Galtieri stepped into his operations room every fifteen minutes to ask if the run-up to the invasion could be stopped.[61] It was during this
window that Reagan acceded to Thatcher's request and telephoned Galtieri on
Thursday evening April 1, He declined to speak to the president for an uncon-
scionable time and then, after forty-five minutes of conversation, refused the
president's counsel.[62] James Rentschler, a career diplomat working at the National Security Council as Haig's aide, was the White House point man during
the Falkland's affair. He kept a diary that describes that phone call and also
captures Washington's attitude towards the whole business:

Yeah, well, the Bell System never had to deal with General Leopoldo
Galtieri. That's the Argentine strongman with whom the President is eloquent-
ly pleading on the long-distance phone line to Buenos Aires, urging him to
call off his country's invasion of the Falkland Islands. Never heard of them,
right? Me neither, at least not until last evening when Prime Minister Margaret
Thatcher sent an urgent message through the Cabinet Line requesting the President to intercede with the Argies. 1800 British-origin sheepherders, pursuing
a peaceful life on some wind-blown specks of rock in the South Atlantic, now

targeted by Argentine amphibious assault units—who, in turn, may soon be attacked by the largest naval armada ever to steam out of British ports since Suez? Yes indeed, the thing certainly does sound like Gilbert and Sullivan as told to Anthony Trollope by Alistair Cooke. But what started out as comic opera now looks to become not only quite serious, but exceptionally nasty. The Argentines have clearly misjudged the British temper, and this guy Galtieri, speaking first in broken mafioso-type English before the State Department interpreter tactfully intervenes, sounds like a thug. I am very proud of the President, but none of his eloquent delivery cuts any ice with the Junta leader, whose machismo, according to the intercepts we have, will propel him forward with his main invasion plans early tomorrow morning (indeed, when we establish a clearer chronology of events just a few days from now, it will appear that the lead elements of that amphibious force were landing at the very moment the two Chiefs of Staff were talking—no doubt explaining that rigmarole we went through earlier this evening when we kept getting all the evasive bullshit from Palace flunkies who told us their President was unavailable to receive the call. . . .) April fool? Unfortunately not, as the text of a Cabinet Line message I do for the President in response to Mrs. Thatcher's plea later tonight makes clear.[63]

Not quite a week later, Reagan told his staff: "Give Maggie enough to carry on."[64]

After that snub by Galtieri and from that hour, the White House, the Pentagon, the US foreign policy community, and the military's working levels switched on. The Argentinian invasion was no longer just a bilateral concern. Not even one for the UN or, domestically, the State Department alone. It moved to and would retain top billing in Washington until the war's end. Reagan's reply to Margaret Thatcher on April 1 made his commitment to Britain very clear:

> *Dear Margaret,*
>
> *I have just talked at length with General Galtieri about the situation in the Falklands. I conveyed to him my personal concern about the possibility of an Argentinean invasion. I told him that initiating military operations against the Falkland Islands would seriously compromise relations between the US and Argentina, and I urged him to refrain from offensive action. I offered our good offices and my readiness to send a personal representative to assist in resolving the issues*

between Argentina and the UK.

The General heard my message, but gave no commitment that he would comply with it. Indeed, he spoke in terms of ultimatums and left me with the clear impression that he has embarked on a course of armed conflict. We will continue to cooperate with your government in the effort to resolve the dispute, both in attempting to avert hostilities and to stop them if they break out. While we have a policy of neutrality on the sovereignty issue, we will not be neutral in the issue involving Argentine use of military force.

Warmest wishes,

Ron[65]

Galtieri's crude dismissal of Reagan personally and of the president's attempt to be an honest broker set the US government on Britain's side. The Americans' very practical responses began immediately. On March 28, even before the Argentinian marines had completed their landing at Port Stanley, and indeed before the president's conversation with Galtieri, the prescient Secretary of the Navy, John Lehman, sent two tankers of oil to Ascension Island in anticipation of British needs there. That sleepy depot, owned by the UK but on permanent lease to the US, was transformed overnight into the main British staging area for its southward flow of troops and supplies. US Secretary of Defense Caspar Weinberger opened America's military warehouses to British requests and immediate aid was sent on a more informal basis.

At some point by Thursday, April 8, the National Security Planning Group had assembled in Washington to handle formally the American side of the war.[66] From that nexus, Secretary of State Alexander Haig began his tedious, albeit quickly concluded, trilateral diplomacy among Buenos Aires, London, and Washington. Straightaway, Mr. Haig climbed aboard Air Force Two and set about preliminary talks in all three cities. Secretary Weinberger said then and later: "I never had any doubt as to where the President stood."[67] From the pickup truck that drove Stinger anti-aircraft missiles from Fort Bragg to a waiting British plane at Dulles airport to Haig's bluff talks with Thatcher, the matter was conducted with no fuss *en plein air*. As the days passed, all concerned, including the Argentinian embassy in Washington knew where America stood. Later, on April 29, in order to legitimize *post hoc* the already-landed assistance at Ascension Islands, the US Senate passed a 99-1 resolution that called for the withdrawal of Argentinian troops from the Falklands and the resumption of peaceful negotiations.

The consultations, messages, and posturing of *haute politique* exerted their own affect on the storm-tossed *Endurance,* even though the only job for its tiny group of Royal Marines was simply to remain afloat and, if possible, undetected in the South Atlantic. As they did that, however, Mills and Barker were absorbing that confusing stream of messages from the British embassy in Buenos Aires as well as from London. The business of preparing mentally and physically for military action only to have it called off remains one of the most irksome torments of junior leaders. After seven or eight days in cramped quarters that pitch and roll every few minutes, the marines' fighting edge might begin to dull, but competent NCOs are alert to prevent or remedy that. While his own stores dwindled, Captain Nick Barker in *Endurance* kept tabs on the Argentinian ships and men that were taking an ever more proprietary interest in South Georgia from their well-provisioned lodgment at Leith. But the police action meant to occur at Leith on March 23 at 1300 was cancelled just as Mills's troops were about to disembark from *Endurance.*[68]

By March 30, two groups of Argentinian ships steamed into foul weather with malice in mind. The larger, amphibious, force made for Stanley. Vice Admiral Lombardo and General Carlos Busser, the Argentine marines' head, had scraped together any floating asset available that could protect and transport their landing force from the mainland to Stanley. Task Force 60, the South Georgia surface force, had lost *Drummond* and *Granville* at the last moment in order to strengthen the amphibious force aimed at Stanley by heading there to keep the combat ships close at hand for what Anaya concluded might end as a major fleet engagement against the Royal Navy. The military logic here is difficult to fathom. No British warship yet lay within thousands of miles of Stanley, and no British naval opposition to the Argentinian landing could be mounted. To the north, Major Mike Norman, the officer in charge of the British marines on East Falkland, lacked large-caliber guns to fire at incoming Argentinian landing craft.

The Argentinian marines who were intended to reinforce their garrison on South Georgia endured a difficult voyage south aboard *Bahia Paraiso,* a new icebreaker built in 1981. It carried one hundred infantrymen and their gear from the Argentinian Marines' 1st Battalion. Task Force 60's sole fighting ship was *Guerrico,* a 950-ton patrol ship built in 1978 at L'Orient for South Africa. Because of an earlier arms ban on Pretoria, the ship was eventually sold under construction to Argentina. *Guerrico* was designed as a coastal patrol ship with a modest range of 4500 miles and a top speed of twenty-three knots. It was neither designed nor fitted out for winter waters barely north of the Antarctic Circle, and it could not break ice.

Captain Carlos Alfonso had little time to work up the ship. *Guerrico* was pulled from dry dock on March 27, and a small crew of eighty-four officers and men was hastily gathered and put aboard. Moreover, there was doubt that such a small crew could efficiently serve so disparate a weapons suite. It carried four MM-38 Exocets, a single 100 mm naval gun, two sets of triple 12.75 torpedo tubes, and light caliber AA guns. The 100 mm gun gave the Argentines an effective offshore mobile artillery weapon with a maximum surface range of 12,000 meters, muzzle to target. The ship did not carry sonar, had never fired its Exocets, and had never seen a sea fight. Captain Cesar Trombetta, TF 60's commander, knew the South Atlantic and South Georgia as well as any other Argentinian naval officer, but he, too, had never fought at sea and lacked any experience in amphibious warfare and ground combat. What was more hobbling from the Argentinian standpoint was that Galtieri's troops ashore at Leith had not, according to BAS reports, ventured out of that settlement or patrolled into the valleys and onto the glaciers. They had no tactical grasp of what enemy, if any, faced them and what British intentions might be. Least visible, but more critical for all of that, the Argentinian troop leaders were unbloodied, their chain of command fuzzy, and their commanders lacking any feel for their place or the struggle they and their troops might hurriedly face.

On the sly, the Junta, that is Admiral Anaya, suddenly found itself wanting South Georgia in addition to Port Stanley, especially if the military occupation might be completed at small cost and little risk. Detailed and competent reconnaissance and staff planning had gone into the Argentinian invasion of East Falklands, but none existed for the capture of South Georgia. The lion's tail could usefully be twisted a bit more. This did little for Nott, who found himself in a muddle of his own making; *Endurance* would come home according to his budget, but Sheridan and his men would go south to accomplish what Captain Nick Barker's crew and ship might have done better, sooner, and more quietly.

On March 28, two portentous events occurred. The first should have been obvious to any bystander in Buenos Aires possessed of vision and smell. Rickety Argentinian landing craft completed their noisy and malodorous load out for the seizure of Stanley. There were roughly nine hundred men, mostly marines, a few small specialist army units, and a gaggle of ramshackle ships. The landing was to be as bloodless as possible, and Stanley was to be occupied within the day. The second was that the British Ambassador to the United States, Sir Nicholas Henderson, sent a note to US Secretary of State Caspar

Weinberger to tell him the Argentinian invasion of the Falklands was underway. That communication, which Henderson mentioned often in public, served to announce a US role.

Yet as the invasion fleet loitered at sea, about to put its troops over the beaches, a storm delayed the mission. Those few hours gave cooler heads the opportunity to end the action, but Galtieri chose to ignore the pressure against his going forward, the troops landed, and the dogs of war romped on British soil. On April 2, the day of the invasion, Governor Hunt was airlifted to Montevideo, Uruguay, and the Argentinian flag flew over Port Stanley. One last mournful message passed between a radio operator in London and one in Port Stanley.

"LONDON: What are all these rumors?

PORT STANLEY: We have lots of new friends.

LONDON: What about the invasion rumors?

PORT STANLEY: Those are the friends I was meaning.

LONDON: They've landed?

PORT STANLEY: Absolutely.

LONDON: Are you open for traffic?

PORT STANLEY: No orders on that yet. One must obey orders.

LONDON: Whose orders?

PORT STANLEY: The new governor.

LONDON: Argentina?

PORT STANLEY: Yes

LONDON: Are the Argentineans in control?

PORT STANLEY: Yes. You can't argue with thousands of troops plus enormous navy support when you are only 1,800 strong. Stand by please.

Then the line went dead.[69]

Mills's tactical situation changed from standing ready to conduct a police operation to one of defense against an outnumbering force supported by a long gun. In short order he received from London three mutually contradictory directions:

> *"When the Argentines attempt to make contact with you, you are not to cooperate."*

> *"When asked to do so, you are not to surrender."*

> *"The Officer Commanding Royal Marines is not repeat not to take any action which may endanger life."*[70]

Mills interpreted the last message to mean that he could not defend himself, his men and the BAS scientists if the Argentinian marines attacked, and he wisely declined not to inform his men of this sad prohibition. Mills's predicament would have tried the cleverest young officer. He worked under time-honored constraints that ruled his professional life as an infantry officer: carry out orders, protect his men, and give his life if necessary. Yet after receiving what amounted to contradictory orders, clearly written by one who lacked familiarity with the realities of conflict, he concluded that *Bahia Paraiso,* armed with a heavy gun that could destroy his positions lurked near him, that a substantial party of Argentinian marines who greatly outnumbered his men were a few miles away, and that they were alone. Unless and until the Argentines attacked his force, he could, of course, obey his original orders of March 31 to maintain a British presence on the island, protect the BAS scientists, and continue surveillance of the Argentines at Leith Harbor. His seniors had left him in a disadvantaged waiting game.

The near anarchy of the command and control system above Mills did not deter him from recognizing several home truths. He knew that the Argentines held Leith and that he could not defend all of South Georgia. Moreover, as the Argentines had not surveyed or plotted a proper landing beach, and given that lengthy reconnaissance would cost them both time and the element of surprise, King Edward Point, with its jetty, was vital ground. *Bahia Paraiso* could dock there handily and unload more troops. The Argentinian marines could also land piecemeal by helicopter. Mills established a two-man post to cover Cumberland East Bay and its barely feasible landing beach.[71] Mills decided to establish his defenses at the northern end of King Edward Point, which stood to the west of Shackleton House and across Cumberland Bay, southeast of

Grytviken. In conducting a necessarily passive reconnaissance of Leith, Barker and Mills obeyed the letter of their seniors' orders but kept themselves and London aware of Argentinian moves.

Any ship entering the bay would pass under his positions, and no civilians would be caught in the crossfire. He wired the jetty and its approaches with demolitions. To guard against the landing craft that *Bahia Paraiso* was thought to carry, he mined the beaches. Because an "all around defense" was impossible even if he mined the few feasible landing points, Mills sited his men's weapons so that any Argentinian boat passing the end of King Edward Point would fall within six hundred meters of his muzzles. He knew that *Bahia Paraiso* had two helicopters that gave the Argentines tactical choices; he had none. He would defend from fixed positions while the invading Argentinian marines had the advantages of concentration, surprise, and tactical mobility. As he explained,

I knew that reinforcements would not be forthcoming, so it would be an impossibility to hold King Edward Point for any length of time. However, my main aim at the time was to ensure that any invasion was met with maximum force, after which we would withdraw at a time of our choosing and then retreat into the mountains. From here it was envisaged that we would continue to conduct skirmishing operations against the enemy. To this end, all our heavy equipment (sleeping bags, food, surplus ammunition etc.) was driven by tractor and trailer about 1 mile to the rear of the old whaling station (Grytviken). It was our intention to pick this equipment up as part of our planned withdrawal.[72]

The young marines put their training into practice with the humor that confident soldiers enjoy. "They set about booby-trapping the shore and fashioning a bomb beneath the jetty that was packed with nuts, bolts and harpoon heads, posing in front of it for one last picture just thirty seconds before they heard the first Argentinian [helicopter] approaching.[73]

On April 2, *Endurance's* signal that an invasion of South Georgia was imminent proved all too prescient. Mills had been briefed that *Guerrico*, with its 100-mm gun, skulked just over the horizon ready to support a landing at short notice. *Bahia Paraiso* did, in fact, sail into Cumberland Bay that same day but because of poor flying conditions, with winds gusting to eighty knots, did not land her party of marines. The same excessively windy weather prevented Mills from retrieving his two-man lookout on Jason Point. By 3:00 pm, Robert Headland of the BAS had burned his cryptographic material, destroyed government seals, and gathered his staff into the old wooden Norwegian church. BAS rifles had their bolts pulled and secured with their ammunition separate from the barrels. Steven Martin of the BAS station sent a message to the

Argentinian government that BAS persons were not combatants and should not be treated as such. A menacing but strangely uninformative message from *Bahia Paraiso* informed BAS to await an important communication the next morning. Diplomatic bleatings from the FCO to the Argentinian government, never successful or predictive, waned during these dark hours to nothingness.

Early that next morning, at 09:40 on April 3, *Bahia Paraiso's* helicopters flew reconnaissance over Grytviken and King Edward Point. At about 10:00, the Argentinian government made good its word and sent a message: "Following the invasion of the Falklands, UK officials there had agreed that all British troops would be sent home and the Argentine flag was to be put upon South Georgia."[74] Martin temporized and replied that he needed time to consider the Argentinian demand and that a British military presence existed that would defend South Georgia. *Guerrico's* skipper, Columbo, sent the grim retort that Martin's contemplation could last no longer than five minutes. That condescension was all of a piece with the Junta's prevailing belief that the Thatcher government would not fight. Later Nott added substance to this shaky conclusion when he declared on April 4 that "12 people [Davidoff's crew] with a valid salvage license" was not sufficient reason in itself for sending such a [naval] task force.[75]

At about 9:40 a.m. on April 3, Mills's Sergeant Major, Peter Leach, retrieved his two marines from Jason Point. Simultaneously, an Argentinian helicopter landed in front of Mills's position and disgorged its marines, who took up combat positions opposite the British marines. Two groups, each of thirty-six Argentinian marines under Lieutenant Guillermo Luna, landed with personal weapons, three 60mm mortars, and two .30 caliber light machine guns [LMG]. Ten Argentinian marines landed at Gull Lake. Shortly afterwards, about noon, Headland informed the Argentines that the British Antarctic Survey civilians were gathered inside Grytviken Church. The Argentinian marines now prepared to assault the British marines' positions at King Edward Point, which they might well have occupied more easily days previous, when Mills's men remained aboard ship. Their delay caused them unnecessary casualties.

Just then, at 10:10, *Guerrico* and its helicopters closed within firing range of both Mills's rockets and his machine guns, even though *Bahia Paraiso's* captain knew that King Edwards Point would be defended militarily. As Mills remembered, "I couldn't have operated both sets of orders; they were too contradictory and time was running out."[76] The moment was not lost on the marine defenders of King Edward Point. Mills answered an anxious corporal's request for instructions: "Well, I've done all I can to stop this happening. Open fire." The shooting started at 10:20.[77] *Guerrico's* commanding officer then committed a felicitous blunder that gave Mills the chance to establish a defense that would go into the textbooks. The ship closed the shore so closely that its very effective 100mm gun could not depress sufficiently to take Mills's position under fire. Columbo had taken his biggest gun out of the fight. Mills's men quickly fired their 66mm and 84mm rockets into the ship. Damage to *Guerrico's* bridge, its engine room, and the Argentines' misunderstanding of their opponents was substantial.[78] This is the first recorded instance of an infantry force defeating a warship from their trenches. Captain Columbo prudently retired his ship out of range while the Royal Marines shifted their small arms fire to his helicopters and quickly brought them down with two Argentinian crewmen killed. Mills won the fight in the short term; he had only one man wounded and plentiful ammunition. His men kept their discipline and executed a brilliant defense from their dug-in positions.

In the longer term, however, Mills could not win. His unit was outnumbered by at least five to one. He could not counterattack with so few men, nor could he fight from a defense in depth. He had, moreover, nowhere to go. He lacked a permanently fortified position in which to hold out, whereas his opponents could reboard their ships. If Barker had tried to reembark the British marines, *Guerrico's* 100mm gun could have sunk *Endurance*. Mills could expect no reinforcements, whereas the Argentinian marines could be reinforced from the mainland.

The *Guerrico*, though badly hit, returned to the fray and began shelling with its 100mm gun, this time from a sufficiently great distance that its rounds jeopardized the British positions without the possibility of retaliation. Mills had no weapon to engage *Guerrico* from a distance, and the Argentinian marines, following US Marine Corps doctrine, laid down a base of fire and began to encircle Mills's positions. They had sufficient numbers to absorb casualties in the attack and ultimately to surround Mills's men.

The brilliant engagement with *Guerrico* would have been a culminating event in any senior officer's career, but Mills rightly saw only one possible outcome: the deaths of many marines on both sides and the Argentinian marines left in possession of South Georgia. Despite his earlier orders from London: "Defend if provoked," Mills parlayed with his opposite number and the firing stopped at about 3 p.m. Mills and Argentinian Lieutenant-Commander Astiz went to the church where Headland had marshaled the local scientists from BAS and completed the formal civilian surrender of Grytviken and King Edward Point. Despite the numbers of Argentinians killed and wounded, the British surrender went smoothly, if any such affair can be so described. Each Royal Marine had an escort as he was placed aboard *Bahia Paraiso* and his remaining personal gear (combs, shoelaces, belts, and so forth) was confiscated. The British marines had lost most of their ashore personal gear and kit before being sent aboard. The single wounded marine, Nigel Parker, was taken for immediate medical care to the ship's medical station. Mills and Astiz discharged Mills's unfired rockets into Cumberland Bay.

. Headland recalls: "There were a number of Argentines wondering about both Buzo Tactico and conscripts. The Buzo were happy and relaxed, but the conscripts were shivering and rather jumpy and unfortunately in order to hand over the civilian surrender I had to come from behind their backs. Fortunately the door of the church squeaked rather loudly." By a *ruse de guerre*, Headland diverted his guards' attention and again managed to destroy yet more cash, seals, stamps, documents, and mail that lay about his tiny post office. Headland conferred with Astiz and willingly gave him the names and locations of BAS civilian field parties still at large in four field huts widely scattered around South Georgia. *Bahia Paraiso*, its prisoners secure in their cabins and holds, left Grytviken for Leith in darkness at 6:30 p.m. on April 3, 1982. The BAS crew was repatriated to the UK within a few weeks, through Montevideo.

Throughout the war, the British Antarctic Survey was held by not a few to constitute a sovereign state of its own with particular rights, needs, and practices that needed neither explanation nor permission. That accusation may have been correct, but the better truth lay in the continued existence of four BAS field parties, those at Bird Island, Schlieper Bay, Lyell Glacier, and St. Andrews Bay. All remained very much alive and constituted the fragments of British sovereignty over South Georgia. The British patrols that later took shelter in their field huts or learned about the ground problems they faced were more than grateful for BAS hospitality. But the BAS went further. In order to maintain real-time reconnaissance, it quickly shifted control of its communications to Signy Island and through its survey ship, the *Bransfield*. Hugh O'Gorman, that ship's radio operator, handled more traffic in the next few weeks than during a normal nine-month tour. Here BAS and their communicators performed that often overlooked but most useful intelligence function of describing what was not happening.[79] As Headland put it later, "The overwhelming memory of those days was the speed with which things developed, how control and organization and diplomacy was lost so quickly." Undeterred by the Argentinian occupation of Grytviken and the capture of its subjects, the British government appointed Alan Hemmings to be the Base Commander of Signy Island and the British Antarctic Territory Magistrate for the South Orkney Islands.[80]

South Georgia's capture by the Argentineans fulfilled Captain Nick Barker's worst expectations. Blood was shed, British territory was lost, and no adequate military response was at hand. *Endurance* had been out of the fight, having steamed out of harm's way to the middle of nowhere. Barker's crew badly wanted food, and their ship needed not only fuel, but also the bits and pieces of materiel that keep a sea-going community content and effective. Until all these became available, the ship remained alone in the Southern Ocean monitoring Argentinian communications and movements in that most unlikely theater of war.

Notes

60-In fact, *Endurance's* decommissioning was announced to the House of Commons in June 1981. *Times* (London), April 2, 2002.

61-Argentinian staff officer during 1982 to the author in conversation.

62-"James Rentschler's Falkland's Diary: 1 April - 25 June 1982," Folio 150, p. 1, Reagan Library.

63-Rentschler's Diary, p. 1.

64-President to officials April 6, 1982. Analysis of Bureau of Intelligence and Research, US Department of State.

65-Rentschler's Diary, pp. 1-2.

66-Rentschler's Diary, p. 2. The group consisted of: Vice President George Bush, National Security Advisor William P. Clark, Secretary of Defense Caspar Weinberger, Joint Chiefs of Staff Chair David C. Jones, CIA Deputy Director Bobby R. Inman, and UN Ambassador Jeanne Kirkpatrick.

67-Secretary of Defense Weinberger in conversation with the author, circa 2001.

68-BAS Chronology, revised, January 7, 1985, p. 3.

69-"Communications Cut With the Falklands," *New York Times*, April 3, 1982, section 1, p. 6.

70-Keith Mills, letter to the author, May 16, 2009.

71-Keith Mills, letter to the author, November 16, 2008

72-Mills, letter, May 16, 2009.

73-George Thomsen, section commander on South Georgia. Aislinn Simpson, "The 22 Royal Marines who took on Argentine Falklands invasion force," *The Telegraph*, April 14, 2009.

74-UK, Ministry of Defence, Release Falklands, October 17, 2008.

75-Sir John Nott MOD, quoted in Michael White, "Carrrington and Nott face humiliation and fury," *Guardian*, April 3, 1982.

76-Mills interview MOD Defence NEWS, May 16, 2009.

77-BAS Chronology, revised January 7, 1985, p. 6.

78-The marines' marksmanship was very good. After 25 meters the 66mm projectile has the ballistic characteristics of a New York telephone book. Author's experience.

79-Robert Headland Interview.

80-BAS Chronology, revised, January 7, 1985, p. 6.

Five

Shadow Boxing

While Thatcher prepared for war, staved off the wets in her cabinet, and prepared the electorate for the shedding of blood, the Junta did little to dissipate the languor that had overtaken it after its brash seizure of East Falkland. A small occupying force for East and West Falkland, South Georgia, and the Sandwich Islands was all that the Junta had envisioned as necessary to transform the Falklands into the Malvinas. The Junta's operating assumption held that the simple military act of occupation, followed by a mainly civilian administration emplaced on the fifth day after the invasion, would settle a nettlesome problem before a distant and unconcerned world, hush a fidgety electorate, and keep Galtieri's circle in power long enough to weather Argentina's current economic storm. Shorn of the Northern Hemisphere's screed, the Southern Cone of South America would then have a new *Caudillo* and a new set of diplomatic practices. It was a majestic view of his country's future with which Galtieri intoxicated himself and his audience by his roseate oratory from the Casa Rosada's balcony.[81] From there, the Junta posited, it would be a short step to deep-sea oil fields that would provide riches sufficient to buy membership in the club of major powers. They disregarded the fact that the fields have only been roughly measured and never tapped. In their presumption about the world's tacit acceptance of their mischief, the Argentinian staff did not bother to write a military plan for the defense of either the Falklands or South Georgia.[82]

All these assumptions proved hollow once the British fleet sailed from UK ports. This dramatic event convinced some Argentinian staff officers in Buenos Aires to believe, even if they could not present an overwhelming military logic for their suspicions, that Thatcher might reinvade the Falklands and that the Junta's forces might first lose South Georgia and then begin a downward slide towards the oblivion of Galtieri's whole scheme. None of the senior Argentinian military or political parties had ever been involved in such matters. They had no precedent for thinking through their awful dilemma to a satisfactory end game.

But there was some negotiating strength to the Junta's position. As Thatcher had stated through her Secretary for Foreign Affairs: "The fact remains that the Falklands are not and never have been part of the United Kingdom."[83] Even so, US Secretary of State Haig impressed the Junta with his face-to-face insistence to Galtieri during his first visit to Buenos Aires that Great Britain would fight and win. His language was resonant: "Do you know what this means? It means war. Do you know what war means?"[84] His word spread like a fevered virus through the interstices of the Junta—but with no voiced or written reply. Dithering dissenters were cowed into glum silence. Negotiation would, they believed, be the only way to end the war without abject humiliation. These thoughtful young officers, most from the Argentinian Navy, missed a logical step, however. The negotiations were transacted among four, not two or three parties: the US, the UK, the Junta, and the imprisoned Kelpers themselves. The last of these remained intransigent, and any solution to the issue of sovereignty could not occur without their agreement. Their resolute stand was to return to the status quo ante bellum. The functionaries of the Palacio de San Martin, the Argentinian Foreign Office, almost certainly missed one crucial point aptly described by Rentschler, who wrote a memo of conversation, or memcon, on April 16, in which he argued that "the talks in Buenos Aires demonstrated more than anything else, the emptiness of our bilateral 'relationship' with the Argies (Ambassador Shlaudeman . . . voiced this same view, heartily seconded by every one of us who had to deal with them)."[85] After it became clear that British forces, abetted by the Americans, had set about retaking the Falklands, by force if necessary, Galtieri put into play stopgap military measures such as reinforcing the Falklands with called-up and undertrained reservists until, he hoped, his diplomacy could extinguish Thatcher's fiery and well-publicized intent. Galtieri, knowing that he held only a tenuous grip on his electorate, did not put the country on a wartime footing.

Anthony Parsons, Britain's delegate to the UN, shepherded UN Resolution 502 through the Security Council. It was approved on April 3. Only Panama voted against it. That skillfully contrived and brilliantly marketed document called for Argentina's immediate removal of its armed forces from the Falklands as a condition precedent to negotiation about the Falklands' sovereignty. Parson's triumphant diplomacy at the UN, a bare few hours after Argentina's invasion, put the Falklands center stage in world affairs and convinced a heterogeneous assortment of Third and Fourth World, industrialized, and non-English-speaking states to oppose publicly the Junta's military adventurism. The Soviet Union failed to veto the British resolution, and for the rest of the war, non-aligned states mutely resisted the Argentinian ambassador's pleas for their help. Much to the surprise of Argentina's Foreign Office, settlement of border disputes by armed force was not a resolution that modern nation-states, especially its neighbors, could stomach. The reasons were clear. Even passive approval of Argentina's invasion would condone military initiatives almost anywhere else, such as along the Amur River, where China and Russia lobbed artillery shells at each other but did not invade one another's territory. Argentina's South American neighbors saw little future in changing their borders through the incursions of a few thousand peasants serving as infantrymen.

Passage of Security Council Resolution 502 gave Thatcher room and time to maneuver, but not much. She could sequester Argentina's holdings in London, stop trade between the two countries, and lobby for other nations' support. Yet no cheap or easy answers to repossession of the islands presented themselves. Thatcher could not attack Argentinian ships on the high seas, her legal advisors warned, because no war had been declared and she was constrained to obey the letter of international law. She could not order the bombing of the Argentinian mainland for the same reason and also because so disproportionate a response would turn newfound allies against her. Worst of all, she could not yet seize the Falklands, because Britain's military was not in place.[86] As dramatic as it was, Parson's victory at the UN gave her only a decaying asset that delay or a false step could quickly squander. Now that Thatcher had negotiating momentum and a moderately approving cabinet that kept Parliament and the country with her, she had to follow Ambassador Parson's triumph with a military accomplishment that could not await the month-long marshaling of Britain's invasion force. The British middle class, whose wrath at Argentina's theft the prime minister had so deftly exploited, could not long exist on rhetoric; they needed at least some blood. In twenty predominantly labor boroughs, twenty-four percent of potential Tory voters considered the Falklands crisis to be an important factor, for some the most important, in the upcoming elections.[87] Moreover, the presence of a woman from the middle class sitting on the front bench still rankled a substantial rump of the Conservative Party. Argentina's capture of South Georgia, its small Royal Marines landing party, and scientists from the BAS were, at first blush, public humiliations for Thatcher. She knew it. She knew her political opponents knew it and would use it against her in Parliament and in the press—if not now, then later.

Yet Argentina's occupation of South Georgia had a perverse and unintended consequence. It presented her a needed benison because recapture of that island became an immediate possibility, with all the public adulation such an event would bring. Defeating ten thousand Argentinian troops on East Falkland and in Port Stanley would take blood, treasure, and time. A hundred or so unwary Argentinian troops skulking out of the wind in ill-found wooden structures was another matter. A fair chance existed in two dissimilar minds, Vaux's and Thatcher's, that South Georgia could be regained by a cheap military operation, just as swiftly as it had been seized. Like Mills's marines, the Argentinian forces on South Georgia were lodged far from home without air cover, artillery support, or a logistics tail. Nott was widely believed to have sought, after due political consideration, a military operation against South Georgia because it would give Thatcher's government a military and public-relations victory that would elevate public enthusiasm until major military efforts provided other more decisive and palpable results, either by sinking the Argentinian Navy or by reoccupation of the Falklands themselves. Nott and others knew that the British fleet was weeks away from Port Stanley and that, at the moment, war was more acceptable to the British public than partisan tittle-tattle. Seen through the prism of cynical public relations, had Argentina's invasion of South Georgia not happened, it would have to have been invented.

In Buenos Aires during the first week of April, several English-speaking junior military officers and at least one officer in the foreign ministry thought along similar lines. Their voices were mute. No follow-up staff study was composed to document their anxieties about possible British retaliation in an environment still ruled by Admiral Anaya's romantic adventurism. Once the British fleet had sailed from UK ports in an almost celebratory mood, these few Argentines believed that the Junta had miscalculated and that it would suffer defeat at the hands of the British military. They based their conclusion on the notion that Thatcher would suffer a greater humiliation by turning back from an anticipated occupation than she had suffered from the invasion itself. Their unpublicized view that the guns of August were being loaded was confirmed to them when Task Force 317.1 (*Antrim*, *Plymouth*, and *Tidespring*) set course for what could only be, in the desolate South Atlantic wastes, South Georgia.[88]

The Secretary of Defence, however, was not sanguine about the possibilities. As Thatcher remembered, "John gave the MOD's view that the Falklands could not be retaken once they were seized."[89] Nott understood just as well as every admiral and sailor the ramifications of his very large cuts to the Royal Navy afloat, to its exercise schedule, to its maintenance, and to its building program.[90] A backward look at British military policy in the 1970s is needed here. It must be recalled that the costs of maintaining large ground and air forces on NATO's central front and ballistic missile submarines at sea had foreclosed solo British operations outside Europe. The men, equipment, and planning for such joint service ventures as recapturing the Falklands could not be included in the Defence Ministry's budget according to the politics of the day. Moreover, they simply no longer existed. As a consequence, the fragile command and control structure for the forces intended to seize the Falklands was an unpracticed one. The military art of opposed landings in distant parts was not there.[91] As a consequence, the recapture of South Georgia burdened a hastily contrived organization, itself unsure of its specific goal, with the need to expel invaders from British territory, a task that had not been tried since World War II.[92]

On April 7, Thatcher ordered Admiral Fieldhouse to reestablish the British presence on South Georgia.[93] The order was based on a false premise, because British subjects, members of the British Antarctic Survey, remained at large, indeed abandoned, at their five posts scattered around the island. Whatever bravado wreathed her order, Thatcher had no military experience and skated over the uncomfortable fact that successful ground warfare was more easily dreamed of than completed. The long-departed whalers had the right idea; South Georgia was an awful place to live and work. To win a fight there was a grail never imagined. Later, Thatcher stated publicly that she hoped the recapture of South Georgia would convince Argentina that the British were "determined in the pursuit of principle. . . . They have had three weeks to start to withdraw their forces and negotiate. . . . We had to retake South Georgia at the best possible time."[94] Yet David Owen, a former Foreign Secretary sought restraint: "It is right to give Secretary Haig a few more days."[95]

Galtieri and the rest of the Junta thought otherwise. Their troops had wintered-in on South Georgia. One thoughtful Argentinian said it best: "Galtieri and the generals are cornered; they have no way to go but forward. If they go backward, they will be swept away."[96] Anaya's obvious predicament may well have been the prompt that Nott needed to draw the public's attention from the Defence Ministry's failure to defend the Falklands while he marshaled forces for retaking the islands. His unwearied sycophancy had brought him around to Thatcher's position that the war was to be fought and won, whatever the cost. Rentschler caught the moment at Downing Street:

very little daylight for a peaceful settlement, especially with John Nott making gonadal noises about the ability of the British fleet to sustain operations indefinitely in the South Atlantic, despite the onset of formidable winter conditions—the ice, the snow, the 60-foot seas, the constant Antarctic gales, and the vulnerabilities of an 8000-mile supply line (Haig will tell us later that Nott is showboating to convince the Cabinet that he is more royalist than the Queen and that the only reason he wasn't offloaded with Carrington was the fear that it would be too chaotic and demoralizing.)[97]

By the end of March, 42 Commando Royal Marines had completed a lengthy winter exercise in Norway, and many of its members were set to go on leave. Its commanding officer, Lieutenant Colonel Nick Vaux, stood out among a small, extraordinarily competent group of senior Royal Marine officers. He had been brought up abroad, became a champion gentleman steeplechase rider, and came to enjoy a reputation as an unusual and very competent officer. He was heading from the exercises in the north for a visit to the United States. His second-in-command, Major Guy Sheridan, was in France with family, and dozens of men had already been transferred to other units, gone off to service schools, or fled to warmer climes. More than a few had hurried off to the merry glens of matrimony. Barely had his Arctic gear been stowed when Vaux was awakened at 0400 hours on April 2 by an order to collect his unit for a trip south. It is a tribute to Vaux's unit that within the week, on April 9, 42 Commando Royal Marines had assembled from all over the world and sailed to war from Southampton.

On April 7, Colonel Richard Preston, Chief of Staff of the Royal Marines' Commando Forces, telephoned Vaux to tell him to set aside one infantry company, equipped for Arctic warfare, with supporting elements for a move on six hours' notice to Ascension Island.[98] Secrecy usually wreaths military moves with importance and sometimes with gains in efficiency, and Operation Paraquat, meant to regain South Georgia, was no exception. Admiral Fieldhouse established a Paraquat cell at Northwood separate from other Falklands communications. Knowledge of ships' movements was restricted to a dozen or so people. From the now-bustling Ascension Island, the tiny marine force, all trained for action in the Arctic, with additions from the Special Boat Service [SBS] and the Special Air Service, was ordered to sail south into winter waters in order to recapture an unfamiliar island from a hostile force of unknown size and capability. A small band of Royal Marines headed for the back-of-beyond eight thousand miles away would, if seen with a cold-roast-beef eye, appear to be on a fool's quest. Success would accomplish little; failure would cost Thatcher her job. The prime minister had never met, let alone scrutinized, Major Sheridan and his lads.

In contrast to the fleet's grand sendoff from Portsmouth, Operation Paraquat was not only conceived but was set in motion under great secrecy.[99] That did not, however, mean that Vaux left for the South Atlantic in the manner he would have liked. Detaching a full company destroyed his Commando unit's tactical integrity, because a Royal Marines Commandos Brigade is scalable upward, but not downward. When the bullets fly, action depends on all three companies plus their attached artillery, engineers, and support troops acting in concert. However, on the way south, the ever-resourceful Vaux scratched up a third company from rear elements and restored his unit to the point that his 42 Commando won the storied Battle of Mt. Harriet, the most elegantly planned and executed combat of the war.[100] Vaux appointed Sheridan, his second in command, as land commander of the force intended to seize South Georgia. In turn, Sheridan selected M Company Royal Marines, commanded by Captain Chris Nunn, as his assault force. Before embarking from the UK, Sheridan and Nunn rounded out Nunn's still-sequestered M Company. They added four signalers, two sections from the Commando's reconnaissance troop, and three medics, including a surgeon. Sheridan was also told that a section of SBS and a troop from the 22 SAS Regiment would join his force later as reconnaissance elements, as they did from *Fort Austin*. Nunn's M Company was still to be the core assault force because it by itself possessed the necessary military skills. The SAS additions were a matter of adding more of what was already there. These additions, especially the reconnaissance troops, were meant to be useful because they could land and reconnoiter from their small boats while the fleet units remained undiscovered, they all hoped, at sea.

This group of about one hundred and ten men was split off from Vaux's unit after its departure parade, sequestered in barracks, and forbidden to communicate with the outside world. Depriving Vaux of a full infantry company did not please him, Sheridan, or Nunn. Marines' combat effectiveness depends on the achievement that is hard won from arduous training together, especially in cold weather operations. Vaux's unit had just finished their winter Arctic exercise at a very high level of competence. Nunn, Officer in Command of M Company, had held his position with distinction for two years. He was considered one of the best helicopter flyers in the British forces, was Arctic warfare qualified, and was a demanding company commander. His grip on tactics was firm, and he had trained M Company to elevated standards. He had flown for three years in Northern Ireland and had led 42 Commando's helicopter flight crew. He had received very high marks for a successful exercise that he had organized and executed against a NATO force from Norway. He was a singular example of the junior and company-grade officers who populated Vaux's 42 Commando. Nunn's hard training of his men bore fruit when M Company, despite being split up among different ships, still acted as a coherent whole in retaking South Georgia on April 25 and 26.

Rear Admiral John (Sandy) Woodward was the overall battle force commander of the ships ordered south. They were to transport, feed, support, and send Sheridan's troops ashore. Among the ships in this task group [CTG 317.1.9] were the very old gunships *Antrim* and *Plymouth*. Woodward selected

Captain Brian Young to be the commander of this small task group. It was not an appropriate choice. Only men, not ships, retake territory. Yet the Defence Ministry's command assignments put navy men like Young and Woodward in charge of Paraquat. For all their successes in their particular career paths, they had no experience delivering combat forces onto, over, and beyond the beach and then supporting them once they were there. Young himself was a successful aviator and commanding officer with no over-the-beach amphibious experience. When ordered to join Operation Corporate, the name given to retaking the Falklands, he and his hard-used ship were both on the point of retirement, he to fishing, the ship to a second life as razor blades. Young had no experience in working with Royal Marines.[101] He had never taken his ship into the kinds of tumultuous waters he would face at South Georgia. His standing orders as a destroyer skipper did not require him to execute anything like a safe, complex amphibious landing of Sheridan's troops a few hundred miles north of the Antarctic Circle. Though a highly skilled pilot, he lacked the ability, one gained only from experience, to order men off his ships in assaults over water and onto hostile beaches. His scant knowledge of such operations came from books and briefings. All this did not prevent Young from enjoying Fieldhouse's confidence and a close relationship with Woodward, his senior officer and ship's rider, during the just-finished spring exercises.

The deficits incurred by Nott's financial cuts were immediately apparent. For example, those who loaded out 3 Commando Brigade and its follow-on, 5 Infantry Brigade, had insufficient familiarity with combat loading for an amphibious assault—with the necessity of stowing the most-needed equipment on top and the least-wanted on the bottom.[102] During the entire war, precious time and helicopter flying hours were consumed getting the right materiel on the right ship for use by the troops at the right time. British forces paid a dear price for their lack of a skilled head of logistics who knew amphibious operations and could on short notice organize and deploy combat materiel for all the services. Sheridan's panoply of materiel intended for occupying South Georgia also had marked deficiencies. His men lacked artillery, armored support, and air support. An opponent possessing weapons heavier than .5 caliber machine guns could isolate and ultimately destroy them. He carried only two medium mortars with limited ammunition.

The remedy, in part, was to come from CTG 317.1.9. If able to close the landing site and if able to act in concert, their 4 x 4.5" guns would cover Sheridan and Nunn with a sustained firing rate of twenty-four rounds per minute and keep the defending forces in their trenches while the British landed. In addition, a naval gunfire support party [22] was assigned to direct the gunfire after landing. This gave Nunn some confidence that M Company would not be out-gunned as long as the weather held.

In toto, Young had four ships: *Antrim*, *Plymouth*, the tanker *Tidespring*, and Barker's *Endurance*, which was already on station. Young had no air support as defined by NATO standards but did have a Wessex 3 anti-submarine (ASW) helicopter on *Antrim*, a Wasp utility helicopter on *Plymouth*, and two Wessex 5 light helicopters on *Tidespring*. The helicopters were purpose-built and fitted out for various narrow tasks. The Wessex 5s were designed as troop carriers for 4 men with kit, a useful but inadequate means for transporting Sheridan's force onto land. Though Chris Nunn of M Company was one of the most skilled helicopter pilots in Arctic flying, he was ordered to command ground troops and thus became a helicopter passenger rather than pilot. If it came to a pitched battle fought over time with a normal number of casualties of men and equipment, Sheridan had serious deficits. He had to win or at least get all his force ashore in daylight quickly. In addition, Young's appreciation of his mission excluded, perhaps justifiably, two valuable assets: the BAS persons ashore were safe, knowledgeable, and willing to share their depth of knowledge about South Georgia, and the failure of the Argentinian marines to patrol aggressively out of their frozen hutches in order to root out these same watchers.

Barker, the commanding officer of *Endurance* was nearly a legend in his own time. Many knowledgeable about the Royal Navy's affairs in 1982 believe that he, with his experience on *Endurance*—the Falklands station ship—should have been chosen to organize and sustain the landing and recapture of South Georgia. He had acquired a navy-wide reputation as an extremely capable CO. Before his assignment to *Endurance,* he had commanded several ships, most valuably *Arrow*, which was equipped with Exocet missiles, a surface weapon the Argentinian Navy would most likely use against the British. Barker had watched from close by the Argentinian buildup, knew its strengths and weaknesses, and knew the Argentinian patch of the South Atlantic, where Young and his ship had never been.

Barker also had that chimerical but priceless advantage, tactical familiarity with his operational area. He had landed on and walked about South Georgia. Only his helicopter pilots could also give the amphibious force firsthand guidance on South Georgia's unique terrain and execrable weather. He personally knew much of the BAS staff, including those few still living free on the island. He had even entertained and been entertained by the very Argentinian naval officers he might face in combat: "Our host ship was the cruiser *Belgrano*. On behalf of Admiral Lombardo I was well looked after by Captain Zaraetiegui with whom I struck up an immediate rapport. We had several evenings together. I learned that he was waiting to be promoted to Rear-Admiral together with a special posting to be in charge of what amounted to the operational base from which a Falklands Campaign could be launched."[103]

In addition, *Endurance* had a full set of communications gear, which Young's *Antrim* lacked. Barker's communications gang regularly intercepted and translated Argentinian military messages. They knew how, when, and under what circumstances the Argentinians spoke with one another. A tactical perspective also argued for Barker. Having successfully commanded a combat ship, Barker knew the kinds of decisions the British sea force commander would face if it came to war. With Barker as the task group's commander, Young could then have managed *Antrim* in combat, a sufficiently difficult task without also having to care for the full squadron. "Nick Barker was a superb example of what a naval officer should be" a senior British officer commented after the war.[104] His crew thought so, too.

The marines were kitted out with only what each could carry. Sheridan's plan to seize the island was crimped from the start because his men could carry very few mortar rounds, had no shoulder-fired rockets to destroy hostile positions, and had no backup if they faced overwhelming opposition. Nowhere in the reports and literature of the day can be found an indication that the Royal Navy staff realized how daunting this job would be. Finally, 132 men and their gear boarded two VC-10 airliners for Ascension Island by way of Dakar. The Senegalese government, almost certainly coached by their French advisors, agreed to refuel the planes but not to allow Sheridan's men to debark. It is hot aboard a crowded aircraft in Dakar.

Before April had seen ten days, the chain of command for *Operate Corporate* had already strained. No air officer had been assigned to plan and coordinate air missions and maintenance for the helicopters carried by Young's force, Task Group 317.1 Each flight commander and ship's CO was left to plan his own sorties as required by the moment and suggested by the marines and special warfare troops. Detached from 42 Commando and from Headquarters 3 Brigade, the command and control problem that was to burden Sheridan and to plague the entire operation emerged as soon as the fleet left its UK ports—there was no central commander aside from the unit commanders, no supremo, no one in a position similar to Eisenhower's in the run up to and actual invasion of Normandy. Petty squabbles went unchecked by a senior captain or colonel. By regulation and custom and as formulated through years of NATO exercises, the Squadron CO, in this case Young (a Royal Navy captain with no amphibious experience) had to direct the entire operation until Sheridan had landed and declared his troops "firm" and able to be deployed safely.[105]

The questions remained: when, where and how was Sheridan to execute his order to recapture South Georgia? There was a marked lack of collegiality on *Antrim's* bridge, and the counsel of his juniors and of Land Force Commander Sheridan to Young seemingly went unheard. Nurtured for a lifetime by the heroic pieties of the RN that commanders are meant to act from bravery, experience, and training, Young's last naval days were embalmed with reluctance, lassitude, and incoherence. That was a pity, because Sheridan's men, not Young's (who stayed safe from air and submarine attacks) would be the ones to run ashore and face a hostile enemy. As matters stood on April 8, the Defence Ministry in London stipulated the missions for all. Woodward, from his flagship somewhere at sea, gave Young such directions as when and where to refuel. Young was the boss on the scene until the troops got safely ashore, Sheridan was the commander of the land force, and Nunn ordered the fighting men who would do the bleeding. But no British officer with any service time in South Georgia's waters directed what would be the most vital aspect of the war thus far: the hour-by-hour coordination of the land, sea, and air assets informed by the best available tactical and eyeball intelligence at hand, all to be accomplished in some of the world's worst weather. With little thought needed, Vaux and his superiors at 3 Brigade Royal Marines concluded that Nunn and his men were best suited for this bone-chilling venture given their experience with mountain and Arctic flying. The Corps of the Royal Marines knew more than any others in the British forces about the perils and dimensions of their mission. They had amphibious training and experience and knew more about rocks, glaciers, snow, and ice than any other British military component.

Fieldhouse's April 11 message to Thompson, CO of 3 Brigade, and Commodore Michael Clapp, the support force commander, dispelled any thought that repossession of South Georgia was to be a sideshow to the Falklands, "as current intelligence indicates clear advantage in landing South Georgia earliest."[106] The sources of that intelligence and the decision making that turned out the order were never provided to Young and Sheridan, who would be executing the findings from that intelligence at spear's point. Nunn was uneasy, and wrote later: "When Guy was identified as the land force commander I could see and welcomed the logic, but had obvious concerns about my responsibilities which I raised with the CO [Vaux] and then discussed frankly with Guy. I received Nick's assurance and then Guy's that I remained" in command of M Company Group and that while "Guy would deal with the political and operational aspects and command the operation, I would undertake the training and tactical aspects of the Coy Group and that 'only I' would give it orders. . . .

'I am pleased to say that from then on the issue was never in question.'"[107] It was a sound arrangement: Nunn ordered the shooters, and Sheridan kept his three marine signalers and a medical team composed of Surgeon Lieutenant Crispin Swinhoe, Chief Petty Officer White, and a Leading Medical Assistant, Woodgate.

Ashore, a ready-made intelligence team from the BAS was monitoring and reporting on Argentinian troops whenever they exited from their warm hutches in Grytviken. Because communications between BAS and *Antrim* had not been thought through, they were sometimes clumsy and not easily used or controlled. If ground action were imminent, the BAS clearly could not return to Grytviken for new radio batteries or provisions. There comes a time in military matters where prudence leads to caution, which then breeds inaction. Such caution was generally practiced but unnecessary on South Georgia Island. The Argentines never did institute aggressive patrols or investigations of their half-conquered land. BAS was able to give Sheridan almost all the reconnaissance data he needed, because there was simply no significant Argentinian military activity in the regions to which Sheridan had to go.

By the middle of April, it became clear to the Junta that the British were committed to retaking the Falklands by force if Argentina did not adhere to the provisions of UN Resolution 502 and withdraw their troops from the Falklands and South Georgia. The Junta's mindset changed; the expectation of easy victory weakened. Combat among ships, planes, submarines, and men had become a real possibility. Yet the military planning to deal with this unsettling situation could not be put into play in Buenos Aires. The Argentinian staff had no precedent for such affairs, and there was little to orchestrate the military arts of communications, logistics, combat support, and so forth into a coherent plan of operations. Galtieri's reinforcement of South Georgia was overly hurried, if not panicky. He had to surmount the following:

(1) The Junta's staff knew little about South Georgia or its surrounding waters.

(2) The recently landed Argentinian marines had come to realize that Grytviken and Leith were the sole habitable settlements, but they failed to keep an effective military eye on even these.

(3) South Georgia had no airport.

(4) High winds made airdrops on the island unreliable and unpredictable.

(5) Amphibious ships could not use what few beaches existed. South George's rocks, shoals, and beaches were uncharted and not reconnoitered.

(6) Surface ships would risk attack from British submarines and planes.

Additional landings by an integrated Argentinian combat force could not be accomplished by using the small and primitive docks. The troopships used for landings on East Falkland sorely needed patching up and not one was available for the voyage to South Georgia. Argentinian heavy guns, their ammunition, crews, and spare parts were never brought to the island. Seemingly small details had major ramifications. For example, lubricants and replacement items for specialized equipment such as small arms and generators intended for use in Argentina or the Falklands would have frozen or been otherwise unworkable in the cold and wet of South Georgia.

Thatcher's dispatch to the South Atlantic of a full combat fleet after Port Stanley's fall prompted yet another turn in Anaya's strategy. He now put forward a plan for a defining sea battle in which Woodward's southbound force would be defeated by Argentina's single carrier task force before the British could land troops on the Falklands. Anaya hastened his combat fleet, especially its single carrier, north of the Falklands to positions from which he believed he could block the Royal Navy. In the ensuing *renversement*, the carrier's planes never engaged the British ships for lack of sufficient wind over the deck. Old and ill-repaired engines threatened to quit if the engines were brought to sufficient power for the planes to take off. The surface-to-surface missiles carried by the Argentinian destroyers that accompanied the carrier never launched. In the event, they might never have fired accurately because they had not been subject to the rigorous testing employed by first-class navies. Anaya's Mahanian epiphany ended in disaster when *Conqueror* sank the *Belgrano* on May 2, and the Argentinian fleet scuttled back to port, never to reemerge.

There is no utility in ascribing responsibility to any person or persons for the Argentinian Navy's abject failure to engage the British battle group in decisive combat. Any idea of defeating the British fleet at sea was chimerical from the outset and has been well treated elsewhere. One fact deserves repeating: Anaya's ruminations on the Falklands rode on the mythos that retaking the Malvinas should be a naval affair, a naval triumph, and a naval contribution to Argentinian grandeur. If Admiral Anaya has explicated the roots and logic of his belief, it is not available now in published form. In any case, the Americans had thought ahead. As Caspar Weinberger remembered, "In some discussions . . . with Mrs. Thatcher and two or three others, some one [sic] jokingly put to me, 'What if we need a carrier' and I said, 'Why of course no problem'. . . . We gave a great deal of intelligence help."[108]

Anaya and Galtieri's thinking turned quickly from grandiose to petty. They decided after their combat fleet's debacle to rely on a covert reinforcement of South Georgia by submarine as the only sure way to retain South Georgia. Why this strategically and tactically useless ice and rock merited such attention is unfathomable, unless they believed its loss would prefigure the Junta's own downward slide. The ancient diesel-powered submarine *Santa Fe* got the call. The Junta's press had crowed that submarines engaged British warships and were major players in the war. In fact, the *Santa Fe* sailed but never engaged any Royal Navy ship, unless escape from British helicopters and anti-submarine warfare ships counts as a sea battle.[109] The casual reader might well ask: "How could a country whose wealth came from land and peasants but was now governed by militarists who had never fought a war or grasped the rudiments of maritime strategy and tactics order ramshackle ships manned by inexperienced crews to fight a professional navy—and hope to execute tricky amphibious warfare with one dilapidated submarine?"[110]

Argentinian planning had not all been slap-dash. For the invasion of East Stanley, Anaya's staff had taken three months to compose and a further two months to refine a good operations plan. Argentinian marines executed that plan clumsily but, in the end, occupied Port Stanley, its environs, Goose Green, and parts of West Falkland. That accomplished, the Junta's staff, or at least a small part of it, was pressed to turn its attention towards dealing with Young's tiny squadron and whatever it intended to do. In the meantime, Sheridan, Nunn, and their professional infantrymen waited in the wings for what they knew not.

Yet a prickly foreboding registered on the dissenters in the staff who, despite their minimal knowledge of South Georgia, saw that they had nearly lost a ship to Mills's few troops firing from land, had lost two helicopters during the invasion of East Falkland, and had suffered several killed and wounded before being able to take control of South Georgia's shabby habitations. If the young men on the Junta's staff sniffed something in the air, US Secretary of State Haig was certain and from Buenos Aires wrote to National Security Advisor Clark that:

I called you on open line with clear recognition that the Argentines would monitor. In order to break impossible impasse this morning on force withdrawal modalities, I created the impression that British military action was about to take place. While somewhat over-theatrical, it has the virtue of being true in the context of first British units steaming toward South Georgia Island. Fortunately, the ploy worked and it is vital that I leave here with an assessment by the Argentines not only that the British are going to attack but we are only hours away from such event. You handled it on the phone precisely as I had hoped.[111]

Notes

81-The Casa Rosada, so named for its color, is unlike the White House and No. 10 Downing Street in that it has a high balcony from which the Argentinian head can address thousands of persons below.

82-Argentine Military Staff Appreciation, Winter 1982. This lament on the part of both junior and senior Argentinian officers recurred in their correspondence and conversation with the author.

83-Lord Trefgarne, FCO Spokesman, July 1981 quoted in Denis Healey, *The Time of My Life* (London: M. Joseph, 1989).

84-Quoted in Edward Schumacher, "Falkland Mission: Haig's Long Days in Argentina," *New York Times*, April 21, 1982.

85-"James Rentschler's Falklands Diary 1 April – 25 June 1982." Reagan Library.

86-40 Commando and the Air Defence Troop were stood down on March 31, 1982 and were told: "no units are required." Michael Clapp and Ewen Southby-Tailyour, *Amphibious Assault Falklands: The Battle of San Carlos Water* (Annapolis, MD, Naval Institute Press, 1996), 14.

87-R. W. Apple, Jr., "Crisis is Expected to Aid Tories in Local Elections," *New York Times*, May 6, 1982.

88-Tuchman's magisterial *The Guns of August* rightly points out that once the German General Staff had pushed the button to start the war, the conflict could not be stopped because the social, economic, military, and industrial sides of the country were dynamically intertwined. Barbara W. Tuchman, *The Guns of August* (NY: Macmillan, 1962). Either side could have ended the Falklands war by a simple withdrawal of the occupying troops or by recall of the British fleet.

89-Margaret Thatcher, *The Downing Street Years* (New York: HarperCollins, 1993), 179.

90-Nott remembered later that "I asked Margaret [January 1981- No 10 Downing St.] 'if she excluded a radical look at the Defence programme'. 'Oh, no she [Thatcher] said . . . by all means you can have a radical look at the Defence programme, and I hope you do.'" John Nott, *Here Today, Gone Tomorrow: Recollections of an Errant Politician* (London: Politico's, 2002), 210. It is difficult to believe that Thatcher knew what Nott intended and what effects his large cuts on the Royal Navy would have if it were ever called to sail off to war.

91-Lord Bramall remembers from his budget jousts with Nott that Nott never considered any funded defense of the remaining pieces of its former empire. See W. G. F. Jackson and Lord Bramall, *The Chiefs: The Story of the United Kingdom Chiefs of Staff* (London: Brassey's, 1992), 398.

92-"We had no advance planning figures whatsoever. . . . Apparently even they (the marines) didn't know what they were to get." Captain Shane Redmond commenting on RFA *Tidespring's* load out for Operation Paraquat in Roger Perkins, *Operation Paraquat: The Battle for South Georgia* (Chippenham: Picton Publishing, 1986), 116.

93-Thatcher, *The Downing Street Years*, 205: "It was on this day (19 April) that the War Cabinet authorized the operation to repossess South Georgia." Given the April 7 order to Vaux's 42 Commando to get up a force to invade South Georgia, Thatcher may be seen to have been marching ahead of her war cabinet.

94-Thatcher Conversation with *New York Times* reporter John Fenton, *New York Times,* April 26, 1992.

95-Thatcher to Fenton, *New York Times,* April 26, 1992.

96-Prominent Argentinian editor quoted in James M. Markham, "Haig's Weak Cards," *New York Times*, April 19, 1982.

97-Rentschler's Diary, p. 4.

98-Vaux was told that the Argentinian forces on South Georgia had "heavy naval support." No capability for heavy support as defined by NATO's standards existed anywhere in the Argentinian Navy. Poor intelligence got Britain into the war and bedeviled it throughout the conflict. Nick Vaux, *Take That Hill: Royal Marines in the Falklands War* (Washington: Pergamon-Brassey's International Defense Publishers, 1986), 17.

99-BAS Chronology, rev. January 7, 1985 p. 20.

100-See Vaux, *Take That Hill*. This book is the best on the Falklands War.

101-When Lieutenant Colonel Richard Eve, the artillery officer assigned to Operation Paraquat, boarded *Antrim*, he was given an admiral's cabin because Young knew him to be senior to Major Sheridan. Eve explained to Young that whatever their respective rank, Sheridan, as land force commander, was automatically senior to all other ground officers. Eve graciously relinquished his spacious quarters to Sheridan, who turned them into his operations room.

102-See Clapp and Southby-Tailyour, *Amphibious Assault Falkland* for Commodore Clapp's heroic efforts to get the logistical side of the Falklands War right. He did.

103-Nicholas Barker, *Beyond Endurance: An Epic of Whitehall and the South Atlantic* (London: L. Cooper, 1997), 96.

104-Senior British officer, in conversation with the author, many years after the war.

105-NATO's Allied Tactical Publication Eight, the Bible for NATO's military operations, lays out these relationships.

106-Clapp and Southby-Tailyour, *Amphibious Assault Falkland*, 54.

107-Nunn, correspondence with the author, April 2012.

108-Caspar Weinberger in Ronald Reagan Oral History Project, "The Falklands Roundtable," Miller Center of Public Affairs, University of Virginia, May 15, 2003, http://web1.millercenter.org/poh/falklands/transcripts/falklands_2003_0515.pdf, 20.

109-Jackson Diehl, "Thatcher Confers On the Next Move in South Atlantic: Galtieri, Uncontested, Upholds Firm Stance," *Washington Post*, April 25, 1982.

110-*Santa Fe's* twin, the *San Luis,* put to sea and engaged the British battle force and the landing ships at San Carlo. It fired four torpedoes: two lost their wires, one ran to its fuel's end, and one came back on *San Luis*. Captain Azcueta was a brave skipper. Knowing that his fire control system was not dependable, he snugged his boat right up close to a British ship, (probably *Alacrity*) and fired two torpedoes, which missed. After these mishaps, the boat returned to port. Retired Argentine Naval officer, letter to the author, April 2008.

111-Secretary Haig to National Security Advisor Clark, April 18, 1982. In National Security Archive, "Briefing Book No. 374." http://www.gwu.edu/~nsarchiv/NSAEBB/NSAEBB374/.

Six

Why South Georgia? The US-British Response

With one glaring exception, the end of the beginning of the American campaign in the South Pacific sixty-five years earlier offers a parallel to the Falklands War. Eric Larrabee, the best historian of that doleful era, explains that:

Strategically speaking, the Guadalcanal campaign was a stepchild. It led nowhere, except to the port and harbor of Rabaul in New Britain. . . . It had no geographical relation to the course the war would later follow. . . . The plan for it was impromptu, a compromise that satisfied no one, and it developed on a pattern its planners had not foreseen and the men who fought it had not been prepared for. Several of the senior commanders involved either disapproved or gave it halfhearted support, and there is some question how many of them really understood it. The logistical backup was at first so mismanaged that essential weapons and equipment were lacking or in short supply. . . . Yet victory when it came . . . was decisive.[112]

Both sides sent their best troops. Both had valid strategic goals, the defense of Australia by the Americans, its isolation by the Japanese. The Japanese lost the better part of an elite jungle-trained army before the Americans gained their bloody victory. What was different in the Falklands War, however, was that the dowdy orchestrations of the Argentinian military stood in sad contrast to the exemplary qualities of the British fighting men. That is not to say, however, that this was a proud hour for either nation's foreign office. Or as one senior State Department official said of the British, "Jesus Christ! How could they have let this happen?"[113]

Mills's stout defense of South Georgia caused the Junta to reexamine the fuzzy assumptions on which they had acted; they began to wonder if Thatcher might preempt the capture of East Falkland by a violent reaction of her own.[114] In fact, Thatcher was caught. The UK had no military capability close enough to the Falklands to reconnoiter Argentinian military moves there, let alone prevent them. Yet by April 6, her wobbly political position in city and shire and among Conservative MPs demanded a military response to the Junta's awkward intervention or surrender to it. The British people, it was clear, blamed her for the disgrace as much as they did Galtieri. "The man on the streets wants some action. Government leaders have allowed us to become a joke."[115] As leader of her party and the government, she could not keep her perch on the House of Commons frontbench without a dramatic riposte to the Junta's adventurism. In the short term, she needed a visible military victory, however large or small, even if the gamble carried slim odds. A dollop of panache would add spice to the headlines and establish her as a successful wartime commander. But there was a hitch. As Thatcher's government and its military heads finally saw that a shooting war had begun, it became clear that Mills and his twenty-one stalwarts on South Georgia had been all too small a force for the military task that confronted them. That a British nuclear submarine had not turned south days, if not weeks sooner, to oppose the Argentinian landings on East Falkland and on South Georgia was a matter of apparent indifference to Admiral Fieldhouse's political masters. Not to have warned the Junta, in explicit terms, that British submarines could sink the entire Argentinian Navy in a few days stands as one of the most glaring omissions of the conflict.

In fact, Galtieri's seizure of the Falklands could not have been more badly timed for Margaret Thatcher. Race riots in English cities, substantial unemployment, High-Tory disdain for Thatcher herself, and the normal rubbings of Parliamentary politics had eroded her dominance over the Conservative Party and the House of Commons. That first week of April, she fired her Foreign Secretary, Lord Peter Carrington, a useful and necessary act under the circumstances.[116] He had, after all, headed the government's foreign policy apparatus while the crisis gestated. The downside to this show of prime ministerial power was her forced acceptance of the much loathed, arch wet Francis Pym as Carrington's replacement.[117] Pym's hawkishness toward Argentina remained in doubt until war's end and beyond.[118] Thatcher and Pym disliked and mistrusted one another, but at least one potential opponent to her policies was close to hand, where he could not babble too loudly against the war. Pym emerged at least temporarily from wetness on April 7, 1982, when in his fig-leaf maiden speech as foreign minister he told Parliament, "Britain does not appease dictators."[119]

Whatever political blather spewed from her ministers and their advisors, Thatcher's own administration in its day-to-day workings had brought her sudden and crushing grief. The Foreign Office had failed to prevent a small difficulty from gestating into a major crisis.[120] She could not rely on her intelligence community after its failure to assess accurately Argentina's overt preparations for war and after the Joint Intelligence Committee's conclusion that Argentina would not opt for an "extreme option" in the immediate future.[121] A new political party, the Social Democrats, had risen to a 40% approval rating in nationwide polls and threatened a major victory over the Conservatives in the looming local elections. Not everyone in her own party was happy with her. Far from it. Few wanted bloodshed. Her whips, working to gain support in the House, found six different shades of opinion about the course to be taken. Some loyal Thatcherites bolted, never again to be allowed into her magic circle. Few saw any particular Conservative charging into the House of Commons on a white horse; it was simply that a menacing minority wanted her to sit quietly on a back bench while it started a new day for the party and the country. The overarching worry in Whitehall, Parliament, and the electorate was that Margaret Thatcher, the master of domestic politics had never participated in a war, let alone been compelled to marshal her country for an armed conflict whose loss would strip the UK from the pantheon of major powers. Her job as PM, as leader of her party, as a voice for the special relationship between the US and the UK, and as the finger on the trigger of nuclear weapons, as well as her moral quest for radical changes in British society were all now in jeopardy. Thatcher could be excused from going to bed convinced that there were few whom she could trust to retrieve her fortunes. She threw the dice.

So on April 1, major fleet units homebound from spring exercises near Gibraltar reversed course, loaded war stores, and sailed southwards. It would take many weeks before troops could assault Port Stanley. In the meantime, Thatcher needed a dramatic event to keep her cabinet with her, to put Galtieri on the defensive, to still her domestic opponents, to preserve US support, to rally the free world to her side, and to convince the captive Kelpers that they might get their freedom back. The needs were immediate, for the sharks were beginning to circle. James Callaghan, Labor's spokesman on defense, accused Thatcher of a "gross blunder" in letting the Falklands fall.[122] From Thatcher's own party, the Falkland Islands lobby shouted, "I told you so" so stridently that a Foreign Office spokesman was moved to retort, "Air Commodore Frow [the lobby's spokesman] has no official standing whatever. The crisis is entirely a matter for the British government."[123] Margaret Thatcher's contingent concern was the Junta, especially Galtieri and Anaya, but her torment of the night was Michael R. D. Foot, who as leader of the opposition kept a ready garrote for the prime minister's throat if she stumbled. There was the Argentinean angle too. If, despite his self-adulatory bluster, Galtieri could be persuaded by the combination of the UN's disfavor, US assistance to the UK, and Thatcher's bellicose speeches that he faced defeat, then the war might end bloodlessly.

Major Sheridan and his men had a valid military mission, but they constituted a pawn, perhaps a rook, in Thatcher's drive to survive.

Once the British fleet had sailed from UK ports, a silent rump of Argentinian staff officers in Buenos Aires believed that the Junta had miscalculated and that it would, in the end, suffer humiliation at the hands of the British military. Their unspoken view was confirmed when Task Force TG 317.1 broke off from Rear Admiral Woodward's force and headed for what could only be, in the desolate South Atlantic, South Georgia. In an unforeseen way, the British government broke the news. After April 4, the BAS Director in Cambridge replied *en clair* to his field parties' concerns: "We have not been idle. Other I cannot discuss."[124] And later to the party on Lyell Glacier: "Moving to Grytviken possibly involves risk of involvement in later fighting."[125] It is not known if the Argentinian military staff read these unencrypted communications, yet by a peculiar turn of logic, some Argentinian officers, mostly from the naval staff, concluded then, and said so later, that South Georgia was worth the fight if only to offer more time for their masters to negotiate the conflict's end. This gambit resembled the mythic Russian practice of throwing the baby out of the sled to distract the wolves.

As soon as the very visible and expensive preparations for war were put in train, Thatcher's allies and opponents alike clamored for quick results.[126] British army and marines trucks filled the highways rolling towards the soon congested southern ports. Sheridan's men, the putative conquerors of South Georgia, were pulled aside from 42 Commando's formation and confined to barracks. But Galtieri's occupation of South Georgia, by itself, was not Thatcher's sole point of concern. It was not altogether clear that Britain's military professionals were of one mind about the chances of success in re-possessing the island.[127] Senior military men abroad issued mordant warnings about an operation for which British forces had neither the equipment nor the expertise to complete. Edward Streator, the American Minister in London and Falklands point man during the war said, "I don't know anyone in a significant position of authority in the UK who was convinced they were going to win."[128] In the face of adversity, Thatcher plunged her dwindling political capital into a distant venture of whose causes and possible results few knew much.[129] A war cabinet was formed, and the dogs of war began to bay.[130] That pervasive confusion, disagreement, and moral feebleness existed at the top of Thatcher's government has never been denied, least of all by the prime minister herself. What is equally true is that that those debilitating antics did not percolate down to the fighting troops. Of all Thatcher's colleagues in this venture, the officers and men of 3 Commando Brigade, the ships' companies, and the pilots were the most competent and resolute.

Notes

112-Eric Larrabee, *Commander In Chief: Franklin Delano Roosevelt, His Lieutenants, and Their War* (New York: Simon & Schuster, 1988), 257.

113-A high-ranking State Department official upon hearing of the invasion. Told to the author in confidence.

114-Retired Argentinian staff officer's private correspondence with the author, winter 2006.

115-Quote from Stan Longhurst, British citizen. Steven Rattner, "Britons, Frustrated and Angered, Assail Failure to Foresee Invasion," *New York Times*, April 5, 1982.

116-Peter Lord Carrington's resignation was crowed to the press as a noble act after a serious lapse in his judgment and performance and in those of the foreign affairs community. One may speculate that he did not wish to remain in the midst of what seemed like a disastrous end to Thatcher's government and did not wish to swing for the defeat. One could also advance the proposition that he had been gulled by his colleagues and could no longer work with them. If he did leave voluntarily, he must have known that his successor would be less sympathetic than he to the war and to the PM.

117-She wasn't sure she was going to survive, took the whips advice and chose Pym—with whom she quarreled incessantly thereafter." Alan Clark, *Mrs. Thatcher's Minister: The Private Diaries of Alan Clark* (New York: Farrar, Straus, and Giroux, 1994), 97.

118-On April 18, Francis Pym told the House of Commons that force would not be used as long as negotiations continued. That would have prevented Operation Paraquat. Either Pym had not been told of the plans to retake South Georgia by force or he had decided to formulate his own policy on the war. The former is more likely. Pym was forced to return to the House later that night and to withdraw his remarks. Margaret Thatcher, *The Downing Street Years* (New York: HarperCollins, 1993), 204.

119-Pym in the House of Commons, April 7, 1982. http://hansard.millbanksystems.com/commons/1982/apr/07/falkland-islands#S6CV0021P0_19820407_HOC_198

120-After the war, Pym referred to it as "negotiations over rocks." Francis Pym, *The Politics of Consent* (London: H. Hamilton, 1984).

121-Peter Lord, Carrington, *Reflecting on Things Past: The Memoirs of Peter Lord Carrington* (New York: Harper & Row, 1989), 367.

122-R. W. Apple Jr., "Britain Imposing War Zone Around Falkland Islands; Haig Plans Mediation Trips," *New York Times*, April 8, 1982.

123-Rita Dallas, "Suddenly the Phones Are Ringing At Falklands' Cramped London Office," *Washington Post*, April 11, 1982, A15.

124-BAS Chronology, revised, January 7, 1985, p. 41.

125-BAS Chronology, revised, January 7, 1985, p. 41

126-"The press was very hostile." Thatcher, *The Downing Street Years*, 185.

127-"John gave the MoD's view that the Falklands could not be retaken once they were seized." Thatcher, *The Downing Street Years*, 179.

128-Edward Streator in Ronald Reagan Oral History Project, "The Falklands Roundtable," Miller Center of Public Affairs, University of Virginia, May 16, 2003, http://web1.millercenter.org/poh/falklands/transcripts/falklands_2003_0515.pdf, 17.

129-Thatcher herself erred when in her opening statement to the House of Commons on April 2, 1982, she mentioned the "Falkland Islands and their dependencies." As noted earlier, South Georgia is a dependency of Great Britain itself and administered from the Falkland Islands. Thatcher, *The Downing Street Years*, 183. British Antarctic Territory Order In Council 1962 (Statutory Instrument 1962/400) created a separate territory for South Georgia.

130-The War Cabinet consisted of: Margaret Thatcher, Francis Pym, John Nott, Willie Whitelaw, and Cecil Parkinson. Sir Terence Lewin, Chief of the Defence Staff, and Attorney General Michael Havers also attended meetings, as did, from time to time, sundry FCO and military people like Brigadier Peter de la Billiere, head of the Special Warfare community. At least one meeting was held each day. Thatcher, *The Downing Street Years*, 188-189.

Seven

Troubles on Fortuna Glacier

Troops, weapons, equipment, fuel, spare parts, and technicians from the UK began to arrive on Ascension Island that first week of April, and the fleet came to crowd inside the harbor. Thatcher wanted military action for political ends, and the men wanted to fight and return home. Sheridan's force, as it arrived at 0830 on April 10, consisted of 132 officers and men and what they could carry. Nettlesome problems arose immediately. The Royal Marines officer who commanded the SBS had arrived at Ascension before Sheridan and set up a small arms range where troops could reset their weapons' sights after the bumpy trip from Britain. There, Sheridan learned from a scrap of paper, rather than from a formal Northwood communication, that Northwood had ordered an entire squadron of SAS (sixty men), D Squadron commanded by Major Cedric Delves, and two more SBS teams to join his force.[131]

> Guy,
>
> 1. Change of plan! [At this point Sheridan had not been told of any plan.]
>
> 2. You will now be supported by 1 x section from 2 SBS and 1 x troop of D Sqn. Therefore I have arranged for all of the D Sqn M&AW stores to transfer to Antrim tonight. Please sight them and arrange for their transfer to Endurance as required. I have not attempted to break the stores down since I have no idea what is required. This will mean that the rest of the Sqn will be minus their stores.
>
> 3. No more news. Col Richard Preston [chief of staff for the entire Corps of the Royal Marines] is now here and is talking to Glamorgan now. I hope the D Sqn plan works – you probably want to mix SBS and D Sqn for their landings – a

tricky problem.

4.   Best of luck

Guy,

Last minute note.

1.   I have just seen a tasking signal saying you are to deploy 7 patrols (I presume this means 4 x D Sqn and 3 x 2 SBS) with the rest of 2 SBS to remain on Fort Austin. I believe you need to have 3 x 2 SBS patrols plus OC and SSM and I hope this is how 2SBS have read that signal.

2.   D Sqn are great at the direct action business – you might have to restrain their 'get up and go' a bit during the recce phase!

3.   I will follow your adventures.[132]

Sheridan had earlier requested the Royal Marines Mountain and Arctic Warfare [M&AW] Cadre as his instrument for reconnaissance because he had commanded them and knew their capabilities and equipment to be better than those of the SAS Mountain Troop. 42 Commando and the M&AW Cadre had just completed very successful Arctic exercises together. The M&AW Cadre knew the marines' shorthand for communications, military planning, and the small ways of going about serious military tasks. Sheridan also had, as a part of Nunn's troops, two sections from the reconnaissance troop of 42 Commando, more than enough capability for the assigned task. These included senior NCO mountain leaders. These men were among the few best Arctic trained soldiers in the British military. Surely it would have been better to let Sheridan use his own snowy colleagues for this dicey task.

No military adventure conducted on the fly eight thousand miles away from where it was planned is without slips, but this unsuitable assignment of reconnaissance troops half as large as the assault force for which it worked had grave portents. The SAS kit was heavy, large, and a burden to every ship on which Delves's men landed. *Antrim* and *Tidespring* were very small ships. From *Antrim* and elsewhere, Delves sent private communications to his regimental commander, Lieutenant Colonel Mike Rose, the commanding officer of 22 SAS Regiment, and to Brigadier Peter de la Billiere, the commander of all British Special Forces. These SAS officers sent and answered messages on special phones lent by the US for use outside the chain of command during Operation Paraquat. These communications were not copied to Woodward, Young, or Sheridan. For example the whole of D Squadron SAS was handed to Sheridan without consultation, approval, or advance notification.[133] The chain of command thus became a shambles before Sheridan's force entered the operating area. 3 Commando Brigade had very precise chains of authority and responsibility. Sloppy practices of the outside world had bedeviled the marines' officers and men during the entire war. Unified command of an operation once broken is seldom regained, and indeed, in the case of the Falklands War, it never was.

Northwood did not consult Sheridan, their appointed man on the ground charged with retaking South Georgia, but went ahead and ordered seven patrols to scout the island. Why seven is unclear. And what did Northwood think they could learn about the operating area that Sheridan did not already know? Once again Sheridan did not receive a formal order, but handwritten directions arrived on the afternoon of April 10 from a fellow officer. Northwood did not disclose what these seven batches of young men were expected to find in the frigid reaches of South Georgia. Any tactical appreciation by officers as experienced as Sheridan and Nunn would have included an assessment of the Argentinian forces as unable to produce a stout or lengthy defense against British troops, backed as they were by the four guns on Young's destroyers, as long as Sheridan was allowed to mount a tactically sound attack in morning light using his entire force. The Argentinian marines had no heavy weapons to station near possible British landing sites, and there were few naturally defensible positions except in the mountains, where the occupiers had not ventured according to the BAS station keepers scattered around the island. Outside of divining Argentinian capabilities within the tight cluster of harbor facilities, common sense shouted that Nunn's M Company Group did not need and would have trouble finding useful tasks for so large a reconnaissance group as had been foisted upon him. That wretched abundance was make-work for the SAS squadron. The SAS's arrival at Task Group 317.1 kicked over any remaining traces of an effective operation executed by an informed professional command structure orchestrating the air, sea, reconnaissance, and amphibious aspects of Operation Paraquat. Then, at 0930 on April 15, an RAF Nimrod flew south from Ascension Island and dropped a pod retrieved by *Antrim's* boat crew, who in this way received the formal order to recapture South Georgia Island.

There is a backstory here. After the SAS had broken the Iranian Embassy siege in 1981, its extraordinary feat of arms was spread across the world's front page, and Brigadier Peter de la Billiere and his men became the apple of Thatcher's eye. 22 SAS Regiment achieved a primacy, at least at No. 10, far above the other military services.[134] When the Falklands War broke out, the theatrical aspects of that victory in London had not dimmed in the public mind, but the glories of Mirbat, Malaya, and the siege caused the SAS to itch from the vicissitudes of peace. The allure of putting his men into a tidy little war and perhaps adding a few more wreathes to the SAS's special history proved too great for de la Billiere, who had remained the SAS commander. That he ordered a full squadron with kit under Delves to join Task Group 317.1.9 without delay and without mature consideration of the resources needed to retake South Georgia Island still needs explaining. All this was consummated without consulting Sheridan or Young, who by this point had some idea of the military resources needed to complete the job. The simple notion that the quickly laid-on reconnaissance unit was fully half the size of M Company, the assault force for which it worked, escaped Northwood's nabobs, if in fact they knew of de la Billiere's precipitate move. But DLB, as he was popularly known, had unusual influence in Whitehall and a proven record of success in sticky affairs. Sheridan owned an extremely fine operational record but was junior in rank and had no influence in the danker recesses of the Ministry of Defence. DLB was given, and readily took, more privilege than most senior officers. Clearly he meant to put his stamp on this conflict and to control the war's narrative. He would leave it to his subordinates to find their way out of whatever woes they might suffer.[135] And suffer they did.

Yet de la Billiere remained an invisible presence throughout the war. His very existence hovered over *Antrim's* bridge, wardroom, and planning cells. He was efficiently served, for his SAS troopers were not kin to the brachycephalic brutes who rescued Wellington at La Haye; they were a well-trained family of technologically aware soldiers who were exceptionally competent in many military fields. Perhaps, too, curiosity about an unplanned war in a place he had never seen had gotten the better of him. Even so, the fractals of small unit warfare were the family business to the exclusion of others, and DLB meant to keep it that way. It made no difference to the commanders at Northwood that Delves's unit, with its independent access to Northwood, to DLB, and to its own chain of command shredded the integrity of Sheridan's hold on the entire operation.[136] War is a serious and bloody business. Families are forever shattered. But one cannot escape the notion that in DLB's interference, there was a schoolboy's whim to play in a rival's sandbox rather than to fill a valid military requirement.[137] The seizure of Grytviken did not ride on SAS troopers mushing across Fortuna Glacier. The taking of Grytviken depended on the crisp execution of a plan to occupy that sullen collection of moribund buildings. *Tout Court!*

Seven patrols slogging around South Georgia, an island which none of the service chiefs in London knew, put into play micromanagement at its most meddlesome and most risky. This practice hounded Julian Thompson, the commander of 3 Commando Brigade, all through his well-thought-out recapture of East Falkland Island and Port Stanley. Seven patrols ashore (instead of two) increased geometrically the possibility of their being compromised. Given their experience and training, any single patrol had almost no chance of being found, let us say a .9 probability of not being spotted. Insertion of seven patrols together meant that the entire patrol effort had only a .48 chance of any given patrol remaining undetected—thus tipping the odds in favor of the Argentines' firing on at least one of the small and off-the-beaten-path patrols. The horrible, virtually unpredictable weather, which changed every hour, could mask the patrols' insertions or prevent the men's exfiltration. When, where, and how many to put ashore were all decisions that might better have been left to Young and Sheridan. Even better still, a joint commander for all the forces connected with Paraquat should have been on scene making decisions about the allocation of forces, their tasks, and boundaries. But there was none. No general officer or decorated naval officer was ever to be found in the far reaches of South Georgia or treading water offshore for the simple reason that most military leaders in London considered Operation Paraquat an all but certain career-ending failure.

Northwood's orders to Young to engage South Georgia not before 1800 on April 21 were stipulated in Young's warning order of April 14 to Sheridan. With minimum damage to facilities and personnel, Sheridan was to:

1. Recapture Grytviken and Leith.
2. Neutralize Argentine Communications.
3. Capture or kill Argentinian military.
4. Arrest and remove Argentine civilians.[138]

That same day, the BBC noted that an operation against South Georgia might soon present itself. Upon leaving Ascension Island, where they had organized themselves after the long flight from the UK, Sheridan's force was split among Young's ships, none of which was purpose-built for amphibious operations or even remotely compatible with them.[139] No single ship in Young's squadron could carry the entire landing force, hoist them quickly over the side, or pack them into helicopters for an amphibious assault. Cranes, davits, and landing craft were missing. Most of M Company, the core assault force, went to *Tidespring*, a tanker, while the mortar crews, communicators, medics, and naval gunfire support team went with Sheridan to *Antrim* because, Nunn said, "I chose to be based with Guy on *Antrim* and not with Coy Main in *Tidespring*. I needed to be present when plans were made."[140] *Tidespring* was put in the unenviable position of carrying volatile fuels, live ammunition, and troops, with the immediate prospect of unloading one or all in rough seas and the distant possibility of being fired at.

By April 12, Young, on *Antrim,* had finally been told through official naval correspondence that three extra troops of D Squadron were to join his force. Delves and Rose continued to engage in black-box satellite communications with SAS headquarters in the UK, messages to which Sheridan was not privy. It was clear to the Royal Marine officers and their senior NCOs that the unrequested SAS manning imposed upon Sheridan had the potential of morphing Operation Paraquat into an SAS operation despite his being the nominated commander of the landing force.[141] Thatcher, Admiral Fieldhouse, the CINC, and Woodward had never experienced infantry warfare in the unique weather and terrain of South Georgia. Minister of Defence Nott had a long-ago term in the army, but withdrew from making military decisions in the war for his own undisclosed reasons. The SAS, wise in the ways of avoiding formal orders from above, wriggled their way around the bland Thameside admonitions and operated without the restraints typically laid upon an expeditionary force by its civilian and military leaders. Firsthand knowledge of the problems at spear's point and a transparent chain of command were never found at the top levels of Operation Paraquat. The mean scrapings and maladroit leadership of Nott's Defence Ministry blanketed some of the best infantrymen. Unwittingly, Thatcher had imposed an unnecessary burden on Sheridan, the man she needed above all others to succeed.

Ships at sea cannot add more room for fuel, food, or bullets. The extra SAS men and their gear thrust an almost intolerable burden onto Captain Brian Young's once tranquil world. *Antrim's* evaporators could not keep up with the demands of the boilers, crews, and surfeit of passengers for fresh water. Rationing began. The improvident glut of SAS bodies and kit fueled speculation among officers and men alike that senior military persons at Northwood, and perhaps Thatcher herself, believed that the Falklands matter could be concluded in Britain's favor by a brief successful attack on South Georgia and that de la Billiere's SAS interlopers, with Thatcher and Northwood's approval, craved and would perform a major part of the military action and take the succeeding credit.

Northwood's interference with decisions that should have been made on scene by the tactical commanders using their eyeballs began a practice that continued throughout the war and did nothing to hasten its end. Putting seven patrols ashore was misguided enough, for example, but finding and retrieving them laid additional burdens on the few available helicopters and on their service crews, who labored on freezing decks to keep their charges flying. All the while, Young lacked a trained air officer to command and allocate economically all air assets in concert with the land force commander's needs. Finally, the effort was plagued by the bane of all clandestine insertions and exfiltrations, helicopter noise from seven patrol actions that could well alert the Argentinian marines at Grytviken and Leith to prospective British military action even though the British ships were hull down over the horizon.

Young's squadron had rendezvoused south of Ascension on April 13. It began its run southward with the bulk of his assault force riding a tanker, while the command elements of the three embarked military organizations lived aboard an ancient destroyer commanded by a naval officer eager for his postponed retirement. Neither Young nor Sheridan had a trained amphibious staff to work out problems that might, and did, arise among the very different organizations that were assigned to them. These junior officers planned the operation and the fighting that would follow by themselves; they had no staff on site, formed as it should have been by Young. So excellent were their training and unit integrity that they coped over the next few days with almost every adversity that fortune, weather, and their faraway seniors threw at them.

No troop reinforcements or logistics support were available to Sheridan. If all went well, he Young, and Nunn would fight the same war together with what they carried. If *Tidespring, Plymouth,* or *Antrim* suffered major battle damage or mechanical failure, the mission would have to be aborted. No unanimous support came from the home front, either. Unbeknown to Sheridan or Young, Admiral Fieldhouse told his task group's commanders at Ascension Island on April 17 that the Army's staff "remained unconvinced of the necessity and likely success of an amphibious operation. . . . He told us he might be required to repossess the Falkland Islands but only when sea control was firmly established and South Georgia recaptured."[142] No one questioned, then or later, the military competence and drive of Young or Sheridan's subordinates. It was their seniors' waffling and the improvidence of the civil servants at Treasury and Defence that put their success in question. Seldom has so much weighed on a disparate military force hurriedly slapped together for a war eight thousand miles from London.[143]

Yet those moving south prepared well while they were en route. A makeshift operations room with adequate ship to shore and ship to helicopter communications was installed in Sheridan's cabin aboard *Antrim*. Maps and charts blossomed ubiquitously around it.[144] The young marines trained incessantly in their cramped quarters and on *Tidespring's* more capacious decks. They consumed months of training allowances firing at targets thrown over the side.[145] Nunn did clever things with the ASW helicopters from 845/846 Naval Air Commando squadrons that were meant to transport his troops. He and the crewmen learned to strip down ASW gear from the helicopters in order to determine how many troops and how much equipment they could carry ashore once Young gave the word.

Sheridan and Young's principal mission lay in getting British boots on the ground on South Georgia. The reconnaissance force drawn from the SAS and their RM counterpart, the SBS, had to go in first. Young's ships carried no watercraft of any description that could be used to deposit and retrieve patrols. The SAS and SBS did use rubber inflatables powered by outboard motors that had performed miserably around Ascension Island. In any case, their short range and vulnerability to a single shot from a medium caliber weapon limited their military usefulness. *Antrim* carried one Wessex 3 (ASW) helicopter; *Plymouth* had one Wasp ASW helicopter; *Endurance* had two Wasp helicopters, #434 and #435; *Tidespring* carried two Wessex 5 troop carriers. These helicopters' normal operation and ASW patrols were normally placid affairs; their time at sea was typically spent chasing down suspected Russian submarines, ferrying a brick [four infantrymen] around Northern Ireland, and on the occasional rescue mission with an almost certain landing at a NATO or UK base. Except for the Wessex 5s, no purpose-built helicopters designed to move troops accompanied Young's force or the additional SAS men, who demanded helicopters for their own unique purposes.[146] This deficit was tolerated by both Northwood and Woodward, the battle force commander, but annoyed Commodore Michael Clapp, Operation Corporate's logistics boss, who owned the helicopters and would have shown a surprising lack of his otherwise mature judgment (had he been asked his opinion) about what would be needed for the successful prosecution of this very unconventional operation. On the voyage south, the helicopters, none built or configured to handle more than few passengers, were severely overworked in cross-decking men and equipment. Clapp, in London the Commodore of Amphibious Warfare, had no hand in the affair at South Georgia, which bled away helicopters he badly needed. He lamented that two-thirds of the assault gear at Ascension Island had to be restored, mostly by helicopter, from a gaggle of ships to those that were to be used in the amphibious assault on East Falkland.[147] In addition, their pilots had to train themselves for the covert insertion and recovery of the SAS troops, as well as the landing, perhaps under fire, of a Royal Marines assault force.[148] Flying low under electronic silence and popping up to do a brief visual and radar search of hostile beaches was as novel for the pilots as was the prospect that they might be fired upon by ground troops hiding behind the next snow-covered hill. Ever-resourceful service crews fitted a few light machine guns [GPMGs] in helicopter doors for self-protection and to provide a modest capability for suppressive fire.

There was a very human side to this expedition, too. Aboard *Antrim*, Young had four commanding officers: in addition to Sheridan and Delves were Lieutenant Colonel Eve, head of the Naval Gunfire Group, and a junior but veteran head of that SBS detachment. *Antrim* also carried a senior helicopter pilot, Ian Stanley, who headed the crews and service crew of the embarked Wessex 3. The marines and SAS troopers, in their informal rough-edged ways, differed dramatically from the fresh-faced seaman who knows his place on board ship and in the naval hierarchy to the last meter. When the skipper or the officer of the watch orders: "Come left 15 deg.," the person at the wheel turns the wheel fifteen degrees to port and no questions are asked. In contrast, ground operations by the special warfare community are more collegial. NCOs have a major, sometimes vociferous role in planning and executing very hazardous missions. Theirs is a special world. Although commanding officers take full responsibility for their missions, they usually seek their sergeants' views and occasional objections. Pilots and their crews also live in their own special domain, where training, operations and risks differ markedly from the rest of their service. The Royal Marines give their officers full responsibility for their missions. Few landsmen understand that a ship's size cannot be increased like a building's. There is no room to take a long walk. Perhaps the harmony of opposites came into play; it is a tribute to the sheer professionalism of these very competent and necessarily strong-minded men that their different worlds did not fatally collide and that they all strained towards the mission's success. "Either Brian Young was in charge or he wasn't. There were times during the operation when it was had to tell."[149]

The Royal Marines' recapture of South Georgia was as untidy as the *Santa Fe's* mission to thwart it would prove precarious. On April 16, Sheridan tasked his reconnaissance force: "to establish covert patrols to determine enemy strength and disposition in Stromness, Husvik and Leith."[150] The SBS was similarly ordered to cover Grytviken and King Edward Point. BAS teams that had been to Fortuna Glacier continued to insist to Delves, the Squadron CO, and to Captain John Hamilton, the SAS troop commander, that Fortuna's peak was impassable, especially given winter's onset. Sheridan, an experienced Himalayan climber who had been head of the Royal Marines Mountain and Arctic Cadre, joined the voices raised against landing on the glacier.[151] Other opponents of this venture, crew and pilots from *Endurance* who had foot-on-the-ground experience on South Georgia, argued that crevasses as big as London buses made it virtually certain that the SAS men could not drag their pulks (sleds) any meaningful distance even in fair weather.[152] Given that winter had just begun, there was the possibility that a storm would leave Hamilton's men no choice but to hunker down for an unpredictable period, perhaps more than the five days allocated for the reconnaissance. But the pragmatic realists did not sway Delves, and he sought affirmative advice where he knew he could find it. Delves used satellite communications to speak with two very experienced Himalayan climbers, Stokes and Lane from the SAS in Britain. They advised Hamilton and Delves that Fortuna Glacier could be conquered. Peacock, who had traversed glaciers in South Georgia and who had been contacted by SAS members years later, said he would not have gone against Sheridan's judgment if he had known that it was indeed Sheridan who opposed taking that route.[153] In the face of this opposition, however, Mountain Troop was put onto Fortuna Glacier as the SAS had planned. Neither Northwood nor Young considered that only one junior SAS NCO participated in the mission atop Fortuna Glacier.

Delves's and Hamilton's insistence that their reconnaissance mission be covert and yet traverse Fortuna Glacier was a function of perfectionism and became a perilous exercise as most such in warfare are. Even more difficult to understand is Young's solifidian blessing for this tricky venture when he himself had no experience in such matters. There was no military reason to ascend Fortuna Glacier even if Young accepted the need for a clandestine reconnaissance of the settlements. Going around the base of the glacier would have given better opportunities for viewing the Argentinian marines, their equipment, and their capabilities. Finally, Delves, the head of the SAS D Squadron during Operation Paraquat, overflew the glacier and ordered his men down onto it against his military and civilian colleagues' objections. That "Shackleton had walked it. . . . to get rescued" was the SAS belief and mantra. There is no evidence in Shackleton's diaries or letters that he did or did not cross Fortuna.[154] US satellites routinely pictured the area with useful accuracy and could have ascertained the Argentinians' strength and equipment, although it is not known if their product reached Delves or if he would have used it anyway.

Moreover, had DLB, Rose, and Delves looked at their military problem from their opponents' point of view, a different picture would have appeared.[155]

If the Argentinian garrison considered a British attack possible or probable, it had three choices besides flight by sea or surrender. It could dig in against an attack. It could be destroyed by gunfire from *Plymouth* and *Antrim* in its trenches or in BAS quarters. Or it could flee without tactical integrity into the mountains and die of exposure and starvation. Delves's requirement for a wholly covert mission fit standard SAS practices. It had a laudable but disingenuous goal, and it did not fit the process of capturing South Georgia. Soviet satellites overflew the area regularly and Nick Barker in *Endurance* took scheduled precautions against them.[156] Admiral Fieldhouse had already warned his subordinates against transmitting when American satellites were overhead. It is a good rule in such matters that when two parties besides the anointed know a secret, many others almost certainly have an inkling of the matter at hand.[157] By April 21, it is very likely that several thousand people of different nationalities, except perhaps Argentinian, knew what was about to happen to the unsuspecting garrisons in Grytviken and Leith.[158] Delves's attempt at secrecy was overkill.

All the commanding officers aboard Young's ship knew almost exactly what the assault force might face once British troops landed. No ships had reinforced the Argentinian garrison, which had no air support and no artillery. The island could not support more than a few hundred persons, in winter probably fewer. The quality and fighting spirit of the Argentines was unknown, but reasonable men could assume that their first-line troops, always in short supply, were posted either on the Chilean border or on the Falklands themselves. It could also be guessed that those few on South Georgia were not assiduously patrolling the mountains now that winter had begun but had instead ensconced themselves in the snug wooden houses of the BAS.[159] Troops could not be flown in, and no hostile naval activity had been noted. No naval fueling facilities, magazines, or repair shops existed for modern warships. The Argentinian occupiers would defend their conquest with what little they had at hand. This was thought to include a winter stock of food, clothes, medical supplies, small arms, and alcohol. Winter would argue against the Argentines' retreating into the freezing hinterlands. Both sides would fight with old iron. In short, South Georgia was a primitive and isolated military outpost with wretched living conditions eight hundred miles from the Falklands that posed no threat to the outside world or to the British plans for recapture of the Falkland Islands themselves. Like MacArthur's isolation of Japanese islands in the Pacific in order to reach essential military goals, the British could justifiably have left South Georgia to freeze its occupiers into submission. The island was scarcely defensible. The assault on South Georgia was an admitted political expedient and not a military necessity. Thatcher and her advisors had that point right.[160]

As Hamilton and Delves planned their covert insertion from the ships at sea, teams from the BAS who were on the ground in remote areas performed their own reconnaissance despite instructions from their Cambridge headquarters to remain in their huts. Northwood erred again; there was small risk that the BAS men who lived in the mountains might be taken for Argentines and targeted. Then too, how could the BAS gather intelligence if they were shuttered inside their huts? The BAS's Peter Stark, who had lived on the island for two years, was flown to *Endurance* for his report and for the singular purpose of dissuading Hamilton's troop from trying the Fortuna route. The BAS parties, thirteen plus two wildlife photographers at Bird Island and Schlieper Bay at the northern tip of the island at Lyell Glacier, and at St. Andrews Bay, south of Grytviken, traversed their areas on foot and met no Argentinian military. On April 20, Tony North and Myles Plant watched Cumberland Bay from Barff Point and discovered nothing. Ian Barker and Damien Sanders stood on the high ground between East and West Cumberland Bay and saw neither Argentinian ground nor naval activity, although their sightings were often obstructed and storms blinded them as frequently as they did the Argentinian marines. But those truly intrepid scientists found no trace of any Argentinian patrols ever having surveyed those likely pieces of useful military ground. Argentinian C-130 planes were heard from time to time, but those flew too high to observe military activity on the ground or to drop supplies. The BAS watchers, although not trained military, had kept a weather eye on much of the area of likely Argentinian ground and naval activity. The BAS patrols, all of whom had capricious and short-range radios, reported their findings back to Northwood with great speed in a complex radio arrangement that sent transmissions through South Orkney to Ascension Island and then to BAS headquarters in Cambridge. There, Dr. Richard Laws transferred the data to Rear Admiral Tony Wheatley at Northwood. Much, but not all of their information did percolate down to the commanders aboard ship. In addition, BAS headquarters had previously entertained a constant flow of visitors from the Royal Navy, SAS, SBS, and various other parties, all eager to learn what the intrepid researchers on South Georgia daily took as normal existence. Counsel was freely given.[161]

It is all the more astounding to learn from Hamilton's orders to his mountain troop that the only acknowledged information came from studying maps, air photos, and the limited local knowledge of BAS personnel and crewmembers of the *Endurance*. This statement, though patently erroneous, formed the basis for the SAS plan to take the hazardous route across Fortuna Glacier, as Delves and Hamilton rejected firsthand information of crucial tactical importance gained by trained scientific observers and by the crew and pilots of *Endurance*. They were bent instead on a short covert trek. The cruel fact is that on board *Antrim* and *Endurance* and buried in the British intelligence system were both good information and mature analyses of it that would have led most reasonable leaders to have changed routes for reaching spots from which to observe Husk, Leith, and Stromness. Success in special warfare demands careful planning and resolute execution informed by prudence born of bitter experience. Rose, Delves, and Hamilton were men of their time and exemplars of a splendid bellicose culture. In the matter of Fortuna Glacier, they went beyond reason and common sense.[162]

At this point, Sheridan, the legitimate land force commander, was dealing with neither a train nor a tree. After lengthy discussions aboard *Antrim* and with Northwood, Sheridan turned, against his better judgment, to Delves's SAS reconnaissance force. Captain John Hamilton commanded 19 Troop (Mountain Troop) of the 22 Special Air Service Regiment (SAS). His mission order stated: "To recon Leith, Stromness, Husvik and E. Fortuna Bay for a Squadron sized attack."[163] No mention of a squadron-sized attack had been listed in Northwood's communications to Sheridan. Brigadier de la Billiere certainly had a synoptic competence, which Thatcher at least partly shared, but which Nott and Captain Young lacked. The mission orders broke down into three different goals. One was to find ways across Fortuna Glacier, Breakwind Ridge, and Konig Glacier. Another was to determine Argentinian strengths and dispositions at Husvik, Leith, and Stromness. The third was to find routes that would best allow a Coy Group to move into position for an assault on Grytviken.[164] All the vague and anxious discussion on *Antrim* boiled down to those few orders. The SBS was similarly ordered to cover Grytviken and King Edward Point.[165] It was then that unrealistic judgments began to threaten the hope for a short swift victory.[166] Nowhere in these orders was it recognized that two BAS persons established on Lyell Glacier on the Grytviken side of Fortuna could observe and report on much, but not all, Argentinian activity below them. Although their communications were sporadic due to an insufficient number of batteries, the reports did usually arrive. However limited their capabilities, the BAS researchers remained cold and valiant as an asset *in-situ* against the unexpected.

The Mountain Troop Commander was eager to work and to reconnoiter the approaches over Fortuna Glacier. In the end, Delves insisted on an eight-kilometer covert approach to the surveillance targets for fear of tipping off the Argentinian garrison. But it could just as well have been argued that a blatant landing preceded and supported by naval gunfire would frighten green, frozen, and isolated troops into quick surrender.[167] At 0930 on April 21, Lieutenant-Commander Ian Stanley lifted off in his empty Wessex 3 from *Antrim* in order to find a landing site for Hamilton's Mountain Troop. Taking Cape Constance on his port side, he flew southeast over Possession and Antarctic Bays and saw no military activity. After vetting Fortuna Glacier, he returned to *Antrim* and loaded up his passengers. Accompanied by the two Wessex 5s from *Tidespring*, which carried the rest of Mountain Troop, they made for Fortuna and were turned back by a snow squall near Possession Bay.[168] It is not only distance that is critical in such insertions but the weather between helicopter and landing site. Five hundred yards behind a snow squall that prevents accurate navigation is as good as a hundred miles in preventing a safe landing. Stanley took Delves and Hamilton on a second reconnaissance run, this time in deceptively decent weather, and Delves ordered a second attempt to land. Day light was fading, and it was best to land the troop and get off the glacier onto firm ground before dark. The second try at landing succeeded. Shortly after 1300, fourteen men from Mountain Troop and three pulks were safe on Fortuna Glacier. Just after the landing, the weather worsened, and the troop progressed barely a half mile before darkness forced a halt to its tortuous slogging.

The night that began with sundown on April 21 saw South Georgia's weather at its worst. Offshore, *Antrim* lashed down its gear as winds rose to one hundred miles per hour. A force 11 sea broke waves over the tired old ship, and the barometer registered 965 millibars, lower than most seamen experience in a lifetime. Even worse, the helicopters secured to *Antrim* and *Tidespring's* decks shuddered almost to their breaking points. On the glacier, Hamilton's men and their kit were safe, but buried cold in the snow. Winds bent tent poles and rent fabric. The horrendous weather continued through the night, and the SAS men's physical condition began to deteriorate. Military operations, even passive reconnaissance, became impossible. At 1100 on April 22, Hamilton radioed *Antrim*: "Unable to move. Environmental casualties immanent [sic]."[169] This time, the SAS sorcery failed. Rose and DLB's golden dream ended at that moment. Snow squalls then delayed Stanley's rescue attempt for forty-five minutes. The storms forced him to order the two Wessex 5s to wait on Cape Constance, eight kilometers from the glacier, while he found the SAS men and a landing site from which it would be safe to rescue them. The weather foiled Stanley's very sophisticated navigational gear, and his helicopter's airframe began to take on ice. Stanley scrubbed the mission, and all three helicopters returned to *Tidespring* and *Antrim*.

Quickly refueled, the three helicopters took off just before 1330 for a second rescue attempt. This time, breaks in the weather and orange smoke grenades brought rescuers and exhausted soldiers together. Tidd, the first pilot to land, quickly loaded his Wessex 5 with six SAS men and their kit and took off. A few minutes later, he ran into the dreaded whiteout. Without Stanley's helicopter to guide him, he crashed into the glacier. Bits and pieces of Tidd's shattered craft flew into the air with such velocity that they came near to hitting the following chopper. His unwanted landing site was cushioned in snow and, by a fluke of fate, the men emerged shaken but not injured from the destroyed helicopter. Ian Stanley, in his Wessex 3, guided Ian Georgeson's second Wessex 5 to the crash site. The crash's survivors, minus their heavy equipment, crawled into the two helicopters and took off for the ships' warm bunks. The Wessex 5 flew close astern Stanley's mother hen but lost sight of it over the glacier's rim. By ill chance, it flew into another whiteout and crashed. Stanley's helicopter, already fully loaded, had no choice but to head back to *Antrim*. By the time the thin Arctic sunlight disappeared, two helicopters had been lost, four of the SAS men had been rescued, and two helicopter crewmen had joined the twelve SAS men stranded on the glacier. All the helicopters that tried to land and recover troops on Fortuna had flown with a single pilot, a military decision either agreed to or not noticed by Young. No second man navigated, searched for suitable landing sites, or kept his pilot safe from whiteouts. Sixteen valuable men found themselves unharmed but unable to perform any military mission and facing another night on the glacier in ever-worsening weather.

Any hope of completing the reconnaissance by night had ended. Young, the amphibious force commander (until the land forces were firmly established ashore), knew no more about his target at the end of the day than he had at its beginning. He did know that some troops under his command had been rescued from lethal danger and that he, a senior and experienced aviator, had lost two helicopters. He knew, too, that the goal of seizing South Georgia was in jeopardy. Sheridan, the land force commander, could do nothing unless and until the SAS problem got resolved. Upon being told of the men marooned atop Fortuna, Thatcher commented: "My heart was heavy. . . . How was I to conceal my feelings? I wondered if the task we had set for ourselves was truly impossible."[170] Gibbon said that; "such events were easier to deplore than to describe." On *Endurance,* Captain Nick Barker was more direct: "In military terms the whole operation had become a monumental cockup."[171]

Young and his operations crew aboard *Antrim* faced calamity. Nunn acted. An emergency rescue team of two mountain leaders from the Royal Marines' Mountain and Arctic Warfare cadre was alerted on *Tidespring,* where another problem had surfaced. "I (a Royal Marine Mountain Leader 1st Class) . . . had checked through their (SAS) kit with them. In my view it wasn't very good. It was standard army issue – not as good as our stuff. There are recognized techniques for getting yourself out of a crevasse . . . it was my opinion those guys just didn't have that sort of gear, that they would not be able to haul themselves up."[172]

A failed reconnaissance operation had degenerated into a rescue operation with a low probability of success. Stanley had few assets: a battered helicopter, the only Wessex left, and less than two hours of daylight (if the weather held) to rescue fourteen men who could not long survive. Taking a new route to the glacier, he landed and found the survivors huddled inside inflated rafts they were using as tents. Time and weather permitted one last attempt at rescue before night. As the weather worsened, he piled in all fourteen — the SAS troopers reluctantly left their kit and weapons except for sidearms — and took off at fifteen hundred pounds above the helicopter's maximum design weight. Stanley made his way back to *Antrim* nicely, his sixth trip from Fortuna Glacier, and landed on *Antrim's* pitching deck in a controlled crash.

Military operations succeed or founder on judgments made about the enemy's strength, equipment, numbers, and location. Not so the Fortuna Glacier affair, for no opposing forces were involved. Delves and Hamilton underestimated the importance and weight of the information they had about Fortuna and overestimated their own ability to assess it. They rejected advice from experts on the climate and terrain of the operation. Most of all, they failed to recognize a new and different enemy, the terrain and weather, and they did not scrutinize it as they would a human foe. This most unusual episode occurred despite the fact that special warfare operatives rank among the best intelligence gatherers and the most realistic analysts of tactical situations.[173] Whatever Rose and Young's incantations to the gods of war, no military objective had been reached during the preceding twenty-four hours. The unlikely figure of the scantily rewarded Stanley had delivered Young and his force from disaster, saved fourteen lives, and spared Margaret Thatcher another acute embarrassment. Special Warfare allows clumsiness or repetitive errors, but not both at the same time. Stanley received the Distinguished Service Order (DSO) for his extraordinary feat of technical flying and for his bravery. His passengers concluded that was little enough. It is not too much to posit that if Stanley had failed in his sunset rescue attempt, then the war, the Iron Lady, and her government would have come clanking to the ground.

The marines of 2 SBS came south on *Endurance,* and it was their turn, after the Fortuna mission had been set in motion to reconnoiter Sheridan's possible landing sites south of Leith and Grytviken, from across Cumberland East Bay, that is. Hound Bay, at the seaward neck of Barff Peninsula, was the insertion point for three SBS patrols. They were to make their way on foot halfway up the peninsula, pick up two Gemini rafts dropped from helicopters, and cross the water to Brown Mountain. That low summit was one of the two pieces of vital ground whose seizure by the assault force was necessary for any attack on Grytviken. The mountain also provided a point from which Argentinian activity, if any, could probably be scanned if the weather allowed. That two BAS men, Myles Plant and Tony North, lived in the proposed patrol area and had seen no Argentinian military activity did not deter the SBS leader from mounting his operation. The orders that Sheridan gave the officer commanding the Special Boat Section were based on advice from Clive Grant, a very competent and experienced SBS operative. Lieutenant Tony Ellerbeck flew his helicopter from *Endurance* to Cindy Buxton and Anne Price's hut on St. Andrews Bay to warn them of incipient military activity. They, too, had seen nothing of the Argentinian invaders. Although staying alert, they lived much as before.

Ellerbeck delivered only one patrol, four men and their kit, before bad weather prevented more flying. The SBS patrol on shore met the two BAS men, Plant and North, who reaffirmed that no Argentinian military lurked in the vicinity. The SBS patrols still aboard *Endurance* were not to be thwarted and went ashore by Gemini courtesy of Nick Barker, who brought *Endurance* as close to shore as prudence allowed — under 1000 meters. The Geminis' motors then failed the three patrols as they tried to cross Moraine Fjord to get to their lookout point atop Brown Mountain.[174] During the night of April 22, the marines attempted a frigid sleep behind rocks on Dartmouth Point. In the morning, the patrol leaders determined that their unreliable outboard motors had ended their military mission and punctured the Geminis' hulls. They decided to be evacuated. A confluence of infelicitous events then occurred. The patrols could not reach either *Antrim* or *Endurance* by radio. Although they could go to ground for days if necessary, the reality was that they were stranded. Unproven reports of an Argentinian submarine's presence had prompted Young to withdraw *Antrim* beyond the SBS's radio's range; *Endurance* lacked the codebooks to decrypt SBS messages anyway.[175] By the end of April 23, an Argentinian C-130 had over flown Young's force, and he had ordered *Tidespring,* with the core of M Company aboard, to clear the area.

Young's decision, or rather the absence of one, showed an excess of concern for an enemy he had not bothered to appraise. Woodward, on *Hermes* far to the north, picked up on the problem. "South Georgia op seems bogged down for fear of Arg submarine (conventional, *Santé Fe*)."[176] *Santa Fe's* few torpedoes, if properly fired, were a potential risk for Young's force, but they did not present a clear and present danger. Fear of these ancient and secondhand weapons was a caution built on dangerous and unwarranted perfectionism. *Santa Fe's* submerged speed was much less than that of *Tidespring's* thirteen knots; it could maintain the same surface speed for only thirty minutes. The tactical offense posed by two twenty-five knot destroyers and their embarked helicopters using active sonar against an ageing diesel submarine with generic electrical problems is lethal. Bicain knew this fact, whereas Young chose not to perform this elementary analysis.

Endurance's radio crew had intercepted messages from an overflying Argentinian aircraft. They knew, therefore, that their position was known to an Argentinian submarine. That made sense, because *Endurance's* loud diesel engines could be easily picked up by the submarine's sonar and because *Endurance* had no sonar of its own to warn of impending attack. Nor could it turn handily to avoid an observed torpedo. Still, any submarine attack seemed improbable because a diesel submarine skipper with an unblooded crew is most unlikely to prosecute an attack that would draw the lethal attention of the British nuclear submarines that were soon to arrive on scene and that were trained to hunt down Soviet nuclear boats.

Amphibious ships, like *Antrim*, purpose-built or not, are meant to sail in harm's way in order to get their troops to the assault area and over the beach. That was Young's sole reason for being in South Georgia's waters. Excessive caution breeds its own potential for disaster. If any British ship had sunk fifty miles northeast of South Georgia, the crew and passengers would have drowned. If disaster had occurred close to Grytviken or Leith, some might have lived. The chances of any British ship around South Georgia being sunk were roughly the same whether they were fifty or two hundred miles from Grytviken. But many seafarers still believe that a ship damaged or sunk going towards the fight causes no dishonor but that harm suffered away from the fight raises questions about mettle, planning, and tactics.

Finally on the night of April 23, *Antrim* picked up the SBS's signal and, after some discussion, *Endurance* was ordered to rescue the isolated marines from Barff Peninsula. Barker's two small utility helicopters, piloted by Ellerbeck and Finding, removed the men to *Endurance's* warmth without their wretched Geminis and malfunctioning motors; a second reconnaissance effort had misfired.[177] The communications debacle that had marooned the SBS team ashore on Barff Peninsula was only a part of the muddle that permeated Young's operations. In separating *Tidespring* from the south-sailing *Brambleleaf,* and in dividing his force up into two units—*Plymouth* and *Endurance* as one and *Antrim* and *Tidespring* as the other—Young lost any defensive advantage against the putative diesel submarine. He also sacrificed effective communications among the forces he was supposed to put ashore as well as the valuable advice of Barker and his pilots. Discreet military accomplishment would have justified this maritime hurly-burly, but by April 24, nothing of value had been gained, no ground reconnaissance had been completed, and no military objective had been achieved. In fact, only the prodigious flying feats of his helicopter pilots (Stanley above all), had saved Young's force from disaster. Sheridan remained on board ship, a frustrated land force commander unable to execute his mission.

D Squadron had one more reconnaissance card to play. At Sheridan's urging, Captain Timothy Burls's boat troop had set out from *Antrim* at 0300 on April 22. They were to reconnoiter Leith, Husvik, and Stromness from positions on Grass Island and go from there to the mainland. A small but potentially bothersome garrison was thought to be guarding Leith Harbor and its disused whaling station. Because the SAS reconnaissance from Fortuna had failed to observe Leith, they considered Grass Island, a few thousand meters west in Stromness Bay to be a good alternative, especially as the presence of kelp precluded other potential landing sites. Fifteen men set out in five boats, because helicopters had come into short supply. Immediately after launching, three motors failed, and the two working Gemini went ashore on Grass Island. A third was probably ashore on a spit of land separating Husvik from Stromness. A fourth boat was found by helicopter at 0830 and brought to safety. When *Antrim* and *Fort Austin* had met at sea on April 14, the boat troop had exercised its Gemini inflatables. Their motors had also failed at that time. The continued failure of these motors in critical maneuvers stymied the efforts of hundreds of millions of dollars worth of complex military equipment manned by thousands of trained operators. It remains a mystery why the SAS chose to go to war with a system of proven unreliability.

The motors had not been warmed prior to launch and acted up when the troops needed them most.[178] Towlines were broken; each crew struggled on its own. By early light, three boats in all, including Captain Burls's, were buried on Grass Island. The nine men then established an observation point from which they could see Leith and Stromness, and Burls radioed his reports back to *Antrim*. By this point, Burls had lost two of his five boats with no knowledge of whether his men had drowned, put up on a distant shore, been blown out to sea, or been captured by the Argentinians. The control team on *Antrim* feared the worst. Because of a waterlogged motor and fierce winds, one lost boat, *Delta*, was blown far off the route to Grass Island and just managed to paddle to safety near Busen Point. Inexplicably this Gemini lacked a SABRE radio beacon and could not transmit the crew's location. The other stray, *Bravo*, its motor inoperative and its crew exhausted, blew steadily eastward away from South Georgia and out to sea. It, too, lacked a rescue beacon with enough range to contact *Antrim* but by luck contacted Burls on the troop's tactical network. He in turn radioed *Antrim*, whose pilots and meteorological officers worked out Bravo's possible position. The ever-resourceful Stanley took off at 0800 in his Wessex 3 and, at altitudes of less than two hundred feet, conducted a classic box search. Just as his fuel supply left him no choice but to return to *Antrim*, Stanley's crewman Fitzgerald spotted the drifting raft, winched up its crew, and returned them to the comforts of *Antrim's* wardroom. There, the Bravo boat's crew owned up to the fact that the troop had enjoyed no pre-mission inspection of equipment.

Yet something had been accomplished. Now one reconnaissance team of nine men could observe in good weather, without discovery, any Argentinian activity in and around Stromness Bay. Still, this view from afar did not afford an accurate count of the Argentinian soldiery. On the night of April 23, Sheridan ordered the nine SAS men to cross a few hundred meters from Grass Island to the mainland. Once again, two of the three motors failed, and the Geminis returned to Grass Island. A second try failed for the same reason, and in the end, the team crossed by paddling. That early morning Boat Troop, or three teams of it, completed the task towards which so much effort had been directed. Doing what it did best, Burls's diminished troop reported the existence of a garrison of sixteen Argentinian marines and no supporting artillery back to Delves aboard *Antrim*. One sentry stood languid watch during the dark hours.[179] Finally, Sheridan knew what did not face him. Yet the lethal mixture of bad weather, uninformed military judgment, poor military administration, inadequate equipment, and sloppy top leadership had come close to crippling Operation Paraquat. And if Paraquat collapsed, there would be no seizure of Port Stanley. There were no reinforcements, no British heavy guns over the horizon, and no acknowledgement that Fortuna Glacier was as much an enemy as any Argentinian marine on its other side.

By the afternoon of April 23, *Endurance's* listeners and Spanish language translators had intercepted transmissions from an Argentinian C-130 to and from a submarine whose signal strength indicated it was a hundred miles from *Endurance* and perhaps closer to *Antrim*.[180] This information prompted Northwood and Young to send his two tankers, escorted by *Plymouth*, two hundred miles northeast and out of harm's way. *Antrim* followed shortly. This decision not only left *Endurance* unprotected, but it also left the main assault force aboard *Tidespring* heading away from South Georgia.[181] Although *Conqueror,* a nuclear attack sub, was headed south to intercept the *Santa Fe,* it would be several hours before its search for *Santa Fe* could begin. Simultaneously, Northwood detached *Brilliant,* with its first-class sonar and two Lynx ASW helicopters and sent it to South Georgia. Further intercepts by Captain Barker's crew disclosed that the Argentinian submarine was meant to attack *Endurance* and afterwards to deliver reinforcements to the garrison at Leith.[182]

On April 23, Sheridan was called to the radio room deep in *Antrim's* bowels and asked what he was doing about the Argentine threat and the reported presence of twenty marines on board who were supposed to reinforce the Argentinian garrison on King Edward Point. Sheridan replied he would do nothing, as no information had been given to him about any Argentinian submarine. Young was *Antrim's* CO and the only officer who could "do something" about *Santa Fe.* Northwood's order to Young's force to clear South Georgia, almost a shriek of *sauve qui peut,* was given at 0300 on April 24.[183] This dispersion of ships carrying all Sheridan's troops to a patch of water two hundred miles from their target remains an incomprehensible error. Even years later, it seems strange that the implications of that decision to disperse NATO trained ASW ships failed to register on Northwood. The truth remains that Young's very adequate ASW force had lost its ability to bring the fight to the Argentinian submarine. Acting in concert, *Antrim, Brilliant, Plymouth* and *Conqueror* could have destroyed or sent away the *Santa Fe* or any other submarine in the Argentinian inventory in very short order. At the very least, Young's ships might better have screened the plodding and defenseless old *Endurance* with its extremely valuable communications gear and helicopter.

Knowing that sooner or later the Royal Navy would have at least one nuclear submarine in the area, the Argentinian Navy imprudently sent only one antiquated submarine without air cover, possibly to target a noncombatant, *Endurance,* when it should have sought to destroy a troop-carrying ship, either *Antrim* or *Plymouth,* that could destroy it. Bicain's boat had unclear orders, which gave its commonsensical skipper leeway as long as the Argentinian marines were delivered. Technically, *Santa Fe's* small size, its slow underwater speed, and the onset of nasty winter weather mandated only one mission at a time, either to transport troops or to find and kill *Endurance,* but not both. As it was, Bicain's boat was not a weapon of war. He knew that unpalatable fact and directed his command in accordance with it. There is little doubt that *Conqueror,* given its excellent speed and sonar, could have made short work of a World War II era diesel submarine even without assistance from its mates on the surface.[184]

On the British side, Young had lost the capacity, at least for the moment, to deliver Sheridan's force to the beach — Young's sole reason for being around South Georgia. At 1600 on April 24, Captain Barker communicated his concern about being the *Santa Fe's* target to Vice Admiral David Halifax at Northwood and was told: "There's really very little to worry about."[185] This time, Northwood was right. It was now aware of the *Santa Fe's* approximate position, and certain that the tankers carrying the force's fuel and assault force lay out of harm's way; it ordered *Plymouth* to return to the proposed area of operations, the waters around South Georgia. Barker's concern for the safety of his ship and crew was justified, but by this time, the six helicopters on *Brilliant, Antrim, Plymouth,* and *Endurance*, however underequipped to prosecute an attack by themselves on a clever submarine skipper, were positioned to search for *Santa Fe* as it brought its troop reinforcements to Cumberland Bay. Their parent ships were still too distant from Grytviken to form the surface anti-submarine warfare (ASW) screen that would bar *Santa Fe* from landing its troops. But the helicopters had an obvious advantage given the paucity of feasible landing sites and patrol areas available to Bicain. The high probability existed that Bicain's passengers would land between Leith Harbor to the north and Cumberland Bay East, which lay to the south. Had *Santa Fe* been truly operational, with freedom to maneuver, to hide under layers of cold and salinity, or to take up an attack position on *Endurance* or any other ships that approached Cumberland Bay, the lack of an integrated tactical plan on the British side would have spelled disaster, at least for Nick Barker's old ship and all who sailed on her.

The failed reconnaissance of Fortuna Glacier, the loss of two helicopters, the proven hostility of the environment, the near death of valuable men, the wear on Young's ships, and the frantic dispersal of his tiny squadron to no avail all induced the dismay and sense of failure that a successful reconnaissance is intended to prevent. After the war, Barker wrote: "We had been on a roll. We had inserted forces without proper preparation or observation and had got away with it. Our best information had not come from any military source but from the British Antarctic Survey."[186] The subtle skills so forcefully applied to the defeat of her opponent for occupancy of No. 10 Downing Street had deserted Thatcher. Mastering the shires and a tumultuous Commons differed from the safe ascent of Fortuna Glacier.[187] Thatcher failed to realize that almost every major military decision in as sharply focused a war as the Falklands conflict is a political decision. She did not balance risk versus reward, a paltry PR victory versus a military disaster. Her SAS troops had not weighed the ramifications of a successful, if unnecessary, reconnaissance from Fortuna Glacier against a likely military disaster. In the end, the SAS and Margaret Thatcher badly needed a rescue operation themselves.

Notes

131-Confidential discussion with the author.

132-Fellow Royal Marines officer to Sheridan as told by Sheridan to the author.

133-"Without any official permission Mike Rose managed to jump the gun...He took D Squadron to Brize Norton...before any one in authority realized where they were...arrived at Ascension Island...half way to their target." General Sir Peter De la Billière, *Looking for trouble: SAS to Gulf Command; The Autobiography* (New York: HarperCollins, 1994), 343.

134-And they, secret in identity and work, gladly soaked up that press and TV notoriety.

135-De la Billiere planned Operation Mikado, which was intended to land B Squadron SAS onto an Argentinian airfield to destroy missile-carrying airplanes. The Squadron CO declined to accept the order because of its 99% chance of failure and the likely deaths of his soldiers and left the SAS. Although political clearance had been obtained, the mission was scrubbed because Argentinian radar coverage was discovered to be greater than had been estimated. A second SAS mission involved landing SAS troops from *Onyx*, a diesel submarine, in order to destroy planes at Rio Grande. The war ended before that mission could take place. Michael Smith, "SAS 'Suicide Mission' to Wipe Out Exocets," *Daily Telegraph*, March 8, 2002.

136-Thatcher's urgency did not always percolate downward to her military staffs. When Captain Nick Barker of *Endurance* questioned the rules of engagement should he meet an Argentinian missile destroyer, he was told: "to phone back after 2 o'clock as that particular staff officer was at lunch." Nicholas Barker, *Beyond Endurance: An Epic of Whitehall and the South Atlantic* (London: L. Cooper, 1997), 184.

137-"All other plans were dropped as we concentrated on how to reach the Falklands before any other British troops." De la Billière, 341.

138-HMS *Antrim* 250/3/1, April 14, 1982, s/ B. G. Young.

139-Ascension Island is owned by the UK and permanently leased to the US. During the war UK forces used the island fully.

140-Nunn, letter to the author, September 2007.

141-It was never made clear to Sheridan that he was the sole commander of all who carried rifles. The normal NATO practice would have been for Delves and Sheridan to receive a message from Northwood saying something like: "You are directed to seize South Georgia Island. You are appointed Land Force Commander for that operation. You will direct and take guidance from such reconnaissance force as will be assigned to you."

142-Clapp paraphrasing Admiral Fieldhouse. Michael Clapp and Ewen Southby-

Tailyour, *Amphibious Assault Falklands: The Battle of San Carlos Water* (Annapolis, MD: Naval Institute Press, 1996), 54.

143-"Apart from the Royal Marines, everyone was learning the amphibious trade as we went along." Captain Brian Young RN in Roger Perkins, *Operation Paraquat: The Battle for South Georgia* (Chippenham: Picton Publishing, 1986), 121.

144-Despite the hundred or so soldiers and marines jammed into his ship, Young paid them scant attention or courtesy during the entire voyage. Young, a graduate of a British Staff College, simply knew almost nothing about amphibious operations or those who risked their lives completing them. Young's sullen discussions with Sheridan, who needed to get ashore, were always conducted de haut en bas. Ignorance was concealed on the surface. It easily flips over to arrogance.

145-It dismayed the young marines and their officers that Captain Young showed so marked a lack of interest in them and their activities during the trip south. He was, until they landed, their commander.

146-The Wessex 5 was built to insert and to retrieve a brick of four troops on anti-terrorists operations in Northern Ireland. Its use in a Coy Group assault showed how scant were resources for force projection. That it was used successfully during the Falklands War was a tribute to its pilots and service crew. In 1982, British forces flew one large helicopter, a Chinook, on the Falklands. It performed very efficiently.

147-Clapp regretted afterwards that the South Georgia operation was a side show, "off the line of march," that contributed little to the war's success, that the SAS had used and lost his two Wessex 5 helicopters without his approval, and that he had not been placed in command of the entire operation. He wrote that the operation was undermanned and underequipped. Clapp and South-Tailyour, *Amphibious Assault*, 71-74. Captain Bicain, the commanding officer of the *Santa Fe,* made precisely the same points regarding the Argentinian occupation of South Georgia to the author.

148-Lieutenant Mike Tidd RN and Flight Lieutenant Andy Pulford RAF had troop experience from Northern Ireland and with commando forces in Norway. Captain Chris Nunn had flown in support of SAS operations in Northern Ireland. Neither the SAS nor the Royal Marines had dedicated combat aircraft as integrated members of their forces. US and Soviet special forces did enjoy this luxury.

149-Barker, *Beyond Endurance*, 178.

150-Lieutenant Colonel Sheridan, interview with the author, October 27, 1998.

151-"I gave him the job and could not tell him how to do it. I advised against the Fortuna route but they thought they could do it." Lieutenant Colonel Sheridan, interview with the author, October 27, 1998.

152-"I could tell right away we were not convincing him (Delves) that the Fortuna Glacier was a rotten option. . . . The truth is that it matters little if you are experienced or a novice. The weather that constantly changes the mood of the glacier is utterly indifferent." Nicholas Barker, *Beyond Endurance: An Epic of Whitehall and the South Atlantic* (Barnsley, Yorkshire: Pen and Sword Books, 1997),

180.

153-Lieutenant Colonel Sheridan, interview with the author, October 27, 1998.

154-Quoted in James Sturke, "The Retaking of South Georgia," *Guardian*, April 25, 2007. Most likely he did not. He was exhausted, wet, cold, and had no equipment to pull himself out of a crevasse should he fall into one.

155-"It is widely accepted that Argentina would not make a significant effort to hold South Georgia against a determined assault." James Markham writing from Buenas Aires in the *New York Times*, April 14, 1982, a week before military action began around South Georgia. James M. Markham, "Argentina Concentrates on a Defensive Strategy." *New York Times*, April 14, 1982. It is not known if this view percolated through the British command structure and, if it did, what was made of it.

156-Barker, *Beyond Endurance*, 184.

157-Argentinian C-130's and a Boeing 707 kept close track of Young's ships plodding towards what could only be South Georgia. An ancient belief holds that there is no such thing as one cockroach.

158-"Argentinian planners concluded immediately (on April 21, 1982) that the British were planning to retake South Georgia. On April 24, it was reported that two destroyers and a tanker were near the island. The Joint Chiefs of Staff assessed that an attack was imminent." Lawrence Freedman and Virginia Gamba-Stonehouse, *Signals of War: The Falklands Conflict of 1982* (Princeton: Princeton University Press, 1991), 219. Professor Freedman has not divulged the source of this information.

159-As the British discovered after they landed, Argentinian troops failed to dig new defensive positions but simply occupied abandoned Royal Marines' trenches.

160-All buildings at King Edward Point had been entered, ransacked, and looted. Great attention was given the tins of food, some of which were opened but not eaten. BAS files were left intact. Sheridan, letter to the author, October 27, 1998.

161-BAS personnel, interview with the author, March 1997.

162-The grand success of the SAS in destroying Argentinian planes on Peeble Island was overshadowed by a tragic accident in which a helicopter exploded over water. Sixteen men, including some of the most experienced members of the regiment, were killed.

163-Hamilton died later heroically defending his men. He was a good and brave soldier.

164-"2SBS a. Your patrols are to establish feasibility of routes from Maiviken for a Company Group to move over.
b. Feasibility of routes from Papua Beach through Echo Pass for a Company Group to move over.
c. You are to locate suitable Landing Sites on both routes in dead ground.
d. To identify if there were enemy OPs on Orca and Hope Points.

<u>DSqn</u>   Your patrols are to establish feasibility of routes over which your Sqn or the Company Group may move prior to the main assault. You are to keep me informed." Sheridan, letter to the author, November 2012.

165-Grytviken was Sheridan's principal target. It was appropriate for the Marine's own SBS to reconnoiter that area.

166-Freedman and Gamba-Stonehouse claim (*Signals of War,* 220): "In this one exceptional case...Britain did have satellite pictures from the United States, taken on a satellite's final orbit. This made it possible to identify the location as well as note the weaknesses, of Argentine defenses." If this statement is true, the entire SAS and SBS reconnaissance effort was duplicative and unnecessary.

167-Delves's decision was faulty. Only one reconnaissance target existed; it could have been overflown briefly, but completely, by a Wessex. The author's direct experience.

168-Mountain Troop inserted from three helicopters, not two as stated in Sunday Times of London Insight Team, *War In The Falklands: The Full Story* (New York: Harper & Row, 1982), 149.

169-Confidential Discussion with the author.

170-Thatcher, *Downing Street Years*, 205. The operative word here is "we." Is this the *Royal We,* perduring and unassailable, the *Committee-Chairman We* that crushes opposing views, or it the *Anticipatory We* that dilutes responsibility for a lurking disaster? The shrouds of time have darkened our understanding of Thatcher's "we."

171-Barker, *Beyond Endurance*, 183.

172-Sergeant Mac Leman, Mountain Leader 1ˢᵗ Class, quoted in Perkins, *Operation Paraquat*, 140.

173-The author's experience.

174-Brown Mountain was with Bore Valley/Mountain a piece of ground whose seizure by Sheridan would be essential to the recapture of Grytviken.

175-These blatant examples of the lack of cooperation and mutual understanding of a joint force show the unnecessary problems that faced the RM land force commander.

176-Sandy Woodward and Patrick Robinson, *One Hundred Days: The Memoirs of the Falklands Battle Group Commander* (Annapolis, MD: Naval Institute Press, 1992), 105. [It is surprising in view of the importance attached to Paraquat's success that Woodward did not order Young to engage the *Santa Fe* with his two experienced destroyer captains in *Plymouth* and *Antrim* and the overwhelming technological superiority of the nuclear *Conqueror*].

177-Barker's statement (*Beyond Endurance*, 184) that: "We, too, decided to call off the operation, and, as darkness fell we recalled the troops" is inaccurate. The

SBS had been trying for more than a day to exfiltrate. Moreover, it was not Barker's decision but that of Young, Sheridan, and the SBS.

178-The boats did not fail completely, but they had not been warmed up in accordance with advice from the SBS's boss. Outboard motors used in New Hampshire were kept in the cows' bank barn where they did not freeze.

179-Whereas Burls's group would, if discovered, have been compelled to fire upon and perhaps kill Argentinian marines, the task group remained under a stern injunction from Northwood not to fire upon the Argentinian C-130s that now shadowed the sea force in what Thatcher proclaimed to be British air space. Here Northwood seemed uncomprehending of war's essential purpose, destruction of the enemy's will to fight.

180-Barker, *Beyond Endurance*, 185. Captain Barker seemed upset at the submarine's presence and omitted the fact that even the plodding *Endurance* could outrun its foe as long as its fuel lasted.

181-Barker, *Beyond Endurance*, 188.

182-Bicain had wishy-washy rules of engagement that permitted him on his own sufferance to attack or lay low. Bicain has written that he would not have tried an attack with his marine passengers still aboard. Bicain later asserted, "We could not use weapons except against immanent attack." Bicain letter to the author, July 2011.

183-Lieutenant Colonel Guy Sheridan, "Operation Paraquat," *The Elite* 5 (Issue 56, 1983), 5.

184-Barker, who had commanded an ASW ship, is adamant on this subject. See Barker, *Beyond Endurance*, 188.

185-Barker, *Beyond Endurance*, 187.

186-Barker, *Beyond Endurance*, 198-199.

187-The time taken to plan fairly simple military operations (ones unlike Kursk) is usually inverse to their success. The US Navy planned a Pacific War against the Japanese all through the 1930s and lost its fleet in three hours on December 7, 1941 at Pearl Harbor. Patton changed the axis of attack and logistics in hours during the Battle of the Bulge in December 1944 and raced three divisions north to save Bastogne.

Eight

Horacio Bicain and the Submarine Santa Fe ARA S-21

As much metaphor as mission, the story of Horacio Bicain and the *Santa Fe* epitomizes the problems that both nations' political captains created for their military leaders. It highlights the Junta's failure to comprehend the military arts. It also demonstrates the particular obstacles Thatcher placed in the way of her amphibious force by deciding to repossess South Georgia Island. As the Argentinian forces were occupying the Falklands, Royal Navy units were completing their annual spring exercises off Gibraltar. On receiving orders to form a task force for a voyage south, half the ships unloaded their stores to the other half. The stocked ships headed for Ascension Island under Woodward; the other half left for their home ports in the UK to reload.[188] By April 8, the Junta's military staff knew from the British press and TV precisely what forces Thatcher had sent south to reclaim the Falklands but had no idea what forces if any she would deploy in order to recapture South Georgia. That information came later, probably in the third week of April, from aerial reconnaissance.

The Junta's reaction to efforts to retain South Georgia against a probable British invasion then centered on one diesel submarine, the *Santa Fe* ARA S-21. The operational head of the Navy, Vice Admiral J. J. Lombardo, opposed *Santa Fe*'s mission. To Admiral Anaya, however, this unseemly choice had a peculiar logic. The Junta could do little to send a balanced military force to South Georgia, because its makeshift troop transports were unequal to South Georgia's weather and because its serviceable warships were deploying northwards in order to block the British task forces heading south. That the Royal Navy could not reach the Junta's invasion fleet before it had seized Port Stanley and that no British troops could arrive in the combat area for weeks stopped the Argentinian military staff from pondering their next move. It concluded none would be needed, and a certain languor, perhaps paralysis, came over the Junta and the staff entrusted to formulate tactics. After the successful invasion of East Falklands and Mills's courageous defense of South Georgia, no shots had been fired or even threatened. Excepting Anaya, the major Argentinean leaders saw negotiation, not combat, as the next step. Haig and his team worked in furtherance of that goal.

During this lull, and in the face of Thatcher's determination to retake the Falklands, Anaya and Galtieri had a political task — they had to be seen by their colleagues, the military, and the public to be acting. Their problem appeared much the same as Thatcher's; they needed to keep the public happy while awaiting the next triumph. The theatrical aspects of this conflict were never far away. To Admiral Anaya, dispatching one troop-laden submarine to South Georgia was a move sufficient to achieve his goal of establishing a garrison large enough to resist a British counter-thrust. To many others, who were fumbling inside the Casa Rosada, this stingy military effort was simply a bargaining chip to delay British efforts while the Junta's negotiators sought a face-saving conclusion to their follies.

What did not happen those first weeks of April in Buenos Aires appears more compelling than the anti-British street parades and nasty slogans addressed to Thatcher. No national mobilization occurred. No troops were rushed to vulnerable seaports. No training against possible British air raids was put in play. British clubs, newspapers, and banks easily carried out their normal routines. In the Argentinian countryside, except for those areas from which the mostly Indian conscripts had been drawn to fill out the occupying forces on East Falklands, no one much cared about the islands, the British, a possible armed response from Thatcher, or any potential interruption of their normal lives. In fact, for all of its skillful seizure of East Falkland, the Junta misunderstood Thatcher's strategic and tactical reach. Notwithstanding Anaya's obstinacy, Sheridan and his tiny band of Royal Marines were headed for South Georgia with hostile intent. Thatcher's bellicosity had jarred the Junta's smugness somewhat but had served even more to swing the British public behind her. Now with the better part of the Royal Navy steaming south at speed, the Junta had to move.

How did ARA S-21 *Santa Fe* come to bob about with hostile intent in these sparsely attended waters? South Georgia had no airport, let alone a modern runway that could handle cargo aircraft. Paratroops dropping in high winds could find themselves blown into freezing waters or onto jagged mountains. The battalion-sized landing beaches that were so easily available on East Falklands did not exist on South Georgia. The Junta, but not the naval staff, acted as though its surface ships risked attack by British submarines. Yet at this early stage of the war, the British subs was still half a continent away. The Junta itched to act, but the irritating snags of conventional war had caught up with it at the least opportune time. The Argentinian ships that had put troops ashore on East Falklands sorely needed substantial dockside supply and installation of the bits and pieces that keep modern navies going. [189] Additional landings from *Buen Suceso* and *Buen Paraiso* by an integrated combat force that included artillery, trucks, communications gear, and the oddments of war were out of the question.

But why *Santa Fe*? Because no other boat was fit or available for a hazardous mission to South Georgia. There were other reasons, too. It is an often-told tale. Major powers usually sell military trinkets to lesser powers because that equipment is outdated and cannot be used successfully against the sellers, because sales raise cash, and because the new users must, in ordinary circumstances, then buy replacement parts, counter-measures, training packages, and add-ons from the original maker. They then play host to crews from faraway lands spending time in Newport, Plymouth, and other spots in northern Europe while training to run their new ships home. Weeks in training tend to lengthen into months and occasionally years, and the crews' experience with these locales grows. New markets and relationships are thus created with the buyers, who sometimes entertain the hope that a *de facto* military alliance now exists and that both parties will eat from the same budgetary table. This condition, gratifying to some and expensive to their navies, explains in part why the two German diesel boats being readied for a fall war remained in Hamburg for the entire conflict.

The Argentinian Junta and its predecessors bought ships, planes, and military equipment from any supplier who would grant it credit. It had no domestic facility that produced world-class weaponry or military gear. Throughout the entire war, the Junta's men at spear's point wore uniforms from Israel and used combat equipment from America, West Germany, Great Britain, Italy, Belgium, and other nations. This recourse to offshore, off–the-shelf procurement produced chaotic logistical, training, and repair problems and, worst of all, bafflement among peasant soldiers who could not in many cases understand the labels on the equipment they were trying to use.[190] The Argentinean diesel submarine *Santa Fe* showed all of that but is intriguing mostly for what it was not, a modern weapons platform that could compete in open ocean warfare.[191] As a centerpiece for a major Argentinian military initiative, the deployment of the *Santa Fe,* despite its manning by a competent crew and a very skilled commanding officer, portended disaster. The Junta's notion of naval warfare had turned to self-indulgence.

The *Santa Fe*, Galtieri and Anaya's weapon of choice to reinforce South Georgia, had once slid down the ways on November 19, 1944 at Groton, Connecticut as the USS *Catfish* SS-339. *Santa Fe's* Argentinian commanding officer in 1982 had barely been born when the boat was laid down. It had been built by the Electric Boat division of General Dynamics, which installed four General Motors (GM) engines rather than the US submarine community's more popular choice, the Fairbanks Morse engine (whose descendant remains to this day the auxiliary engine in US nuclear boats). Among the last of 121 Balao-class submarines, the design of *Catfish* was a response to lessons learned in the Pacific war, with the principal remedies being the installation of six torpedo tubes forward, four aft, and reliable fire control equipment. In 1948, the still new *Catfish* received a Guppy 2 conversion that raised her displacement from 1500 to 1800 tons. In addition, better batteries were installed in place of one GM engine, and the metal sail was replaced with a plastic structure in order to lighten topside weight. This conversion enabled the boat to make twenty knots surfaced and eight knots submerged. Safe submerged depth was four hundred feet. The days of easy pickings from among slow Japanese merchant ships were long past, and *Catfish* completed her Korean War service without sinking a ship. *Catfish* typified the workhorse boat of the post-World War II US Navy and made its six-thousandth dive on September 5, 1968.[192]

But after years of noble use, *Catfish* became a tired ship. Her GM engines, never sailors' favorites, threw oil from shafts and bearings at awkward times, and her electrical system required undue attention on lengthy patrols. Suddenly, in early 1971, rumors of her deactivation became fact, and her skipper, Commander Clyde van Landingham, was ordered to transfer her to the Argentinian Navy "as is where is." USS *Catfish* was struck from the US Naval Registry on July 1, 1971. Under its new owners, *Santa Fe* then made a war patrol in 1978 against the Chilean Navy without engaging in combat. *Santa Fe* never fired a torpedo in anger and, for a warship, led an easygoing existence. Its American torpedoes were lightly maintained, seldom tested, and uncertain of firing on command. The Argentinian Navy gave the old ARA S-21 several overhauls in dry dock and also relied on pierside repairs to keep the boat fit for occasional patrols. This meant that every dent, hole, and panel below the waterline got an eyeball or hands-on inspection. In 1980, under its prewar skipper, Julio Eneas Grasso, *Santa Fe* bottomed out and lost its bow sonar dome. Captain Bicain, the wartime skipper, had to make do with a scavenged and well-used replacement from another Argentinian submarine, *Santiago del Estero*.

By spring 1982, *Santa Fe*, through no fault of the very competent engineer serving as its skipper, was no longer a fighting ship according to US Navy and Royal Navy standards. It was old and tired. Nonetheless, Anaya ordered that it remain an operational combat ship carried on the roles of Jane's Warships and Lloyds of London because there were no immediate replacements for it. The two diesel submarines being built in Hamburg were not yet fitted out and ready for combat. *Santa Fe's* mate, *San Luis,* was in equally poor condition and made such loud engine and hull noises that it was used before the invasion only for peaceful patrols off the Straits of Magellan. *San Luis* did carry twenty-two torpedoes, a mix of American anti-ship and German anti-submarine weapons.[193] Twenty-two stable torpedoes in the hands of a competent skipper, although an inherently potent weapon, were useless when carried by *San Luis* because its hastening to a firing position would produce enough noise to make it the hunted rather than the hunter. Earlier, *San Luis* had reported to Captain Moya, the submarine squadron's commander, that its wire-guided Special Surface Target (SST) torpedoes, weapons also carried by the submarine *Salta,* had failed during exercises, as they would later when engaged against British ships.[194] These two ancient boats were in fact the less-favored orphans of the Argentinian Navy. So erratic were the electronic communications among the Argentines that the captain of *San Luis*, Fernando Azcueta, had only learned of the Argentinian possession of the Falklands by commercial radio rather than via his navy's chain of command.[195]

On April 2, ARA *Salta* (S-31), a third Argentinian submarine with water under the keel, lay alongside Puerto Madryn, the Argentinian submarine base. The boat was a type 209 built by German designers to control the Baltic against Warsaw Pact forces. The successful design required a small crew of thirty-two and used easily fixable diesels that gave a surface speed of twelve knots and a submerged speed of about twenty-three knots with a clean bottom. Some sixty boats of this class had been sold abroad. Against expectations, *Salta* suffered the very lethal flaw it was designed against. Under Argentinian care, it had become unacceptably noisy, and on the day the war began, French technicians were working to put the boat back to sea in combat shape. They failed; the boat still made excessive noise whether surfaced or submerged. Captain Moya then ordered *Salta* to dry dock for a complete examination. At the same time, the French technicians left Argentina with their job unfinished. In addition, *Salta's* CO was relieved because of illness. On April 13, Captain Roberto Salinas, a naval aide to Galtieri, got the job. He had never seen combat and, as a further measure of Admiral Anaya's failure to plan, there was no tactical doctrine for fighting British surface ships or submarines.

In dry dock, *Salta's* propeller and axel were removed and repositioned with repaired bushings and bearings. Tests at sea again proved the boat unacceptably noisy, and it again returned to port. The Argentinian naval staff intended the boat to intercept and sink any British ship that could carry reinforcements, such as Sheridan's cramped crowd of infantrymen, to South Georgia. By any standard except Anaya's romantic logic, *Salta* was ineligible for a mission to South Georgia. The most junior naval officer might without much rumination conclude that these creaky old boats, *Salta, Santa Fe,* and *San Luis,* could not engage the Royal Navy with any chance of success.

Woodward disagreed. Argentinian combat potential as seen through his eyes prompted changes in British defensive dispositions around East and West Falkland, in Young's already unnecessarily cautious tactics around South Georgia, in the time a logistic ship could spend unloading in San Carlos Bay, and in amphibious operations there on East Falkland. Woodward's excessive and unjustified response prolonged the war.[196] Among the Royal Navy's upper command, it was axiomatic that the British were not prepared to fight a battle whose loss in ships could sunder the Anglo-American relationship, which Britain's seaborne nuclear deterrent was meant to preserve. Woodward and Young's disposition of their ships carried that caution a step too far. On the other side, Anaya and Lombardo realized that their submarines, especially *Santa Fe,* could neither flee nor fight. Their crews knew that, too.

When the Falklands conflict began with the seizure of East Falkland six months earlier than the Junta had planned, Bicain was forced to go to war in a ship that was unfit for combat against a NATO navy. In spring 1982, *Santa Fe's* radios worked randomly, bilge pumps operated only at periscope depth, the GM engines threw ever more oil, a main hatch cover leaked, and batteries gave only twelve knots for four hours submerged. When this charge was exhausted, the boat had to run at two to four knots, to surface or at snorkel depth until it had replenished its batteries. The batteries could not, in any case, keep a full charge. Communications between Bicain and his headquarters were frequently down. Oil slicks from the wonky bearings could be seen from a distance by a trained observer.[197] *Santa Fe* was an easy and natural target if it were ever to be engaged.

Upon taking command of *Santa Fe,* Bicain put to sea with his senior officer, Captain Grasso, aboard. Once in open water, the boat refused to submerge, owing to a defective water valve, and had to return to Puerto Belgrano for emergency repairs. The boat had enjoyed at least two spells in dry dock after the transfer of ownership, but in January 1982, when the astern steering system failed, *Santa Fe* returned for a further stay. That Admiral Anaya's blue-water ships were scheduled to train and to repair that summer for an autumn war did not console a competent and loyal crew three hundred feet in the deep on a terminally unsafe submarine. Yet Bicain survived all of this. He had made his career as an engineer-officer and until the end, he and his crew dealt very competently with their boat's defects.

On March 24, Captain Moya, head of the Argentinian submarine force, passed a warning order to Bicain that *Sante Fe* was to carry a reconnaissance party of marines to the shores of East Falkland. An operations order followed, and Bicain put to sea from Mar del Plata at 2230 on March 27 in order to practice unloading drills with Lieutenant-Commander Alfredo Cufre's tactical divers, who were to plot the landing sites on East Falkland. This fact alone belies Thatcher's remark that the invasion was sudden and unpredictable, for submarines do not leave port in plain sight without a palpable military mission. The drills succeeded, but foul weather postponed the Argentinian beach reconnaissance and landing from March 30 to March 31. Just before midnight on the thirty-first, Cufre's men debarked from *Santa Fe* and completed a very successful survey of the landing beaches on East Falkland. They cut the airfield at Stanley and the Cape Pembroke Lighthouse from the list of possible landing sites and put Mullet Creek and York Bay into play. Cufre's beacons marking the landing areas were accurately placed, and Argentinian forces landed precisely onto their intended locations. Cufre's work was the most professional Argentinean military exploit of the war. Bicain retrieved his landing party and headed his barely operating ship back to port as the Falklands were acquiring new, if temporary, owners. It was this very success in landing the beach reconnaissance team that got Bicain nominated to carry reinforcements to South Georgia and to confront Sheridan and his men, whose careers had not, until now, included dealing with barely operating submarines.

Santa Fe, the most operational Argentinian submarine, had limped back to its home port, Mar del Plata, and returned to sea despite unusually serious defects.[198] Yet the voyage to East Falkland had exacerbated all the boat's known flaws to the point of breakdown, and a few more hitches were discovered *en route*.[199] To be sure, the boat dove and surfaced, and its essential systems often worked. But they did so raggedly, not always on command or up to the demands of battle. The US Navy's three American torpedoes, which had accompanied the boat's transfer to Argentina in 1971, had never been used and had been only been tested pierside. Few aboard had confidence that they would leave their tubes if armed and fired, let alone that they could sink a British ship.[200] Still, on the trip home from the Falkland beaches, none of that truly mattered to skipper and crew because all assumed that no combat would ensue, that Thatcher would not fight a war, and that *Santa Fe* would soon be scrapped. Bicain and his crew, mostly engineers, knew their business. They had patched up a basically unseaworthy warship and performed a successful military mission. They could tie up alongside after their last voyage with satisfaction and relief.

Bicain had another problem, though. Imprecise rules of engagement cloaked all of his meanderings during the Falklands War.[201] He had vague orders not to engage British combat units for fear that such an act would scuttle negotiations with Haig and give Thatcher reason to open submarine warfare against the Argentinian Navy.[202] He could, however, engage on his own judgment in the face of imminent danger. Lombardo wanted the rules relaxed, but Anaya refused to change Bicain's orders and prevailed. Bicain never achieved a fire-control solution on a British ship and no torpedoes left his tubes with hostile intent.

By the middle of April, the Junta approached its end game, which was neither skillfully planned nor executed. Galtieri and Anaya had few cards to play. In part, this was because Thatcher faced political constraints. Any kind of conciliation on her part, either before the war or after, foundered on the Kelpers' demands for self-determination. The Junta's Foreign Office understood that large fact, even if the Junta did not admit it or act upon it. That perduring conviction, Argentina's ramshackle governmental machinery, Galtieri's arrogance, and Admiral Anaya's undampened adventurism virtually guaranteed American support for Britain in a conflict that would first desiccate the bravado of Galtieri and the Junta and then humiliate Argentina. When British forces set to sea that spring, Galtieri acquired two enemies: Thatcher and the head of his own navy.

The Junta now warred in the dark. It had no Wellington to bark, no Nelson to turn a blind eye, only newspaper hacks to trumpet an offense that did not exist. Every military move by the Junta became a jittery affair. Collywobbles started at the top. On the other side, an ocean away, there was no such trepidation. As a British officer on the scene wrote of the South Georgia operation, it "was a risk worth taking and I was prepared to put my life on the line to execute it."[203]

While Sheridan and his men sweated their way southward and Bicain made for sea, Rentschler attended Thatcher's dinner for Secretary Haig on Thursday, April 8 at No. 10 Downing. He recorded that:

Her position — strongly supported by Defense Minister John Nott and Admiral of the Fleet Lord Terry Lewin, somewhat less so by Francis Pym – calls for the status quo ante, period. High color is in her cheeks, a note of rising indignation in her voice, she leans across the polished table and flatly rejects what she calls the "woolliness" of our second stage formulation, [it was] conceived in our view as a traditional face-saving ploy for Galtieri: "I am pledged before the House of Commons, the Defense Minister is pledged, the Foreign Secretary is pledged to restore British administration. I did not dispatch a fleet to install some nebulous arrangement which would have no authority whatsoever. Interim authority! – to do *what*? I beg you, I beg you to remember that in 1938 Neville Chamberlain sat at this same table discussing an arrangement which sounds very much like the one you are asking me to accept; and were I to do so, I would be censured in the House of Commons – and properly so! We in Britain simply refuse to reward aggression – that is the lesson we have learned from 1938."[204]

Poltical bravado or not, this statement presented an extraordinary display of courage—especially since two years earlier she had wanted to dump the islands and its people to Argentina through the Ridley sale-and-lease back arrangement. No great forces of history were at play here. No missiles were put on alert. No tank armies glowered at each other across the European plain. It was, at its barest, a case of a grocer's daughter, hardly a figure of war, despised by a few, doubted by many, and questioned by all. Her foreign affairs servants had failed her, and she entered the Commons the morning of April 3 to plead for her job, her political future, and her place in history.

Neither Bicain nor Sheridan nor the twenty year olds who would suffer the bleeding knew that Thatcher had drawn a line in the sand as they headed for their meeting in the South Atlantic. One senior British officer later summed up the status quo in mid-April: "For the first time in the war Argentine intelligence correctly divined British intentions and capabilities."[205] Haig's insistence to Galtieri after his talks with Margaret Thatcher, that Great Britain would fight and win, spread like a fevered virus through the interstices of the Junta—with no good results.[206] Once the British fleet sailed from its home ports, some Argentinian staff officers in Buenos Aires believed, but could not argue to their superiors, that Thatcher would reinvade the Falklands and that the Junta's forces would lose. Almost simultaneously, in the second week in April, Minister of Defence Nott retreated publicly from his narcissistic pessimism and now favored recapture of the islands by force.

At this point in the conflict, Galtieri, Anaya, and Bicain could not be said to act in response to Thatcher's determination. They sat and waited. Thatcher's icy resolve and Anaya's burden of hubris and diplomatic incompetence had all become palpable. The war's momentum began to change in Thatcher's favor. By this time, too, Thatcher's military fell in line with her rhetoric. Nott's unwearied sycophancy closed the circle around the prime minister, and Thatcher could wage war without an abnormal concern for her back. Her new cabinet colleague in the Foreign Office, Francis Pym, mewed forlornly and in vain.

When a small British task force, TF 317.1, struck for South Georgia, her cabinet understood that Thatcher had put a lot of straw into her bricks. This was the point at which some Argentinian officers, mostly middle-grade and from the naval staff, concluded with a peculiar turn of logic that South Georgia, the clear target, was worth fighting for to gain time to negotiate the conflict's end. They did not understand. As Thatcher said later: "I have not sent British troops and British treasure 8000 miles from England to establish a UN trusteeship."[207]

Upon its return to port, *Santa Fe,* was reprovisioned and repaired, contrary to its crew's hopes and expectations. But given that Santa *Fe* was imminently to be decommissioned, no spare parts had been purchased or machined for it. Eleven store-bought, untested torpedoes and four tons of food and water were struck below while the yard's workers fixed what defects they could. Even with the yard help and the competent crew working furiously, the boat could make only thirteen knots on the surface for less than an hour before needing to cut speed to under ten knots in order to cool the diesel engines. Despite frantic efforts by yard technicians, the crew could not use automatic controls but had to fire the torpedoes manually.

Shortly after *Santa Fe* was combat-loaded, Bicain received new orders to jettison all but three torpedoes and to take onboard nine marines as garrison for South Georgia and eleven technicians to keep safe the island's power supply and buildings. The after torpedo room and much of the forward torpedo space were opened for the marines and their bulky weapons. How twenty persons with military equipment were to sleep and eat aboard an already cramped boat was left to Captain Bicain.[208] If it came to fighting, an already dicey submarine with untrained passengers aboard would be a demanding affair. Bodies jumping over bodies is not the normal way for a crew at general quarters. Bicain was ordered to land these men on South Georgia after a covert transit in order to strengthen the Junta's legal and military position as sovereign of the island. At least that is what the Junta told itself. As a shining example of the Junta's inexperience with the artifices of warfare, Bicain was also ordered, on the side, to command the South Georgia garrison upon his arrival there.[209] Clearly a vast gap existed between *Santa Fe's* military capabilities and the mission set by Admiral Anaya.

Bicain's trip was not intended to include attacks on British combat or supply ships. Only two Argentinian boats ever came anywhere near British ships, and their design, manning, and meager operational characteristics made them targets rather than hunters in a war at sea. Their negligible abilities could be gleaned at the time from a reading of unclassified information. For example, it was a truth universally acknowledged at Mar del Plata, an Argentinian submarine base, that those officers and crew who were thought to be politically reliable, to have lengthy careers before them, and to be the most competent had gone to Germany for training on its new Type 209 submarine. Two such boats were due to be commissioned only that late summer and then made ready for a fall war. The Argentinian submarine force as it stood on April 1 could not ready for an offensive war at sea.

The acid test for a submarine's seaworthiness lies in the answer to the question: "Would you go down in her?" The most junior naval officer might ruminate that these creaky old boats, *Santa Fe, Salta,* and *San Luis* could not engage the Royal Navy with any chance of success. Weeks into the war, with none of his ships having been attacked by Argentinian submarine or surface forces, Woodward continued to view the sea war as one where a strictly defensive posture remained utterly necessary. But his defensive tactics failed. He lost five ships to a third-rate air force. *Atlantic Conveyor,* after *Canberra* the most important ship in South Georgia's waters, was sunk, taking with it with the transport helicopters and supplies that would have shortened the war and saved lives.

While Sheridan pled his case to Young for an immediate landing on South Georgia, British intelligence divined *Santa Fe's* approximate position as being close to the island. The boat's mission to bring troops there had been ordered by Admiral Anaya despite the opposition of J. J. Lombardo. *Santa Fe's* transit to South Georgia's operational area was a tribute to its commanding officer and his crew of engineers. The crew was not told of *Santa Fe's* mission until it was well at sea. Professional seamen that they were, they carried on without hesitation. Of course with marines and technicians newly packed into a fairly small submarine, it was not difficult to determine that the submarine's mission excluded the classic assignment of sinking enemy surface ships. The weak batteries that did not take a charge compelled frequent surfacing, occasionally at thirty-minute intervals, where bad weather and high seas slowed *Santa Fe* to a maximum of thirteen knots.[210] Overheated diesels had to be cooled after less than an hour of high speeds in rough waters. Once arrived in South Georgia's waters, Bicain remained surfaced, against his military judgment, because his maps gave an inadequate picture of the rocks and shoals on the bottom approaches to Grytviken. In addition, his night-vision periscope had malfunctioned, and his radar played tricks when used against South Georgia's ice and mountains. His problem on May 23 was to remain undetected by British surface radar and to land his passengers safely. Bicain passed King Edward Point, reached calm waters, and late on May 24 discharged his marine passengers and their equipment in three boatloads onto Gryvtken. The offloading was delayed because of disparities in communications between *Santa Fe* and the shore-based marines, and Bicain ended up using BAS radio frequencies to contact his mates on dry ground. He intended to leave empty at 0400 on the twenty-fifth, but tests and repairs delayed him for an hour. Once underway, Bicain ordered full speed on his diesels in the hope that *Santa Fe* could reach deep water and dive before the diesels had to slow and cool down. The delay in reaching deep water before sunup proved fatal.

British helicopters began their search for the submarine anew at false dawn on the twenty-fifth. They flew over the entrance to Cumberland Bay and found Bicain surfaced and five minutes from deep water, where he might dive. Though whether he could have remained protected from Young's sonars at his maximum safe depth of one hundred fifty meters is doubtful.[211] Cavitation noise from water rushing past the large holes in the sail would almost certainly have given him away. Stanley, in his Wessex 3 from *Antrim,* found the target on the surface, dropped two old-fashioned depth charges, and damaged the *Santa Fe* sufficiently to prevent her from submerging. Her ballast tanks were terminally damaged, and she lost her ability to communicate. As Bicain described it later,

Just as we reached open water in the false dawn and five minutes before diving, a Westland Wasp Helicopter came out of the clouds and dropped a depth charge that exploded near the safety ballast tank. The explosion not only rocked the boat, but disrupted propulsion and cut off communications. I ordered a course change towards the coast while more aircraft [Lynx from *HMS Brilliant* dropped 1 Mk 46 torpedo] launched homing torpedoes, which were ineffective because of shallow water.[212]

In fact, a British observer reported that the *Santa Fe's* entire stern was lifted out of the water.

Bicain could not break off the action: "Feldman and Muracioli, along with Ghiglione, Macias still carrying his steward's towel, Silva, Mareco in his chef's apron, Bustamente, the sonar operator [crew men in the sail] got FAL rifles and began firing at the attackers."[213] ASW torpedoes fired at *Santa Fe's* screws proved ineffective because the weapons do not operate properly unless the target is more than thirty feet underwater, and *Santa Fe* had lost the opportunity to submerge safely. Bicain recounted later, "my second in command, Lieutenant-Commander Michelis suggested to me that we edge the sub away from the coast and sink it, because the ship still had the capacity to move. I ordered him to wait until the night to assess damage and, if possible, to withdraw under protection of darkness."[214] Battered into unseaworthiness, the boat was taking on water. Many hours from night's protection, *Santa Fe* turned back to King Edward Point and, while en route, was hit by British helicopters' AS -12 missiles. Their fuses did not detonate the warheads because the sub's plastic sail did not offer sufficient resistance. One seaman on board wrote, "I had never seen a missile launch, but I can assure you that with two coming at you, one becomes an expert."[215] The British helicopters peppered the boat with fire, and Bicain concluded that he must have lost several crewmen from his control room. In fact, the only injury was to Alberto Macias, who lost a leg to a passing missile. A quick-witted NCO medic, Arnaldo Funes, applied morphine, stopped the bleeding, and saved the young sailor's life. Macias was later flown to *Antrim*, stabilized, and underwent surgery to remove his right leg.[216] At this point, Bicain could not fight, hide, or run; he was a sitting duck. At 1700, Lieutenant-Commander Lagos, who was in charge of the Argentinian marines on South Georgia, informed Bicain that surrender was the best and only course because of the overwhelming superiority of the British. He could honorably strike and did so by radio. Later Bicain regretted not sinking Santa Fe as his Number One had suggested. "It was a difficult decision when one still cherishes some hope to save it" he explained.[217]

Northwood considered codebooks and live prisoners more valuable than bodies lying in metal on the sea bottom, and the helicopters broke off their attack in order to allow *Santa Fe* to continue surfaced back into Cumberland Bay. Under cover from the Argentinian marines ashore, who fired their personal weapons and launched anti-tank missiles at the British helicopters, Bicain's well-punctured ship limped back into Grytviken harbor and tied up alongside the BAS jetty at King Edward Point. *Santa Fe* did not sink to the bottom but kept a meter or so of water under her keel.[218] Bicain never did order his crew to abandon ship, only to tie up alongside as usual. They did so and left their ship in an orderly fashion. For the first and last time in their careers, Sheridan's marines took a submarine crew as prisoners of war. Later, when night had fallen and before the crew left the *Santa Fe,* Michelis asked Bicain if they might sneak the boat out into deep water using only electric power and then scuttle it. Bicain declined. The crew was taken as POWs, inventoried, and given food, cigarettes, medical assistance, and warm quarters. Sheridan's men followed the Geneva Convention very closely.

This drama fit the bizarre side of the Falklands War. Submarines are accurately typed; in war zones they navigate under water where layers of differing salinity and temperature protect them from direct observation and hostile sonar. Fate ruled that Bicain could not take advantage of these normal protections. In those dark hours, his crew of mainly engineers fought as rifle-firing infantrymen—shooting at air targets they had never before seen. The British helicopters attacks proved equally old fashioned. As became apparent upon inspection the next morning, Bicain's boat had been terminally damaged by depth charges, which function best at depths where an explosion close to a hull causes water pressure to burst that hull. They are simply barrels filled with explosives and a primitive fuse.

The next day, April 26, Bicain watched as *Santa Fe's* flooded stern sank deeper while still tied up alongside the wharf at King Edward Point.[219] *Santa Fe* never again took to open water under its own power. British inspection of that sad derelict showed only its dismal and unequipped state. There were no special codebooks, no innovative torpedoes, no unusual communication equipment. All that was left her were the trappings and leavings of a demoralized crew and twenty-five cases of beer.

Notes

187-The time taken to plan fairly simple military operations (ones unlike Kursk) is usually inverse to their success. The US Navy planned a Pacific War against the Japanese all through the 1930s and lost its fleet in three hours on December 7, 1941 at Pearl Harbor. Patton changed the axis of attack and logistics in hours during the Battle of the Bulge in December 1944 and raced three divisions north to save Bastogne.

188-Rear Admiral John Sandy Woodward, lecture to National Defense University, November 19, 1982.

189-James Rentschler noted that while the palace guards' boots had a glassy sheen, the toilets stank. See Rentschler's diaries for many enlightening comments in this vein. "James Rentschler's Falkland's diary: 1 April - 25 June 1982," Reagan Library.

190-British soldiers envied Argentinian boots and night-vision equipment and eagerly sought such.

191-James Mandelblatt, a former crew member of *SS-441*, has graciously supplied the pertinent information on *SS-339*.

192-Much of the data on Balao-class boats come from lengthy exchanges between the author and James Mandelblatt, a crewman on that class of submarine. Mandelblatt was curator of the SS-*Requin* Foundation, which was, until it lost funding, dedicated to that submarine's restoration.

193-*Argentine Naval Review*, No. 45 (June 1997), 116.

194-Both 209s carried the SST4 wire-guided battery-powered propulsion system. The weapon's 550 lbs. of explosive was meant to kill Russian ships with one shot. The torpedoes were almost certainly aimed at *Alacrity*.

195-Jorge Bóveda, Argentine naval historian, letter to the author, October 2, 2000.

196-This problem is addressed in David J. Kenney, *2 Para's Battle for Darwin Hill and*

Goose Green (Upperville, Virginia: Oak Square Press, 2006).

197-Bicain Interview, *DeySeg: Defensa y Seguridad Mercosur* (November 2, 2010), 1-2. Available as "Operacion Georgias, Por El Com andante Del Submarino 'Santa Fe,'" at the site of Historia y Arqueología Marítima (www.histarmar.org/Malvinas/OpGeorgiasxBicain.htm).

198-*Santa Fe's* twin, *San Luis,* put to sea and engaged the battle force and the landing ships at San Carlo. It fired four torpedoes: two lost the wires that kept the torpedoes headed for their target and fell short of the British ships, one ran to fuel's end, and one came back on *San Luis*. The British ships were unaware that they had been targeted and attacked. Captain Azcueta was a brave skipper. Knowing that his fire control system was not dependable, he snugged his boat up close to a British DD. Both shots that lost wires had probably been intended to hit *Alacrity* at around midnight on May 1. After these mishaps, the boat returned to port. Letter from retired Argentinian naval officer, April 2008.

199-Bicain could receive messages but could not transmit during most of his time at sea.

200-Notes from an Argentinian submarine commander on *Brilliant* web site, June 20, 2008. http://www.hmsbrilliant.com/.

201-Bicain, letter to the author, February 21, 2012.

202-Bóveda, letter to the author, October 2, 2000.

203-Senior British Infantry officer, who did just that, in confidential conversation with the author, April 2007.

204-"James Rentschler's Falkland's Diary: 1 April – 25 June 1982,", p. 4, Reagan Library.

205-Senior British Infantry officer in confidential conversation with the author, April 2007.

206-See Rentschler Diary, passim. At several meetings with his Argentinian interlocutors, Haig stressed that Thatcher would fight and, aided by the US, would win.

207-Rentschler Diary, June 3, 1982.

208-See the *USS Requin* site for a picture of the after torpedo room where the passengers were intended to stay. *Requin* and *Santa Fe* were similarly built Balao-class boats.

209-Captain Bicain's crew list, and, his list of Argentine marines, their equipment, and the garrison numbers on South Georgia. Courtesy of James Mandelblatt.

210-Bicain, letter to the author, February 15, 2012.

211-Bicain, letter to the author, February 15, 2012

212-Quote from Bicain AviacionArgentina.net February 7, 2009. The author's Translatio

213-Bicain, interview Dey Seg, February 7, 2009. The author's translation. After leaving the navy, Feldman became master of his own fishing boat.

214-Bicain, interview Dey. Seg. on AviacionArgentina.net. February 7, 2009. The author's translation.

215-Jorge Bóveda, *Malvinas: la odisea del submarino Santa Fe* (Buenos Aires: Instituto de Publicaciones Navales, 2007).

216-Macias lives on with his family and three children in Cordoba. Communication with the author, December 2012.

217-Bóveda, *Malvinas*.

218-Bicain, letter to the author, February 15, 2012.

219-Bicain was harshly treated by his own government after the war. He suffered a brief period of house arrest. His crew thought and acted differently. They have an annual reunion and picnic at which Bicain is the honored guest.

Nine

Well-Planned – The Seizure of Grytviken

Prior to the dramatic diversion of the *Santa Fe*, Northwood had taken Sheridan to task for his lack of progress in recapturing South Georgia. Under political pressure to get matters underway, Northwood had perversely ordered the bulk of Sheridan's landing force away from the landing sites to protect it from the *Santa Fe* before it became the abandoned jetsam of the Argentinian Navy. Sheridan's reconnaissance of feasible landing sites for the marines had not been completed, and two of Young's helicopters had been lost on an imprudent mission that Sheridan had opposed. Up to this point, Sheridan had not had *Antrim* and *Plymouth* together for firing on Argentinian positions. The unnecessary loss of two helicopters meant that the M Coy Group was compelled to land in waves rather than in integrated tactical formations.

The reasons for Sheridan's exasperation were obvious. Young, the force commander responsible for the safe passage and landing of Sheridan's troops, had declined to put them ashore and had dispersed his ships over hundreds of square miles of ocean. Sheridan could not legally order his men on his own over the side and onto the beaches. In conferences aboard *Antrim,* Young was seen to be more impressed with Delves (probably for reasons of personality alone), the reconnaissance force commander, than Sheridan, the land force commander. Young's *de haut en bas* relationship with Sheridan never changed during the entire operation, even though the land force commander was the most important member of the military on *Antrim*. Lack of resolve was concealed on the surface.

Young, ever ruminative, never pushed aggressively for a landing, but instead encouraged unneeded and lengthy reconnaissance that drained his resources, dulled the marines, and delayed the war's end. Northwood had stipulated the recapture of South Georgia as a condition for the recapture of the Falklands themselves, but the word *urgency* was seldom bruited in Young's cramped circle of counselors. There was also no sense on *Antrim's* bridge that ground operations must have a beginning, a middle, and a discreet end, as opposed to maritime operations that can last for months of staring at the sea with little or nothing accomplished. There was no understanding on *Antrim* that it was Young, and nobody else, who had to kick off the operation. Even before it was damaged, no one could claim that *Santa Fe* seriously threatened anyone except her own crew. But with the beaten sub a few thousand yards in front of him, Young had no further excuses for his temerity, no logical or imagined reason to fear attack by submarine or by any other Argentinian weaponry, whether by sea or air. His ships could safely coalesce. The noose of silence was loosened in Antrim's chart room. For his part, Sheridan sensed that the defeat of the *Santa Fe*, now a prize hulk at Grytviken, likely demoralized the original Argentinian garrison and that the trifling reinforcements just debarked from *Santa Fe* would be in no condition to fight. His own men, crammed aboard a variety of ships fundamentally unsuited to carry combat units for long, might lose their edge if Young loitered any longer.

It was then that Sheridan moved with verve. He presented his plan for the landing to Young at 1000 on April 25, having been delayed for three and a half hours while Young and Coward, *Brilliant's* skipper, lingered to replay the attacks on *Santa Fe* and ascertain who engaged first. (It was Stanley.) Sheridan's patience was fortuitous, because the helicopters had to be readied to lift the scratch force of seventy-five men from the SAS and marines in tactical order to Brown Mountain and because Young's gunships had to be drawn up and positioned to give the fire that Sheridan needed to neutralize any positions the Argentinian marines might have dug. Remember that half of Sheridan's landing force remained out of the fight on the distant *Tidespring*.

The helicopters had returned victorious from their attacks on *Santa Fe* by 1030. Thanks to Nunn's having trained them for their transport role, they were ready within a few hours to load the troops and their equipment for a run onto land. In Young's world, three and a half hours was a trifle. In the domain of the young marines, it could well mean defeat instead of victory. But it was not until 1330 that Young, tethered to rank and position, opened a vein and bled out the long awaited formal order to put the landing force ashore. The tedious dialectics aboard *Antrim* ended. Freed from the sapping fug and ferrety conceits of Young's chartroom, Sheridan set about doing what he had been sent to do.

Even if the SAS and Young's behavior had curdled the run up to Sheridan's mission, South Georgia's military world had morphed in his favor by 1100 on April 25. Neither Young nor the SAS men could deny that. The weather and terrain had remained the same for days, but the military situation facing Sheridan, or at least the perception of it aboard *Antrim,* had changed. With *Santa Fe* out of the picture, Young's appreciation of the scene that forenoon permitted him to order the completion of his mission: the reoccupation of South Georgia by Sheridan's previously shackled troops. *Plymouth,* with its twin 4.5" guns, stood nearby *Antrim.* Yet Sheridan knew that disabling the *Santa Fe* was only an intermediate step and not the victory he had been sent to obtain. Until his men took positions on the ground, he remained the tip of a misused spear. Whatever he accomplished or failed to fix would define all the chatter and illuminate the planning inadequacies of Thatcher's government and military and of Captain Young's odd behavior.[220]

Militarily, the SAS patrols and the BAS watchers, valiant as they were, counted for little as an occupying force. The jackpot was the ownership of Grytviken by British infantrymen. *Tidespring,* carrying Sheridan's main assault force, was two hundred miles away, and the remnants of Boat Troop remained ensconced on Grass Island. These men could not be brought into play for at least a day. If the one hundred fifty or so Argentinians chose to fight the seventy-five-man landing force and keep a battle going over the night, the odds would shift towards the Argentinian defenders. Sheridan judged that his command element, the mortar teams, Delves's few SAS men, the SBS section from *Endurance,* and the SAS men from *Plymouth* could break the Argentinian defenses if landed quickly under the support of naval gunfire. It was a judgment made without computers or any other form of high technology; rather it was the gut feeling of a longtime infantryman, comfortable in his own skin, who knew what heartens or demoralizes green troops holding positions against whom or what they could not know. Delay in landing British troops could mean hardened Argentinian defenses. This moment was an inflection point in the whole operation, and Sheridan answered the moment. For all the chatter and scribblings about who did what under which awful circumstances, for the first time in this war there was a direct instrument of Thatcher's will—Sheridan's band of riflemen, who thus became creatures of history. The layers of torpid management designed to hide possible failure (if it came) and to reap reward (if it arrived) all jelled a few days later.

Sheridan needed no encouragement to act. Without the formality of an O Group [orders given to juniors], Sheridan gave hasty commands to his officers at 1345. His plan was simple and quick of execution. The seventy-five men of his landing force were less than half as many as intended and many fewer than the number of defending Argentinian marines. Young had not thought to keep his entire assault force ready at hand. So much of M Company lay aboard *Tidespring,* miles away, and the core of the marine landing force remained scattered about Young's squadron. Because he had only three helicopters of his original fleet left (after the loss of the two on Fortuna Glacier) and two small

Lynx, which had arrived later on *Brilliant*, he could not land the entire force in any case. The enormous tactical disadvantage of landing small groups of only twenty men at a time destroyed surprise and made tactical unity a tricky affair. Landings are best made at dawn to let those newly on shore use a full day of light; Sheridan had at most five hours from takeoff in which to win the battle. He had, however, regained one precious asset: the four naval guns on *Antrim* and *Plymouth*.

The plan focused on two pieces of vital high ground; Brown Mountain is eleven hundred feet high, lying south of Grytviken and a few hundred yards across King Edward Cove, and Bore Valley Pass lies west and behind Grytviken. Seizure of these two dominating points would virtually guarantee Grytviken's submission. Sheridan ordered Delves's SAS group to secure the landing site on the southern side of Hestesletten, flat rocky terrain two and a half kilometers from Brown Mountain's slopes. Delves was then to advance to contact, that is to engage hostile forces. Hestesletten was the higher point, defensible and suitable for landing a helicopter and disgorging its troops. At this distance, the landing site was secure from small-arms fire in the event that Argentinian troops had dug in on the mountain's slopes. But they had not — a surprising omission committed by a first-line Argentinian unit. Captain Chris Nunn then led two groups of infantry in the next two waves and Sheridan followed with his command element, signalers, and medics. Nunn immediately set up a base plate for the sole .81mm mortar carried by the landing force and began registering targets. Finally, Ian Grant landed with a smaller group. As soon as the second wave had landed and established its position, Delves was to "advance to contact" and occupy the line ridge descending from the mountain's top, from which Delves should already have pushed off. At this point, helicopters would lift the remaining troops from *Plymouth* and *Endurance* to Bore Valley Pass in order to give supporting fire to the main body as it advanced from Brown Mountain into Grytviken. Sheridan's calculations had a certain grimness. The plan was bare bones: secure the landing site, bring in the attack force, and push through to the main objective, Grytviken.

Sheridan's fire plan, written with Lieutenant Colonel Eve, was critical to his plan's success.[221] The four guns on *Antrim* and *Plymouth* were his only artillery. At 1435, ten minutes before H Hour, 4.5" British shells rained in rapid fire on Hestesletten, the landing site, a flat patch of rocky earth at the foot of Brown Mountain. Hestesletten, though small, was the only flat surface close to Brown Mountain suitable for helicopter landings and assembly. It had to be cleared so that the British marines could land unopposed and head quickly in the falling light to meet and defeat their opponents. Accurate firing had soon made safe that patch of ground, which was at that moment the most important strip of British holdings. Twenty minutes later, the fire switched to the long ridge that sloped down from the top of Brown Mountain to the sea as the SAS men emerged from the helicopters to secure the landing site. No enemy fire greeted Delves's men then or later that day. The naval gunfire killed no one and destroyed no occupied positions, but it was a precisely timed demonstration of accurate shooting, seen and heard by the Argentinian garrison.[222]

Meantime, Sheridan ordered in his second group of Royal Marines, instructing them to push on behind and through Delves's group to Grytviken. He then arrived himself at 1535 with his command element, signalers, and medics. Already short of daylight, he was enraged at Delves, who had not obeyed the orders Sheridan had given on *Antrim* before the landing, orders to advance to contact enemy forces in the direction of Brown Mountain after the second wave had landed. Delves was meant then to secure the ridge that ran from the mountain's top to the sea. In reply to Sheridan's queries, Delves claimed that an Argentinian position lay at the peak. Sheridan again ordered Delves to advance, and Delves moved forward over stony ground onto and up Brown Mountain. As a preliminary to their attack, the SAS men fired Milan missiles at a suspected enemy position only to discover that they had killed two seals who were disporting themselves on the banks of the Penguin River. No Argentinian troops awaited Delves and his men on Brown Mountain.

Sheridan's advance on the ground met no opposition, and no hostile shot greeted the advancing British troops. While the British scurried to the top of Brown Mountain, naval gunfire shifted to its third phase. Since Sheridan had been ordered to avoid, to whatever extent possible, damage to BAS buildings and any civilians that might be present, his fire plan's third phase directed the ships' gunfire to land over and behind the BAS buildings and the Argentinian defensive positions at King Edward Point so to explode on the opposite shore, where it would exert decisive effect on the defending Argentinian troops. It was made clear to them that an adjustment of only four hundred meters downward would put them on the receiving end of accurate, heavy, and sustained fire. Young's gunnery officers and men had done their job well. By the end of the engagement, *Antrim* had fired sixty-nine 4.5" rounds and *Plymouth* had let off one hundred sixty-six 4.5" rounds. At the end of the day, that accuracy and volume, as well as the presence of aggressive infantrymen, compelled the Argentinian marines to quit.[223] Before South Georgia, the Argentinian marines had never dug in under an artillery barrage, let alone that of accurately registered naval guns. At 1705, ninety minutes after his arrival, Sheridan saw two white flags fluttering from the main buildings in Grytviken. He called off the landing in Bore Valley Pass and began the three-kilometer march to Grytviken. Delves's SAS men leaped forward, and Delves did not answer Sheridan's call to halt.

Sheridan called *Antrim* for a helicopter, and Tony Ellerbeck was given the assignment to fly him into Grytviken to accept the surrender from the Argentinian commanding officer on South Georgia, Lieutentant Commander Luis Lagos.[224] Sheridan took the surrender himself as light failed at 1605. All the confusion, dilatory behavior, back and forth niggling, consumption of resources needed elsewhere, physical exhaustion, and outright bravery ended in a few minutes of applied common sense. On April 25, at 1745 on King Edward Point, Lagos and Captain Bicain surrendered themselves, their men, and their equipment to Major Sheridan.

This most infrequent ceremony occurred in the BAS base at King Edward Point. Barker, Young, and the SAS commander were not present. On April 26, Captain Young gave Sheridan a typed instrument of surrender, which was finally signed by Lagos and Bicain on the twenty-eighth and then backdated two days by an unknown hand on *Antrim*. Bicain behaved honorably toward his one-time enemies and warned them that the helicopter landing pad and the path leading to it from Grytviken were mined. Despite the delays, the Navy's unfamiliarity with amphibious operations, the failed reconnaissance on Grass Island, the threat real or not of submarine attack, the ramshackle command structure, the dispersion of his assault force, the faulty motors on the SAS Gemini boats, and especially the near disaster of Fortuna Glacier, Sheridan put the best face on the nasty business of war. He had completed his mission with no casualties to his own men or to the enemy, either.

Just after Lagos's surrender of all 137 of his men on South Georgia, Lieutenant-Commander Astiz, who commanded the fifteen or so Argentinian marines at Leith, was told to lay down arms prior to the arrival of a British force on the morning of the twenty-sixth or to accept the consequences. Barker radioed Astiz from *Endurance*, with Surgeon Lieutenant Neil Munro's assistance. He told Astiz to stay put and to muster himself and his men the next morning for their surrender. Astiz, who commanded only fifteen marines, had observed the precision of the British guns from afar and complied with British demands. The collapse of the Argentinian garrison, the sound and fury of British naval guns, and the certain presence of British troops extinguished Astiz's prolix bravado, and he yielded. As happens in war, the picture shown in the world's press of Astiz signing an instrument of surrender aboard *Endurance* in Leith gave a false impression that Astiz was surrendering Argentinian forces on South Georgia. In fact, the garrison's surrender under law had taken place the previous day at King Edward Point. Astiz signed only for the fifteen or so Argentinian marines in Leith, and his act unnecessarily duplicated Bicain and Lagos's capitulation to Sheridan of all the Argentinian forces on South Georgia the day before.[225] Even in defeat, Astiz sought and was granted the limelight.

The next day, aboard *Antrim,* Sheridan was amused to receive from Northwood a message asking for a list of those to be decorated for the victory. But South Georgia was not a victory for which combat decorations might be issued; there had been no ground combat. Sheridan's landing force had received no incoming fire and suffered no casualties.[226] Neither had any aboard ship or in the reconnaissance teams been hurt. Still, 190 Argentinians were behind the wire. Thatcher held a jubilant al fresco press conference outside No. 10 Downing Street: "Just rejoice at that news and congratulate our forces and the marines . . . . Rejoice."[227]

However well received the victory, it was quite clear that the Royal Navy lacked the resources and the experience to prosecute small, independent amphibious operations. In fact, the operation was a string of blunders rescued from utter disaster, mainly by the steadfast leadership of Sheridan, the coolness of Barker, and the bravery and skill of Stanley. Little mentioned in the press reports that followed were Nunn's young men from M Company who, although scattered around the South Atlantic, retained enough cohesion and basic military habits to execute a quirky operation with great skill and precision. Had they failed to force the Argentinian marines into surrender that afternoon and given them the night to reorganize their defenses, a dark shadow would have fallen over the war and called into question Thatcher's leadership of it. Simply put, owing to ships' guns and Sheridan's quick execution of a dicey plan, there had been no military opposition and no blood. That would come later.

Operation Paraquat was a slipshod affair conducted by a high command that did not pair adequate human or material resources to the task. The goal was an important political one, but even the scant resources devoted still diverted assets from the main goal, the seizure of Port Stanley. The excuse could be made that a first try at amphibious warfare was bound to be difficult, but that does not explain dispersing the task force before a World War II diesel submarine and sending the assault force away from its target beach. Nor does it explain the poor decision making that went into the Fortuna Glacier incident or the Grass Island reconnaissance. The SAS failed in South Georgia because they used equipment known to be faulty, because they did not credit mountain men with more experience than their own, and because fate and nature do not care how clever or strong humans claim themselves to be.

Some systemic flaws surfaced in the British military, too. The reconnaissance practices of the special warfare units needed refinement of their practices, especially in little-known combat areas, and equipment up to their tasks. The SAS was willing to overman an operation, override the chain of command, go behind the legitimate commander's back, overburden ships and logistics, take incomprehensible risks, and snarl impotently at Fortuna Glacier in order to gain a place in the sun. The Royal Navy did not have a grip on the essence and purpose of amphibious operations — getting troops ashore in order to seize and hold ground from which they could not be expelled. Yet these shortcomings did not overwhelm. Down deep in the corps of the Royal Marines, far from desks and parade grounds, junior officers and enlisted men found a competence and an obduracy that would overcome enormous obstacles, the worst of those posed by their own side.

There were many possible reasons for Thatcher to undertake this mission: to begin the reacquisition of the Falklands, to bloody the Junta's nose, to get her sea-weary soldiers on the move, to keep Reagan, Haig, Pym and Parliament behind her, to spite her domestic opponents, to prove her mettle, to remain prime minister. Take your pick. Sheridan and Nunn's sequestered band of riflemen were given the job. Sheridan's capture of Grytviken and Leith showed the many sides to this small war. Thatcher was not yet the Warrior Queen. That coronation would come with blood, time, and the seizure of Port Stanley. She could, however, hold a cabinet together long enough to gain a victory, because she insisted that UK forces take the initiative and win a bizarre military engagement eight thousand miles from home. She had never waged war before, let alone with a military that her own treasury had savaged. Nonetheless, she made the biggest bet of her life; she threw the dice into the tumultuous waters of the deep South Atlantic, and she won. For the first time since Suez, a British prime minister undertook diplomatic and military responsibilities outside NATO, risked blood and treasure, and prevailed despite a clumsy military command and control system that at first failed to connect the interstices of British intelligence with political necessities and military resources. Members of the armed services, especially pilots and infantry, displayed high competence, heroically in some instances, despite their seniors' lapses. The Argentinian military, on the other hand, had no rationalized plan for the defense of their new holdings. In the meantime, the Argentinian Navy's not fighting surface and submarine engagements demonstrated both strategic and tactical incompetence and gave the British time to remedy their own inadvertencies. The loss of *Santa Fe* only lengthened this dismal tale and foretold to Thatcher and the outside world the inevitable end of this unnecessary affair.

Notes

220-In May 1996, Sheridan, by then retired, seemed unaware of the political weight that had been thrust upon him and his men. Interviews with the author (in Europe), August 2006 and September 2009.

221-Sheridan's fire plan depended for its base time on the moment the helicopters lifted off plus five minutes for the flight to the island. That minute was H Hour. There were three phases: H minus ten to H plus ten for *Plymouth* to neutralize Brown Mountain, H to H plus five for *Antrim to* sanitize the marines' landing site on Hestesletten, and the time after H plus ten for both ships on call to begin for a creeping barrage ranging from Brown Mountain's slopes to Gull Lake.

222-The naval gunfire spotters, one aloft in a Wasp from *Endurance* and another at Dartmouth Point, called the fall of shot very accurately. The job is not glamorous but is extremely important.

223-Argentinian marines occupied the Royal Marines' former holes. The Argentinians chose not to fight building-to-building where they could have caused considerable casualties.

224-A report to his superiors contains the surrender document itself and Lagos's comments on the entire affair on South Georgia. See Lieutenant Lagos [Argentinian marine CO on South Georgia], Battle Report, May 12, 2012, and Annex C to the Official Report of the Surrender 1069. Both in author's possession.

225-Thatcher was also confused about the garrison's head: "A certain Captain Astiz had been in charge of the garrison there (Grytviken)." Margaret Thatcher, *The Downing Street Years* (New York: HarperCollins, 1993), 208.

226-In *Looking For Trouble: SAS to Gulf Command; The Autobiography* (London: HarperCollins, 1994), 344, General Peter de la Billiere wrote: "a combined force of Royal Marines, SAS and SBS fought their way into the former whaling base of Grytviken and recaptured South Georgia in the first victory of the war." This is a wholly erroneous statement because disabling the *Santa Fe* was the first victory and because there was no fighting on South Georgia leading up to its recapture.

227-Thatcher, *Downing Street Years*, 209.

Ten

The Death of Felix Artuso

No flagons of ale, no welcoming crowds of the newly freed greeted Sheridan and his men at Grytviken's whaling station. Only confused and ill-clothed prisoners who had so defiled their buildings that Sheridan's immediate task was to order their cleanup in the interest of upholding the terms of the Geneva Convention. The Argentinians, who had an hour earlier not decided whether to kill the British marines or to surrender, found themselves engaged with mops, brooms, cleaning fluid, and the oddments of decontaminated life. The captives outnumbered their captors two to one. A few watching patrols were established on high ground above Grytviken to prevent mischief by Argentinian stragglers.

On the evening of April 25, Young invited Sheridan, Bicain, and Lagos for dinner aboard *Antrim*. Leith and Astiz's fifteen Argentinian marines would not surrender until the next day. Sheridan mentioned to Young that *Santa Fe* still had one meter of water under its keel, but that margin was slowly disappearing. He wanted the boat moved away from the King Edward Point jetty, which would soon be needed for British supply ships. Sheridan further advised Young that the submarine, which Young's men had been trying to sink earlier in the day but now wished to save, should and could be moved under its own power and scuttled in Cumberland Bay's deep water. This evolution would have been cheap, solved any legal problems about the boat's future ownership that might arise after the war, and allowed British forces to get on with retaking the Falklands.

But since the UK was not formally at war and could not dispose of the *Santa Fe* as a prize of war, Northwood ordered Young to move the ship intact to Grytviken, several hundred meters away from its present berth. It was also suggested that the existence of the torpedoes aboard *Santa Fe* and the emission of noxious gas could provoke an explosion that would kill or harm those in the vicinity and destroy the wooden structures alongside the dock.[228] But by the morning of the twenty-sixth, *Santa Fe's* stern rested only a few inches above the mud of Cumberland Bay, and if fired, its torpedoes could not have exited their tubes, armed themselves, or run off to anywhere but land. The boat could not have maneuvered into a firing position from which it could aim at British ships. No competent officer or sailor was aboard the sub to perform the complex operation of loading, aiming, and firing a torpedo.[229] The ship was not, that is, a military threat.

Also that morning, Sheridan allowed rotations of Argentinian sailors under close marine guard to remove their personal belongings from the *Santa Fe*. The guards kept their weapons loaded but not cocked and were instructed not to fire unless attacked. The Argentinian prisoners, most cheerful, a few sullen, were otherwise busily engaged in cleaning up their new digs and were easily handled. In the afternoon, Coward, CO of the frigate *Brilliant* and a successful submarine captain arrived by Lynx helicopter at King Edward Point by order to assess the captured boat's condition and decide on its prospects as an abandoned derelict. Early the next morning, he returned to King Edward Point, having again received a repeat of his firm orders from Northwood to ensure that *Santa Fe* be moved to the Grytviken jetty some few hundred meters from its present position. Sheridan was not told what authority had given the order and was not given a copy of it. Coward ordered a skeleton crew drawn from among the Argentinian prisoners to man critical stations below decks during the move. They refused.[230]

After discussions among the crew, Bicain, and Coward, five former crew members of the submarine volunteered to work under Captain Bicain's supervision and descended into the sub's hull in order to get their former boat under way. Bypassing its damaged diesels, *Santa Fe* had just enough charge in its batteries to proceed on electric power. Two Argentinian sailors remained topside to handle the lines. Armed Royal Marines with loaded weapons, all made safe, attended each Argentinian sailor. The marines had orders to shoot to kill if they were threatened or if the Argentinians threatened to sink or damage the boat. Overnight the boat had become mired in the mud and took ten minutes to get released from the bottom and achieve some forward movement. During that time, structural damage from the British missiles and depth charges had let water into the boat's bottom and through the shafts' glands. *Santa Fe* began to list. The Argentine crew, slogging through water and debris below decks, had head sets that transmitted orders to them from Coward and Bicain on the bridge. The marine guards lacked communication with the bridge and heard nothing from either Bicain or Coward or any words in English. Bicain remembered the horror later:

When we were sailing the submarine began listing, then with the approval of Coward I ordered to blow the tanks with the LP compressor. Artuso opened the correct valves, by the noise caraterísticos I heard from the bridge. It really was a terrible mistake by Coward. He knew the Guppy submarines, but one where the immersion valves were on starboard and the LP compressor valves in port, inverted with respect to the *Santa Fe*. Coward's orders were that Artuso could not touch any valve on the starboard side.[231]

Artuso's response to a legitimate order happened in seconds. A Royal Marine standing guard who could not hear the order and would not have understood the Spanish even if he had, concluded that Artuso was about to sabotage the boat and shot him four times. Artuso died instantly. The young marine had executed the proper move as ordered and the boat passed quickly to its new berth with a corpse aboard. *Santa Fe* then sank into 20 meters of muddy water. Only the well-holed sail showed.

Artuso's body was moved to an unused side of the sub's control room and covered with a sheet in order not to alarm the other Argentinian sailors, who had obviously heard the shots.[232] On April 28, Sheridan, his medical officer (Swinhoe), and a senior NCO removed the body to shore where Swinhoe and the Medical Officer from *HMS Brilliant* performed an autopsy on Artuso that same afternoon.[233] The report of the Royal Navy of Inquiry (presided over by Barker) and the comments made on it are detailed and instructive. They conclude that once the movement of the submarine to its new berth was undertaken, no culpable actions ensued.[234] The fundamental cause of this awful and unnecessary death was the fabled order from Northwood to move the boat, complicated by having non-English-speaking sailors man critical stations with non-Spanish speaking British marines by their side. The precipitate cause was one British marine's failure to hear and to understand a legitimate order given to Artuso in Spanish. Coward had not taken an obvious precaution in that instance.

It would have been better to wait for a professional salvage crew to perform whatever actions Northwood deemed necessary after the euphoria of the surrender had exhausted itself. The young marine who shot Artuso believed that the Argentinian sailor was trying to scuttle the boat. The marine's belief was honest; he concluded that a hostile act had occurred that might endanger him and the other marine sentries. But no one had informed him and the other guards that *Santa Fe* scraped the bottom and could not have sunk. The same report admits that the submarine was not in immediate danger and Artuso's move in starting the air compressor had righted the submarine, prevented it from tipping onto its side in the mud, and allowed it to continue to its new mooring.[235] After hearing shots fired, Bicain called in vain for help on an international distress frequency. Upon hearing of the incident, Young on *Antrim* demanded that the marine in question be arrested and confined. Nunn, the marine's superior, refused to surrender the young man until inculpatory facts had been put forth that showed the boy's unmistakable guilt in this matter. In any case there was no place to which the marine could escape with any chance of survival.

Bicain thought later about how he might have altered events that day: "I must say that the death of Artuso is something that I have on my conscience, because if I had refused to maneuver it [the death] would not have happened."[236] The naval board concluded that no further action was necessary. On South Georgia, the matter was handled with grace. Bicain writes: "I must add that the burial of Artuso was made with full military honors, seriously; by decision of Captain Young, who was present, I presided [over] the ceremony. The tomb of Artuso always is well cared, for approximately two years ago I received a photo of the crew of the HMS *Lancaster* doing an honors there."[237]

Artuso's death was a terrible end to an operation that until then had been bloodless. *Santa Fe* waited several years before an extremely expensive towing and salvage operation delivered this sad boat to the depths. *Santa Fe's* crew remains in touch with each other and holds periodic reunions with Bicain as the honored guest. M coy under Nunn remained unhappily as garrison for South Georgia throughout the entire war, and after Port Stanley's surrender finally retook South Thule Island under hazardous circumstances from the Argentinian group that had illegally established a weather station there.

In retrospect, the entire operation's risks seem obvious. In addition, Sheridan annoyed Young at various stages of the mission by his aggressive plan to reoccupy Grytviken, by his opposition to the Fortuna Glacier mission, by his admonitions on the fateful moving of Santa Fe, by his honest response to Young's request for gallantry recommendations, and probably by his mere presence. Young, however, knew little about amphibious operations and less about air or ground warfare, whereas Sheridan knew all the nuts and bolts of going at an enemy on the ground and in this event winning an engagement without losing a life. That was obvious to those who participated in this strange episode. It was clear to many that Young wanted to see his land force commander's back. Without formal notice or even an order, Sheridan was given two hours to board a Lynx helicopter that would bring him to Coward's *Brilliant,* which was then heading at best speed to the Falklands. Sheridan returned as executive officer to his parent unit, 42 Commando, where he participated in the assault and capture of Mount Harriet on East Falkland Island, the best planned and executed battle of the war. He behaved valiantly then and later, but never again captured an island or a submarine.

Notes

228-"Report of the Inquiry into the Death of Argentine Prisoner of War Suboficial Primero (SIMQ) Felix Artuso," April 30, 1982. http://rna-10-area.co.uk/files/boi_felixartuso.pdf.

229-The "Report of the Inquiry" states on page 2 that "potentially explosive mixture represented a significant threat to both land and sea elements of the British forces." This is nonsense. All that was necessary was to stay a few hundred feet from the hull.

230-Whether these particular Argentinian crewmen knew it or not, they were legally entitled to refuse Coward's order, because they were not POWs given that no war had been declared between Argentina and the UK.

231-Bicain, letter to the author, February 17, 2012.

232-Sheridan, letter to the author, April 14, 2012.

233-Sheridan, letter to the author, April 14, 2012.

234-In offering mitigating circumstances for that sad affair the Board of Inquiry report mentions that "none[marines] had never encountered the enormous pressures etc." That statement is disingenuous.

235-Sheridan, letter to the author, April 14, 2012, p. 5.

236-Bicain, letter to the author. February 17, 2012.

237-Bicain, letter to the author. December 17, 2012.

Captains Bicain and Coward on *Santa Fe*'s deck after surrender.

Royal Marines taking charge of *Santa Fe*.

Moment of Silence at Artuso's grave.

Military Honors rendered at Artuso's funeral ceremony.

Sheridan now retired at Artuso's grave.

MG Nick Vaux salutes the dead of his 42 Commando RM.

Santa Fe being towed to its grave.

Santa Fe down by the stern before transfer to new docking.

Santa Fe in an
undignified
position during
a failed salvage
attempt.

Santa Fe showing battle
damage after surrender.

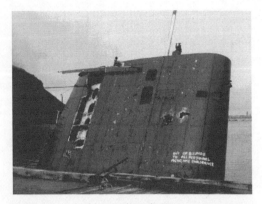

Santa Fe holed by rocket shots.

Santa Fe being snugged
up to tug.

Santa Fe snugged up and underweigh.

KEP and *Santa Fe* from Brown mountain Grytviken from across the bay.

Grytviken at peace. Note the old Norwegian Church bottom right.

Grytviken harbor probably 1895.

Grytviken late 19th century.

Nimrod dropping orders for repossession of South Georgia Island.

Santa Fe's crew at reunion.

First wave of landing force loads up.

Argentine prisoners marshalled on South Georgia's beach before assignment to quarters.

Sloane, Thwaites(CO), Kinsella-Bevan, GS, Op Lance Dhofar, July 1969

SecNav John Lehman sent oil to Ascension Island before the UK went to war.

An exhausted Sheridan and his radio operator atop Brown Mt. before their entrance into Grytviken.

Sloane A&SH (centre) Kinsella-Bevan RIDG, GS RM,C Coy MR Offrs sharing meal Op Lance 2

Sheridan's command team atop Brown Mt. April 25th 1982.

Sheridan on secondment commanding troops in hard country.

Lcdr Astiz surrenders fifteen Argentine Marines.

Sir Henry Leach   Captain Brian Young

John Nott UK
Minister of Defense
before, during and
after the war.

Francis Pym, Thatcher's Foreign
Minister during the war.

Sir Antony Acland Head of the
UK Joint Intelligence Committe
before, during and after the war.

Funes and Family

Macias minus right leg and his rescuer
Funes debarking at Ascension Island.

Arnaldo Funes

Rex Hunt Governor of the
Falklands before, during and
after the conflict.

SAS wrecked Wessex 5
crashed on Fortuna Glacier

General Leopoldo Galtieri   Admiral Anaya

Captain Bicain in retirement and daughter.

Secretary of State Alexander Haig

Keith Mills at the site
of his victory.

Reagan and Thatcher

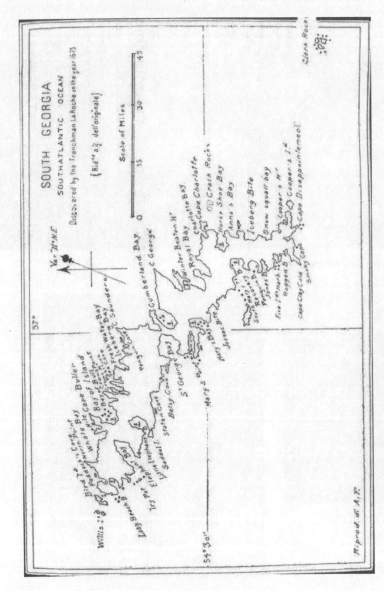

Old (early 19th century) map of South Georgia.

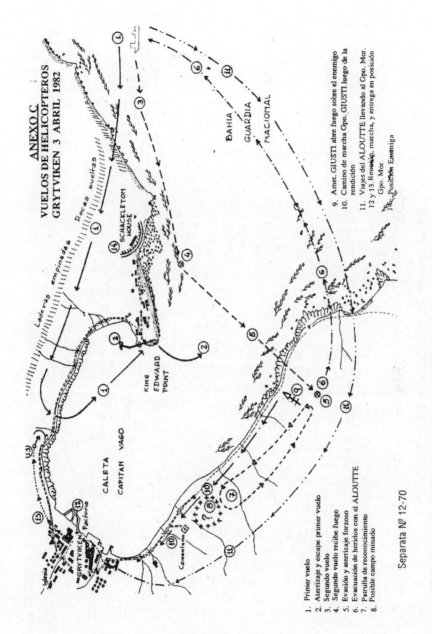

ANEXO C
VUELOS DE HELICOPTEROS
GRYTVIKEN 3 ABRIL 1982

Rocas sueltas

Laderas empinadas

SCHACKLETON HOUSE

KING EDWARD POINT

CALETA CAPITAN VAGO

GRYTVIKEN Factoría

Iglesia

Cementerio

BAHIA GUARDIA NACIONAL

1. Primer vuelo
2. Aterrizaje y escape primer vuelo
3. Segundo vuelo
4. Segundo vuelo recibe fuego
5. Evasión y aterrizaje forzoso
6. Evacuación de heridos con el ALOUTTE
7. Patrulla de reconocimiento
8. Posible campo minado

9. Amet. GIUSTI abre fuego sobre el enemigo
10. Camino de marcha Gpo. GIUSTI luego de la rendición
11. Viajes del ALOUTTE llevando al Gpo. Mor. 12 y 13. Reunión, marcha, y entrega en posición Gpo. Mor.

Posición Enemiga

Separata Nº 12-70

British helo attacks on *Santa Fe* as charted by an Argentine officer.

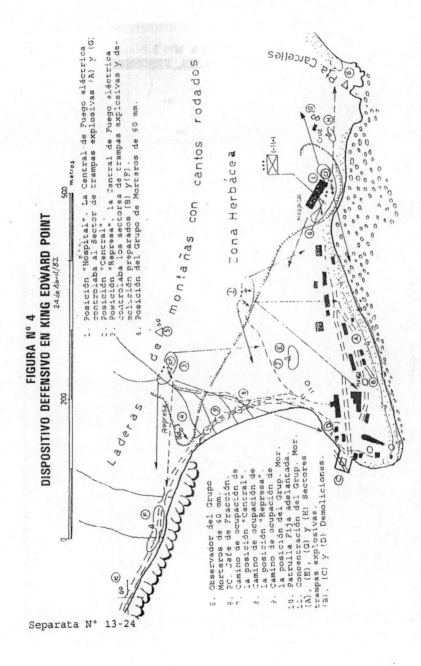

Chart showing Argentine defense positions, the same holes as used by Mills' marines.

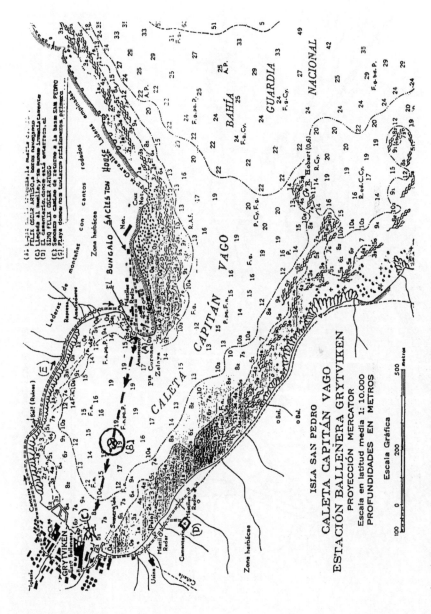

The chart used by Bicain in attempting escape from UK attacks.

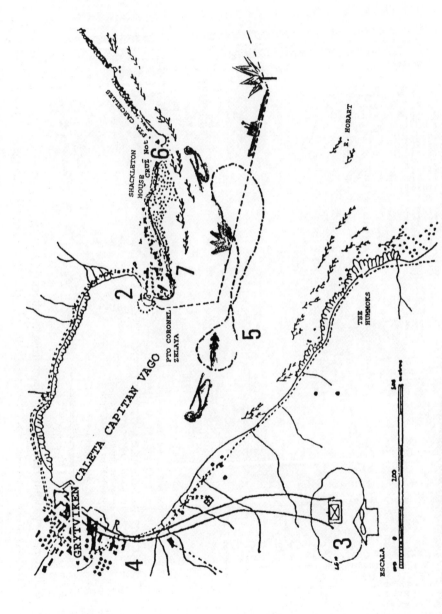

Santa Fe's plot and UK attacks at Cumberland Bay.

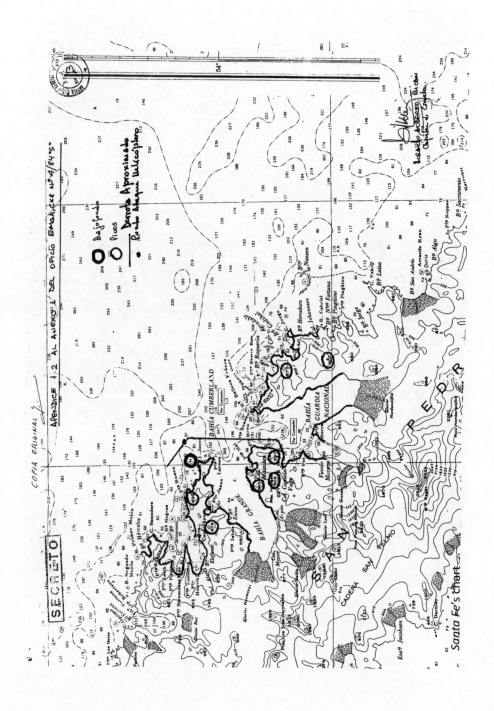

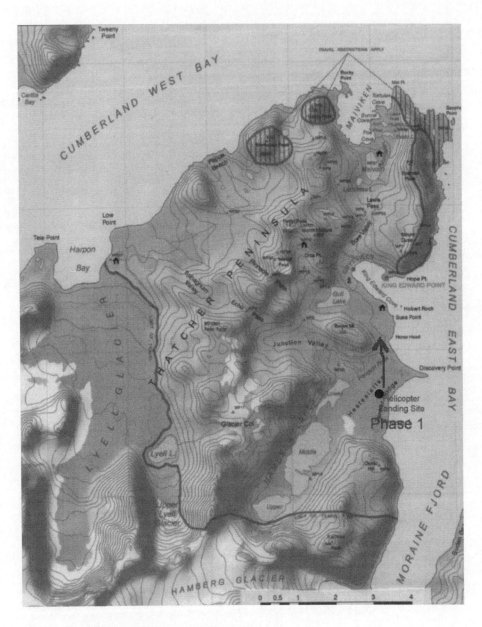

Major Sheridan's attack plan as it turned out.

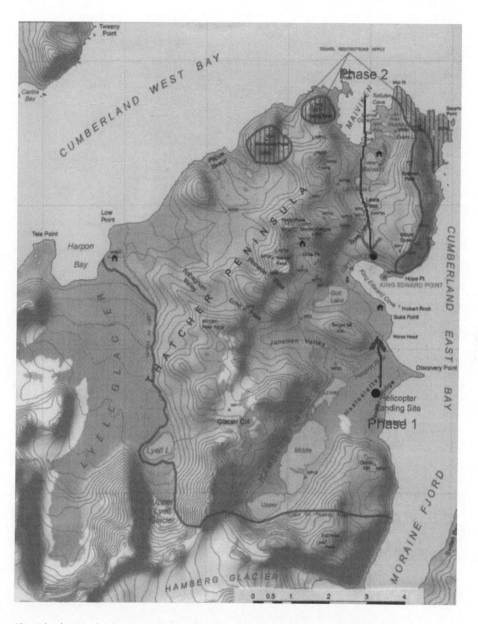

Sheridan's attack plan as intended before the Argentines surrendered.

Afterword

This narrative is incomplete because answers to serious questions have yet to be found. Did Thatcher and her cabinet colleagues discuss the Falklands with de Hoz in 1980? If so, did Thatcher agree to give them up? If not, why not say so? If the subject was left unmentioned, Thatcher chose not to intervene after that discussion and missed one of the larger opportunities of her career. Why were irrefutable and prescient warnings of the Argentinian invasion buried at the British Intelligence Community's lower levels there to molder unseen by Carrington and or No. 10? What did Sir Antony Acland, chairman of Britain's Joint Intelligence Committee know, and when did he know it?

Why was a military supremo not sent to *Antrim* to supervise and coordinate all the components of a land, sea, and air operation against South Georgia instead of the *primus inter pares* Young who, as the event played out, showed he knew almost nothing about combined operations or about amphibious assaults? Why did DLB send (or why was he allowed to send) his meddlesome troops? True, he bet that he would win, but in so doing he made himself a stake holder in a possible disaster. The Royal Marines were not infirm of purpose, and DLB was not a mountebank, as was his opponent Anaya. Both worried the same bone from different ends. Or was DLB stiffening Nott, Fieldhouse, and Young's spines? Why did the Royal Navy pay such deference to *Santa Fe* when open source materiel described its true condition and when the British naval attache in Buenos Aires could have lunched near its yard and seen that it was not a first-class military asset?

Why did Galtieri, who was trained in part at a US military school, conclude that the 150-man garrison on South Georgia could be strengthened by a nine-man addition to it? What went into Galtieri's decision to continue fighting after Sheridan had occupied Grytviken and Haig had given up negotiating? Why did Nott change his mind, coming to support Thatcher's determination to reconquer the Falklands a few days after he had stated in a cabinet meeting that reoccupation could not be achieved?

Sheridan's luck and skill, and Ian Stanley's, too, rescued Thatcher's present and opened up her prosperous future. They excised from public consciousness Young's timid, dilatory, and sclerotic responses to the exigencies of war and SAS's insouciance towards impassable glaciers. Young's intellectual fatigue in the midst of conflict, while it showed how a wartime commander should not behave, was let go as lapsarian consideration of his alternatives.

Those who know the events of that April 1982 understand that after battle, bits of metal and ribbon seldom tell the truth.

APPENDIX A

Table of Abbreviations

ASW..... Anti-submarine warfare

BAS ..... British Antarctic Survey

DSO..... Distinguished Service Order

FCO ..... Foreign and Commonwealth Office

GM ..... General Motors

LMG..... Light machine guns

M&AW .. Mountain and Arctic Warfare

NATO.... North Atlantic Treaty Organization

OCRM ... Officer in Charge, Royal Marines

SAS ..... Special Air Service

SBS ..... Special Boat Service

SIS ...... Secret Intelligence Service

SST...... Special Surface Target

APPENDIX B

INSTRUMENT OF SURRENDER

I *Cap Corb M* LAGOS Commander of the Argentinian Forces in occupation
of the islands of SOUTH GEORGIA, hereby unconditionally surrendered those
Forces under my command including landed Naval Detachments and the crew of
the submarine Santa Fe to the Commander of the British Task Group, HMS ANTRIM.

This Instrument of Surrender is understood to have been proffered
by the hoisting of a white flag at KING EDWARD POINT at 1705 Z 25 April 1982
and to have been effective at 1715 Z the same day.

I order all Forces under my command to surrender as at 1715 Z 25
April 1982 and those Forces with whom I am not in direct contact to surrender
immediately on notification of this instrument.

I understand that I am obliged to make safe and to notify the
Commander British Task Group any dangerous defence measures for which my
Force is responsible or of which they are aware, such as mines, booby traps
and similar latent explosives.

It is understood that my Forces will be treated as Prisoners of
War and afforded such rights as are applicable under the appropriate Article
of the Geneva Convention provided the above conditions are complied with.

Signed.   Commanding Officer
                                     Argentine Submarine SANTA FE

Countersigned.   Commander Argentine Land Forces

Signed.   Commander Task Group 317.9
                                     HMS ANTRIM

Countersigned.   J N G SHERIDAN   Second in Command
                  Major Royal Marines 42 Commando Royal Marines

Dated this 26th day of April 1982

COMANDO DE LA FUERZA DE SUBMARINOS

TRIPULACIÓN DEL SUBMARINO A.R.A. "SANTA FE" AÑO 1982

UL GR	APELLIDO	NOMBRES
CPET (RE)	ACEVEDO	JUAN CARLOS
SSCO (RE)	ACOSTA QUIZAS	NÉSTOR
SPMQ	ALBORNOZ	FRANCISCO
SICO (RE)	ALDAO	RODOLFO HÉCTOR
SPAM (RE)	ALFARO	ISIDORO FRANCISCO
SSMQ (RE)	ALFONSO	MARCIAL TOMÁS
SIMW	ALTAMIRANO	ZACARÍAS RENÉ
CIOP (RE)	ARES	JOSÉ ROBERTO
CC (RE)	ARGAÑARAZ	BENJAMÍN JORGE
SIMW	ARIAS	JAVIER
SPMQ (F)	ARTUSO	FÉLIX
CSCO	AVENDAÑO	WALTER DANIEL
SPOPSO	ÁVILA	JOSÉ FEDERICO
CIEL	BALDONI	RICARDO HÉCTOR
CFCD (RE)	BICAIN	HORACIO ALBERTO
CIMQ	BUSTAMANTE	NORBERTO ARNALDO
CIMQ	CANO	JORGE
CIAM	CIOCHI	JUAN JOSÉ
CISVCM	COCCO	DANIEL GILBERTO
SSMQ (RE)	CORTEZ	LUIS ENRIQUE
TNCD (RE)	CROCCI	CARLOS HUMBERTO
SMMQ (RE)	CUEVAS	FRANCISCO
SPAM (RE)	CHAVARRÍA	RAFAEL DALMACIO
SPMQ	ENRIQUE	JOSÉ
CPMQ (RE)	FELMAN	OSCAR
SPCO (RE)	FERNANDEZ	MANUEL
CLCD	FERNANDEZ OSUNA	OSCAR CÉSAR
SPEL (RE)	FRANCESCONE	DANTE
SIEN (RE)	FUNES	ARNALDO
SSMW	GALIER	FRANCISCO
SMMQ (RE)	GALVÁN	GUIDO ROBERTO
SIMW	GHIGLIONE	JORGE OMAR HORACIO
SISVCM	GONZALEZ	CARMELO
SPCO (RE)	GORDILLO	OSCAR
SMCO (RE)	GUARDIA	RAMÓN FRANCISCO
SMFU (RE)	GUDIÑO	CLARO
CIOP (RE)	HERNÁNDEZ	JOSÉ A.
SIEL	HOMES	LUIS NÉSTOR
SSAM (RE)	IBALO	DELMIRO

Place	Chief	Fire power	Number
Grytviken (King Edgard Point)	Teniente de Navío Guillermo Luna	Fusiles 2 MAG 3 morteros 60 mm	2 grupos de tiradores (-) (36 infantes de marina y 5 suboficiales de marinería) *(2 muertos y 2 heridos el 03.04.1982)*
Leith	Teniente de Navío Alfredo Astiz (Grupo ALFA	Fusiles 1 lanzacohetes 3,5" 1 MAG	15 buzos tácticos y comandos anfibios

Refuerzos transportados en el submarino "Santa Fé" el 24 de abril de 1982:

Place	Chief	Fire power	Number
Grytviken (King Edgard Point)	Capitán de Corbeta Luis Lagos (Grupo GOLF)	Cañón s/r 105 mm (20 proyectiles) 6 misiles Bantam y dos guiadores 5 lanzacohetes de 3,5" 300 kg de trotyl y 1000 detonadores Granadas PDEF, PAF y de mano	20 oficiales y suboficiales

Otros argentinos en Georgias

Place	Chief	Fire power	Number
	Submarino "Santa Fé"		77 tripulantes
	Grupo Davidoff (personal civil)		Aproximadamente 50 hombres

Figure 3.1 Command Chain Falklands 1982 100-A

Before 20 May 1982

Commander Task
Force (CfF) **317**
Admiral Sir John Fieldhouse
HQ at Northwood throughout

Air Commander *Air*
Marshal Sir John Curtiss

Land   Deputy   (advice)
Major General Jeremy Moore

Command er
Carrier Task Group
CTG 317.8
Rear Admiral John Woodward

Commander
Amphibious Task
Group.
CTG 317.0
Commodore Michael Clapp

Commander Landing
Force Task Group (3rd
Commando Brigade (+»
CTG 317.1
Brigadier Julian Thompson

After 20 May 1982
CITF 317
Admiral Sir John Fieldhouse
HQ at Northwood

Air Commander *Air*
Marshal Sir John Curtiss

Land Deputy (advice)
Lieutenant General Sir Richard Trant
GOC South-East District

Command er
Carrier Task Group
CITG 317.8
Rear Admiral John Woodward

Command er
Amphibious Task
Group
CTG 317.0
Commodore Michael Clapp

Commander Land Forces
Falkland Islands
CTG 317.1 *Major*
General Jeremy Moore
See note below

3rd Commando Brigade (+)
_ _ CTU 317.1.1
Brigadier Julian Thompson

5th Infantry Brigade
CTU 317.1.2
Brigadier Tony Wilson

Note:
General Moore joined the liner Queen Elizabeth II off Ascension Island on 20 May,
but was out of touch with events, and 3 Brigade in particular, because of comms
problems on the ship until he came ashore at San Carlos on 30 May 1982

March   82.

To the Master of the Bahia Buen Suceso.

        I have been instructed by His Excellency
the Governor of the Falkland Islands and Dependencies
to restate Her Majesty's Government's strong
displeasure with your illegal and irresponsible
actions which could have escalated into a serious
incident with far reaching political consequencies.

                        S. Martin.
                        Magistrate.

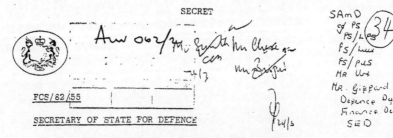

SECRET

SAmD
cd PS
PS/LPS
PS/hui
PS/PuS
MR Ure
MR Gifford
Defence Dy
Finance Dc
SED

FCS/82/55

SECRETARY OF STATE FOR DEFENCE

Falkland Islands: HMS Endurance

1. As you know, we may be at a critical stage on the Falklands
dispute. I am minuting separately to the Prime Minister and OD
colleagues, setting out the present position and seeking
political and financial authority to carry our civil contingency
planning forward. In advance of an OD meeting on the Falklands,
you may wish to consider whether it would also be helpful at
this stage to circulate to colleagues the contingency paper which
your officials have prepared on the defence aspects.

2. While we may still hope that a continuation of negotiations
with Argentina will be possible, we must, I think, accept that
this is unlikely. Information from secret sources indicates that
the Argentines may be prepared to take early action to withdraw
Argentine services to the Islands. If they do, there will be two
main problems: how to replace them; and how to demonstrate to
public opinon here and to the Islanders our commitment to support
them. Detailed arrangements for a replacement of Argentine
services will inevitably take some time. We must recognised that
we could face criticism if we appear unable to step into the breai
quickly.

3. There is one action we could take which would be an immediate
demonstration of our support for the islands: that is to maintai
HMS Endurance on station in Falklands waters for the time being.
This would serve as a visible sign of our commitment, would be
an appropriate signal to the Argentines and could allow us to
provide practical assistance if necessary. I appreciate that
this would cause difficulties, not least for the captain and crew
of the ship at the end of their long season, and that such a
solution could only be temporary. But the latest incident, on

/South Georgi

SECRET

168

South Georgia, indicates how vulnerable we are and how important a role HMS Endurance can play. I think therefore that it would be of the greatest assistance if contingency plans could now be made for HMS Endurance to remain on station in the area of the Islands after the rotation of the Marine Garrison is completed at the end of this month. Indeed I suspect that our position, both here and in the Islands, would become politically untenable if HMS Endurance were not to remain on station beyond the date of her scheduled departure.

4. This of course leaves on one side the broader question of HMS Endurance's future. As you know, I believe that it must be retained for at least another year. The South Georgia incident has obviously reinforced the case for this. This is something we shall need to look at in OD fairly soon.

5. I am copying this minute to the Prime Minister and to the Chancellor of the Exchequer.

(CARRINGTON)

Foreign and Commonwealth Office
24 March 1982

S E C R E T

30679 - 1

ZE TEL AVIV

GRS 445
SECRET
FM FCO 311240Z MAR 82
TO FLASH TEL AVIV (FOR PRIVATE SECRETARY)
TELEGRAM NUMBER 100 OF 31 MARCH '82.

Aw 040/325/12		
RECEIVED IN REGISTRY NO. 18		
31 MAR 1982		
DESK OFFICER		REGISTRY
INDEX	PA	Action Taken

FALKLANDS CRISIS

1.   FOLLOWING IS PROPOSED REPLY TO BUENOS AIRES TELNO 126.
BEGINS
WE ARE GRATEFUL TO YOU AND TO THE AMERICANS FOR THIS REPORT OF
US/ARGENTINE EXCHANGES ON OUR BEHALF. WHILE WE SHALL CONTINUE
TO BE GRATEFUL FOR AMERICAN EFFORTS TO PERSUADE THE ARGENTINE·
GOVERNMENT AWAY FROM HASTY OR VIOLENT REACTIONS, WE DO NOT
SEE THAT WE CAN USEFULLY ASK THEM TO UNDERTAKE NEGOTIATING A
SOLUTION OF THE SOUTH GEORGIA PROBLEM ON OUR BEHALF. FOR YOUR
OWN INFORMATION WE FEAR THAT WE WOULD END UP WITH THE AMERICANS
ALSO EXERTING PRESSURE ON US TO REACH A SOLUTION WHICH WAS
POLITICALLY UNACCEPTABLE TO US.
YOUR TUR WAS DESPATCHED BEFORE THE PROMINENT UK MEDIA STORIES
ABOUT NUCLEAR POWERED SUBMARINES AND OTHER SHIPS BEING
DESPATCHED TO THE FALKLANDS. WE MUST ASSUME THAT THESE
SPECULATIVE REPORTS (PARTICULARLY TAKEN IN CONJUNCTION WITH
OUR OWN LATEST SECRET REPORTS INDICATING ARGENTINE JUMPINESS)
WILL GIVE AN IMPRESSION IN BUENOS AIRES THAT WE ARE SEEKING A
NAVAL RATHER THAN A DIPLOMATIC WAY OUT OF OUR DIFFICULTIES.
THIS COULD BE A VERY DANGEROUS IMPRESSION TO LEAVE - EVEN FOR
A FEW DAYS.
WE THEREFORE THINK IT IMPORTANT THAT WE LAUNCH OUR DIPLOMATIC
INITIATIVE WITHOUT FURTHER DELAY, EVEN IF THE ARGENTINE
RESPONSE TO THIS AND THE DESPATCH OF OUR 'EMISSARY' IS LIKELY
TO BE LESS SPEEDY (INDEED THERE WOULD BE SOME ADVANTAGE IN NOT
HASTENING UNDULY). WE THEREFORE WISH YOU TO DELIVER THE
MESSAGE IN MY TELNO 116.
HOWEVER WE ARE VERY CONSCIOUS OF THE SKILL AND FIRMNESS WITH

1

S E C R E T

WHICH YOU HAVE BEEN HANDLING THESE EXCHANGES SO FAR AND WE HAVE
OF COURSE NO WISH TO RISK UNDERMINING YOUR POSITION AS AN
INTERLOCUTOR. IF YOU FEEL IT WOULD BE HELPFUL YOU MAY THEREFORE
INSERT INTO THE MESSAGE A SENTENCE TO THE EFFECT THAT 'THE
EMISSARY WOULD BE COMING TO SUPPORT OUR AMBASSADOR BY PUTTING AT
HIS DISPOSAL SOMEONE WITH AN UP TO DATE KNOWLEDGE OF MY OWN
THINKING ON EVERY ASPECT OF THIS PROBLEM'. WE WOULD RATHER NOT
DROP THE REFERENCES TO 'CONSTRUCTIVE PROPOSALS' BECAUSE WE THINK
IT IMPORTANT THAT THE ARGENTINES SHOULD NOT THINK WE HAVE RUN
OUT OF ANY IDEAS EXCEPT MILITARY ONES.
AS REGARDS YOUR FURTHER SUGGESTION (YOUR TELNO 128) THAT THE
EMISSARY SHOULD BE SOMEONE LIKE LORD CARVER OR LORD HILL-NORTON,
WE THINK THAT NEGOTIATIONS WOULD MORE EFFECTIVELY BE CARRIED OUT
AT WORKING LEVEL AND THAT IN ANY CASE SOME OF THE PRESENTATIONAL
OBJECTIONS WHICH WOULD APPLY TO SENDING A MINISTER TO BA WOULD
ALSO APPLY TO SENDING A PROMINENT PUBLIC FIGURE.
ENDS
2. WE SHALL OF COURSE AWAIT SECRETARY OF STATE'S COMMENTS BEFORE
DESPATCHING THIS FURTHER TELEGRAM WHICH REFLECTS MR LUCE'S VIEWS.

CARRINGTON

NNNN   X
DISTRIBUTION:
STANDARD   ADDITIONAL DISTN
S AND D   FALKLAND ISLANDS
CABINET OFFICE

THE HANDWRITTEN REPORT OF THE LANDINGS AT GRYTVIKEN

SOUTH GEORGIA ON 25 APRIL 1982

As the Commander of the Land Forces that repossessed South Georgia for the Crown on 25 April 1982, I was required by duty to submit a report of the proceedings. This would normally have been typed by a clerk and would have been submitted to the overall Commander of the entire operation - in this case the Commander of Task Group (CTG) 317.9, Captain Brian Young Royal Navy, HMS Antrim. However, because Captain Young showed no interest whatsoever in the events that occurred ashore (see Appendix I, 'Letter from Grytviken', in **Taxi to the Snow Line**, by Guy Sheridan, ISBN 2-9525255-0-1) I unilaterally decided to address my formal report under a covering letter to my Commanding Officer, Lieutenant Colonel NF Vaux RM (later Major General NF Vaux CB DSO), the Commanding Officer of 42 Commando Royal Marines. At the time I was his Second in Command and had no access to secretarial staff. My report was therefore written in longhand but not completed until 7 May 1982 due to my movements on the high seas attempting to rejoin the Commando for the main Falkland's conflict that still lay ahead. The report was left in my briefcase in the cabin of the Amphibious Operations Officer (Major MGC Gosling RM) aboard HMS Fearless at anchor in San Carlos Water on 1 June 1982. It remained in his cabin on the ship until 18 June 1982 when I was able to retrieve it to give it personally to Lieutenant Colonel Vaux near the ruins of Moody Brook Barracks after the surrender of all Argentine Forces at Port Stanley. The report was then taken by him to Major General Jeremy Moore OBE MC* who had established his Headquarters at Government House in Port Stanley. The original report is held in the National Archives.

The original handwritten report with its annexes was photocopied on HMS Endurance at South Georgia before I left the Island on 26 May 1982. There was only one copy made by me and this is it – as the author it is my personal copy. There are seven Annexes to the report. Of particular note is Annex A. This is the **Original** Warning Order to mount reconnaissance patrols and to commence planning for the repossession of South Georgia. The Order was signed by Captain Young and personally given to me by him on board HMS Antrim on 14 April 1982. Annex G is a copy of the surrender document. The document was back-dated to 26 April 1982 on the instructions of Captain Young. Details of this document and how the Argentine signatures were obtained on 28 April 1982 can be found in Appendix I, 'Letter from Grytviken' in **Taxi to the Snow Line.**

1 November 2009   **JMG Sheridan**
                                                                 Lt Colonel OBE RM

of OC A Sqn by Wx3 and two Lynx in the first wave on HESTESLETTEN GR 6379. Thereafter the two small rifle troops under command of Capt NUNN RM (OC M Coy) and LT GRANT RM (OC Trials Team SB Sqn) respectively would stream ashore. I was able to retain my Tac HQ with communications to the ops room in HMS ANTRIM together with the MO and his party. Although I was able to deploy the mortars into a base plate position on HESTESLETTEN, I also had one NGSFO party attached to the first wave and one NGS officer airborne in a Wasp helicopter to direct the pre bombardment. Tac HQ would be in the last aircraft.

8. My fire plan was totally influenced by my original order to limit loss of life and damage to property and was as follows

ANTRIM a. ⟹ H to H+5 — Neutralise landing site on
           ZJ 1027   HESTESLETTEN

PLYMOUTH
b.   H-10 to H+10 — Neutralise BROWN MOUNTAIN slope
       ZJ 1026   GR 6281 where Argentinian troops had been seen moving earlier.

c.   From H+10 — On call for a creeping barrage across the open slopes of BROWN MOUNTAIN and GULL LAKE GR 6282.

The gun line for para 8c would pass over the settlement at KING EDWARD POINT and the purpose of the creeping barrage was to demoralise further the Argentinians who were also in a position to see the fall of shot some 500 metres away on the opposite side of the cove.

9. My plan also included the landing by helicopter of the SBS and two SAS Tps from HMS ENDURANCE and HMS PLYMOUTH in BORE VALLEY pass GR 6284 once the slopes of BROWN MOUNTAIN were secure. Their tasks were to move to the high ground above GRYTVIKEN and KING EDWARD POINT and provide covering fire for the advance to contact from BROWN MOUNTAIN through GRYTVIKEN to KING EDWARD POINT. Their orders were sent by radio

10. This plan was put before CTG who agreed to the concept but the timing remained open. I was extremely keen to maintain the momentum and exploit the state of shock that the 140 or so Argentinians were undoubtedly in, and I assessed that if this was done as soon as possible there was every chance that their resistance would be minimal. It was 1000 when I proposed

- 4 -

ARTILLERY FIRE PLAN PROFORMA

FIRE PLAN PEA SOUP .... SUPPORTING M COY/42 COO .... ORIGINATOR .... MODIFICATIONS BY ....

.... SUPERIMPOSED .... H HOUR .... SHEET .... OF .... DATE/TIME GROUP ....

		TARGET INFORMATION			
	(a)	(b)	(c)	(d)	(e)
LINE	TARGET No.	DESCRIPTION	LOCATION	ALT	REMARKS
1	ZJ 1026	BROWN MOUNTAIN	625818	250	PL POSN H-10 to H + 10
2	1027	LS ANDLE	627796	100	LS H to H + 5 12 RPM
3					= 60
4					
5					
6					
7					
8					
9					
10					
11					
12					

SCHEDULE

	(f)	(g)	(h)
LINE	REGT OR PLAN	FIRE UNITS	TIMINGS
1		PL Y	ZJ 1026 BROWN MOUNTAIN ON CALL / AIR OBS 105A
2		AH T	ZJ 1027 ON CALL / AIR OBS 65A
3			
4			
5			
6			
7			
8			
(j)	REMARKS		E-1

174

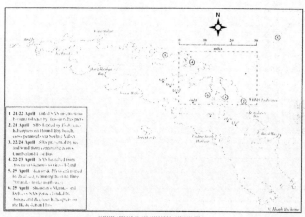

N. Hugh Basheete

OPERATIONS AT SOUTH GEORGIA

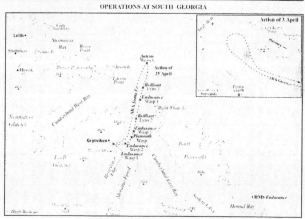

Hugh Basheete

the comma...' of Lt Cmdr Astiz refuse to surrender.

, "Endurance" and "Plymouth" sail along to Leith and the marines give in. "Plymouth" and "Brilliant" leave on to join the CVBG, but "Tidespring" now with nearly 150 Argentine POW's and the 40 civilian workers from Leith embarked, and escorted by "Antrim" does not head north for Ascension until . A disappointed M Coy 42 Cdo stays on to garrison South Georgia, and "Endurance" remains as guardship.

SOUTH GEORGIA. OPERATION PARAQUET - SUMMARY OF RECAPTURE

Destroyer Antrim, 2x4.5in, 1xWessex HAS.3
Frigate Plymouth, 2x4.5in, 1xWasp
Ice patrol ship Endurance, 2xWasp
RFA Tidespring, 2xWessex HU.5's

joined by frigate Brilliant, 2xLynx

- 250 from:

M Coy 42 Cdo RM,
No.2 Section SBS RM,
D Sqdn SAS,
148 Bty 29 Cdo Regt team

Commanders:
Capt B G Young   RN of Antrim, Task Group
Maj J M G Sheridan RM, Landing Forces
Maj C N G Delves   , D Sqdn SAS
Capt C J Nunn RM, M Coy 42 Cdo

Al CIEL QUIROGA FELIPE RUBEN

La dotación del submarino S.E.D SANTA FE navegando en condición de prisioneros de guerra a bordo del H.M.S TIDESPRING te dedica este humilde presente en tu 23° cumpleaños

CTE CC BICAIN

2do Cmo CC MICHELIS	CTEN ZAGUEZ	CISO SALTO
TN FERNANDEZ DAVID	CPET GUARDIA	CICO SCHULTZ
TF CROCI	CIMA ZECALDE	CICC SANTA CRUZ
TF MARTIN	CIMA TAPIA	CIEL HOMES
TF SEGURA	CPEL VERGARA	CIMQ ENRIQUEZ
TF BROGNOLAZ	CPAS FELMAN	CIMS GALIER
TC IGLESIAS	CPSE GODILLO	CIEL DELSONI
SPRI GUDIÑO	CPSE PAEZ	CIMQ LEDTEROS
SIMQ ARTUSO	CPMQ SANTILLAN	CIMQ ORREN
SIAS CHAVARRIA	CPMQ LOPEZ	CIEL NAGEL
SIMQ MARQUEZ	CPCE MORECO	CIEL SILVA
SIEL ONTIVEROS	CPAS IBALO	CSMQ ALBERNOZ
SSEL FRANCESCONE	CPSO AVILA	CSCC MILANO
SSMQ GALVAN	CIEL VILLA	CSMQ PRATO
SSRT ALDAO	CPET ACEVEDO	CSCM COCCO
SSEL SILVERA	CICM JORGE	CSAS RODRIGUEZ
SSCP ACOSTA	CIET ALTAMIRANO	CSAS CIOCHI
SSMQ ALFONZO	CIMQ CORTEZ	CSAS GIGLIONE
SSEL RUIZ	CIAS MARACIOLE	CSAS ARIAS
SSAS LONDON	CIOP HERNANDEZ	CSRT AVENDAÑO
SSMQ CUEVAS	CIMQ CANO	CSSO ARES
SSAS ALFARO	CIMQ POTES	CSEL RIOS
SSSE FERNANDEZ	CIMQ REGGIARDO	CSEL NUÑEZ
SSEM FUNES	CIMQ RUBIOLO	CSCM MACIAS
	CSMQ BUSTAMONTE	CSEM JAIME

1 de mayo de 1982.
Cap. BICAIN

Captain Bicain's own log.

177

1O DOWNING STREET

THE PRIME MINISTER   11 June 1980

Dear Mr. de Hoz,

    I very much enjoyed our meeting last Thursday and I am sorry that it was so short.

    I am extremely grateful to you for your lovely present and hope that you will accept my sincere thanks.

    With all best wishes.

Yours sincerely

Margaret Thatcher

Dr. Martinez de Hoz.

SECRET

Treasury Chambers, Parliament Street SW1P 3AG

Rt Hon Lord Carrington PC KCMG MC
Secretary of State
Foreign & Commonwealth Office
Downing Street
London SW1A 2AL

29 March 1982

Handwritten annotations in the top right margin:

SAM D 28
cc FS
PS, LPS
...
PS, PUS
...
...
...
...
...
...
MH
29/3

Stamp over the address area:
Aw 540 / 3 25/9
-1 APR 1982
INDEX

FALKLAND ISLANDS

I have seen your undated minute (ref.PM/82/23) to the Prime
Minister drawing attention to the possibility that the Argentines
may cut off some or all of the essential services which they
now provide for the Islands.

I have no objection to contingency planning for a sea service
being carried forward on an urgent basis. However, I cannot
agree that, in the event of the plans having to be implemented,
such financial provision as may prove necessary should be found
from the Contingency Reserve. I am conscious that the programmes
for which you are responsible will total some £1.6 billion in
the new financial year, and I find it hard to accept that the
cost of a sea service for the Falklands (even if it were to
exceed the £1.5 million annual cost of the service to St Helena
as your officials expect) could not be accommodated within these
programmes. Before 1982-83 has even begun, I should have thought
there must be sufficient flexibility in your programmes to absorb
relatively small claims of this kind.

If extra costs were incurred in order to keep Endurance in the
Falklands (as proposed in your letter of 24 March to John Nott)
these costs should be met without recourse to the Contingency
Reserve.

I am copying this letter to the Prime Minister and other members
of OD, to the Secretary of State for Energy, the Attorney-General
and Sir Robert Armstrong.

LEON BRITTAN

APPENDIX C

American Aid to the United Kingdom During The Falklands War

"It was the right thing to do."[1]

When asked why, in his opinion, America rushed to Britain's side at war's inception and provided millions of pounds of aid a retired Royal Navy officer answered: " Blood is thicker than water."[2] During the first few days of the war two US tankers were diverted to Ascension Island in order to provide fuel for the task forces steaming south "without which the Task Force could not have made it to the Falklands."[3] A system already existed by which navy to navy communications, operating practices, weapons transfers etc had been accomplished regularly farther back than anyone then serving could remember. Such things were simply done with a wink, a blink and a nod. Very early in the war three hundred AIM 9 L Sidewinder missiles were shipped to British forces. Close friendships between the special forces of both countries resulted in Stinger ground to air missiles and bits and pieces of that community's military oddments being handed over immediately. The paper work for that elegant military administration caught up much later if at all. The transfers accumulated to such large amounts that an as yet unidentified monitor of such things in the Pentagon cried out for at least a truncated accounting. As Lehman remembers: "the requests were handled routinely, without reference to higher authority."[4] It surprised many here that some abroad might think this practice excessively casual. It is a nonsense that America and Great Britain speak different languages. At their peril a few abroad had dismissed the idea: "It is a truth universally accepted;" that the Special Relationship meant much to both.[5]

Secretary Weinberger, a man of very precise habits, ordered the transfers made with a pay later proviso and put in place a short administrative chain. The military supermarket remained open twenty-fours per day seven days a week for the war's duration. Still when Lehman visited London on May 31st he suffered resentment from MOD over the US lack of enthusiasm for supporting Great Britain, all this after US fuel had kept the task forces steaming. Thompson was not the only person to suffer from MOD's and Nott's ignorance about what was happening where it counted.

Sir Nicholas Henderson claimed that Secretary Weinberger: "had under-taken to give us anything we wanted militarily. I'm sure Haig did not know of this."[6] On this matter Sir Nicholas was incorrect. Haig knew. Henderson also gives credence to the notion widely bruited in the US Navy at the time that Weinberger could and would provide a carrier if asked. What was not widely known is that the RN was given its choice of two such. Henderson's summa-tion says it best although it omits the willingness and good cheer of those bid-den to the feast: "the Americans provided us with equipment and intelligence facilities from their satellites. …the Prime Minister has conceded that, without the new Sidewinder missiles that the Americans provided, we would not have won the war. We have a lot to be grateful for, even if there were difficulties along the way."[7]

Nott's statement that: "In so many ways the French were our greatest al-lies."[8] is not only wholly untrue and defamatory but also testament to the poor judgement that got Great Britain into a war that cost two hundred, fifty-six British lives and kept the plastic surgeons of that country busy for their profes-sional lives.[9] It is difficult to conclude, though it may be true, that Nott knew less about his friends than he did about his enemies.

The following list of items sent or given to British forces by and from America is incomplete:

- Use of Wideawake Airbase on Ascension Island.
- 12.5 million gallons of aviation fuel
- 300 Sidewinder AIM 9 L air to air missiles.
- Shrike radar seeking missiles
- Stinger shoulder fired AA missiles
- Long Range Patrol Packs (many)
- Mortar rounds (copious)
- Data on countermeasures and disarming of US made bombs.
- Intelligence information.
- Use of US communication satellites.[10]
- Matting for Harrier landings
- Medical supplies and equipment. (Copious)
- All USAF equipment at Wideawake from screw drivers to electronic parts was made available to British forces.
- 12 F-4 Phantom jets were sold post hostilities at inconsequential pric-es to the British for Stanley's protection.

NOTES

1-Caspar Weinberger. Conversations with author.

2-Retired British Naval Officer and veteran of the Falklands War. This expression is credited to Commodore Josiah Tattnall USN who during the second China War pulled British boats out of danger and gave this expression to Sir John Hope the British commander as his justification for this benign interference.

3-Secretary of the Navy John Lehman. *Daily Telegraph* March 30, 2002.

4-Ibidem. Many who served under Secretary Lehman remain amused at his working defintion of the words: "routine or routinely."

5-Any sailor worth his salt knows that helping a British service man, especially a sailor, to get his bed and board and perhaps more is part of naval life. The practice is well reciprocated.

6-ibidem

7-ibidem

8-Nott

9-"The British operation to recapture the Falklands in 1982 could not have been mounted, let alone won, without American help." Goose Green and the entire Falklands war were the first such to be won by British forces fighting alone.The Economist March 7th, 1984. Not a few asked during and after the Falklands War if Nott had known the Falklands' location.

10-*The Economist* March 7th, 1984 and others.

INDEX

Page numbers in *italics* indicate illustrations.

A

Acland, Sir Antony, 21, *146,* 159
Air Defence Troop, 67n86
Alacrity [British ship], 69n110, 118n194, 119n198
Alfonso, Carlos, 43
Allied Tactical Publication Eight [NATO], 68n105
Anaya, Jorge, *148*
    anti-British sentiment, 24, 37
    chain of command, 36
    East Stanley invasion, 66
    misjudging British reaction, 35–36, 57, 113
    political need for action, 106
    press leak, 20
    public voice, 25
    reasons for war, 37
    romantic adventurism, 27, 56, 65–66, 110, 112
    rules of engagement, 112
    Santa Fe's mission, 105, 108–109
    South Georgia Island invasion, 43, 66, 115
    war plans, 24, 25, 65, 109
Antrim [British gunship]
    Argentinian threat, 93, 97
    artillery, 68n101, 124–125
    attack on *Santa Fe,* 116, 117
    commanding officers, 60, 85, 95, 97, 102n176
    communications, 62, 64, 94
    D Squadron, 77, 95–96
    en route to South Georgia Island, 56
    Grytviken seizure, 124, 125, 126, 129n221
    helicopters, 61, 84, 90–91, 92, 98, 126
    lack of collegiality, 63
    leadership needs, 159
    onboard training of marines, 84

Hope, Sir John, 183n2
Hound Bay, 93
House of Commons [UK]
    decommissioning of *Endurance,* 50n60
    Kelpers' sovereignty, 23
    reports to, 75n118, 76n129
Howe, Geoffrey, 23
Hunt, Rex, 17, 18, 19, 34, 44, *148*
Husvik, 85, 89, 95

I

Inman, Bobby R., 50n66
Iranian Embassy siege [1981], 80

J

Japan
    World War II, 71
Jason Peak, 19
Jason Point, 34, 46, 47
Jerez, Gregorio, 10
Joint Intelligence Committee [UK], 73
Jones, David C., 50n66

K

Kelpers, sovereignty of, 27, 29, 54, 112
King Edward Point, *141*
    Argentinian forces, 47, 97, 125, *152*
    Argentinian reconnaissance, 47
    Argentinian surrender, 126, 127
    BAS facilities, 34, 101n160
    British forces, 34, 46, 47–48, 89
    British reconnaissance, 85
    British surrender, 48–49
    Santa Fe, 131, 132
    strategic location, 45, 46
Kirkpatrick, Jeanne, 28, 50n66
Konig Glacier, 89
Kotzebue, Otto von, 15n13

L

Lagos, Luis, 117, 126, 129n224, 131, *163*

Mountain Troop [19 Troop], 89, 90–91, 102n168
Moya, Captain, 109, 111
Mullet Creek, 111
Munro, Neil, 126
Muracioli [Argentinian submariner], 116

N

National Security Council [US], 39
National Security Planning Group [US], 41
NATO
    Allied Tactical Publication Eight, 68n105
Naval Gunfire Group, 85
Navigation, 10
Norman, Mike, 42
North, Tony, 88, 93
Northern Ireland
    SAS operations, 100n148
Northwood. *see* Military Operations Command, Northwood
Nott, John, *146*
    decommissioning ships, 37, 43
    defence budget, 20, 29–30, 32n48, 56–57, 60, 67n90, 68n91
    Endurance, 21, 29–30, 43
    Falklands actions, 35, 47, 56–58, 113, 159
    meeting with de Hoz, 23
    officers, 32n48
    situational ignorance, 35, 38, 89, 181–182, 183n9
    South Georgia Island actions, 47, 56
    support for Thatcher, 112
    Thatcher's War Cabinet, 76n130
    withdrawal from making military decisions, 82
Nunn, Christopher
    845/846 Naval Air Commando, 84
    aboard *Antrim,* 82
    Artuso's death, 134
    chain of command, 63–64
    competence, 59
    difficulty of position, 24
    Fortuna Glacier mission, 91–92
    Grytviken seizure, 124
    helicopter skills, 61, 100n148
    M Company Group, 59, 79, 127
    South Georgia Island garrison, 134

support gunfire, 60–61
training of helicopter pilots, 122

O

Official History of the Falklands War [Freedman], 23
O'Gorman, Hugh, 49
Oil fields, deep-sea, 53
Onyx [British diesel submarine], 99n135
Operation Alpha [Argentina], 18, 20, 22
Operation Corporate [UK], 60, 62
Operation Mikado [UK], 99n135
Operation Paraquat [UK]
    chain of command problems, 79, 81, 82
    command failures, 96, 127
    commanders, 60, 68n101
    intelligence failures, 68n92
    mission, 58
    Northwood cell, 58
    Pym's knowledge of, 75n118
    as SAS operation, 82
    secrecy, 58–59
    summary of recapture, *176*
    US equipment loan, 79
Operation Tabarin [UK], 13
Overseas Defence Committee [UK], 21, 23
Owen, David, 24, 57

P

Palacio de San Martin [Argentinian Foreign Office], 21, 54
Paramour [ship], 10
Parker, Nigel, 49
Parkinson, Cecil, 76n130
Parsons, Anthony, 54–55
Patton, General, 118n187
Peacock [glacier traverser], 86
Pearl Harbor, Hawaii, 118n187
Peeble Island, 101n162
Plan Alpha. *see* Operation Alpha
Plant, Myles, 88, 93
Plymouth [gunship]
    artillery, 124–125

torpedoes, 69n110, 109, 118n194
Sanders, Damien, 88
Santa Fe [Argentinian submarine], 105–120, *141*
    Argentinian surrender, *136*
    battle damage, *140*
    British attack on, 97, 102n176, 116, 117–118, 122, *151, 154*
    chart, *155*
    commander, 12
    communications, 115–116, 119n199
    crew, *143, 164*
    Cumberland Bay reinforcement, 98
    danger to British forces, 93–94, 97–98, 121, 159
    disabling, 129n226
    disposal, 131–135, *139, 140*
    East Falkland reconnaissance, 111
    missions, *165*
    passengers, 119n208
    removal of personal belongings from, 132
    South Georgia Island invasion, 66, 105, 106–107, 114, 115
    torpedoes, 108, 109, 111, 112, 114
    as unfit for combat, 108, 110, 111, 114, 115
    weaponry, *165*
Santiago del Estero [Argentinian submarine], 108
SAS. *see* Special Air Service
SBS. *see* Special Boat Service
Schlieper Bay, 49, 88
Scoresby, William, Sr., 13
Sealers, 11
Secret Intelligence Service [UK], 26
Senate, US, 42
Shackleton, Ernest, 86, 101n154
Shackleton House, 34
Shaw, Neil, 18, 19, 25
Sheep, 12–13
Sheridan, J. M. G. [Guy], *143, 144, 145*
    42 Commando, 59, 134
    aboard *Antrim,* 82, 84, 85, 97
    Arctic training, 58
    Argentinian surrender, *163*
    Artuso's death, 133, *138*
    chain of command, 63–64, 68n101, 79, 80
    chain of command problems, 62–63, 97, 99n141

204

South Georgia Island, 84
SS-*Requin* Foundation, 118n192
St. Andrews Bay, 49, 88, 93
Stanley. *see* Port Stanley
Stanley, Ian
    bravery and skill, 127
    D Squadron rescue, 96
    defeat of *Santa Fe,* 116, 122
    Distinguished Service Order, 92
    Fortuna Glacier mission, 90–91, 92
    role, 85
Stark, Peter, 19, 26, 88
Staveley, Vice-Admiral, 30
Stokes [Himalayan climber], 86
Storki [Russian tug], 26
Streator, Edward, 74
Stromness Bay
    British reconnaissance, 19, 85, 89, 95, 96
    French assistance to Argentinians, 26
    whaling facilities, 18
Swinhoe, Crispin, 64, 133

T

Task Force 60 [Argentina], 42, 43
Task Force 317.1.9 [UK]
    en route to South Georgia Island, 56
    reconnaissance, 80
    ships, 59–60
    weaponry, 60
Task Force 317.9 [UK]
    en route to South Georgia Island, 74, 113
    helicopters, 62
    reconnaissance, 79
Tattnall, Josiah, 183n2
Thatcher, Margaret, *149*
    advisors' doubt about military success, 31n26, 56, 74
    defence budget, 20, 29–30, 67n90
    diplomacy, 22–23, 159, *178*
    on Falklands Islands sovereignty, 29, 54
    favor toward de la Billiere, 80, 82
    Fortuna Glacier mission, 91, 102n170
    Franks Report, 23–24

excessive caution, 93–94, 96, 110, 115, 121–122
experience, 60
experience deficits, 60, 62–63, 100n144
Fortuna Glacier mission, 86, 91
Grytviken seizure, 123–124, 125
on inexperience of troops, 100n143
intellectual fatigue, 159
loss of helicopters, 121
Operation Corporate, 61
Operation Paraquat, 60
personnel deficits, 83
relationship with Delves, 121
relationship with Fieldhouse and Woodward, 60
relationship with Sheridan, 100n144, 115, 121, 134, *172*
Santa Fe conquest and disposal, 122, 131, 134
SBS mission, 102n177
ships, 61
situational ignorance, 89
South Georgia Island recapture, 84, 98, 122–123
tactical errors, 94–95
transportation of Sheridan's forces, 81–82

Z

Zaraetiegui, Captain, 62

12156850R00124

Printed in Great Britain
by Amazon.co.uk, Ltd.,
Marston Gate.